DATE DUE

SEP. 2 6 1989			

SHAKESPEAREAN
ICONOCLASM

SHAKESPEAREAN ICONOCLASM

JAMES R. SIEMON

University of California Press
Berkeley
Los Angeles
London

University of California Press
Berkeley and Los Angeles, California

University of California Press, Ltd.
London, England

Library of Congress Cataloging in Publication Data

Siemon, James R.
    Shakespearean iconoclasm.

    Includes index.
    1. Shakespeare, William, 1564–1616—Style.
I. Title.
PR3072.S53   1985   822.3'3   83–17923
ISBN 0–520–05031–2

Printed in
the United States of America

1   2   3   4   5   6   7   8   9

For Alexandra

The nature of the human mind is more affected by affirmatives and actives than by negatives and privatives; whereas by right it should be indifferently disposed towards both. But now a few times hitting or presence produces a much stronger impression on the mind than many times failing or absence: a thing which is the root of all vain superstitions and credulity. And therefore it was well answered by one who when the table was shown to him hanging in a temple of such as had paid their vows upon escape from shipwreck, and he was pressed to say whether he did not now acknowledge the power of Neptune, "Yea," asked he in return, "but where are they painted that were drowned after paying their vows?"

(Bacon, *De Augmentis Scientiarum*)

Contents

Acknowledgments

As in any long-term project, the debts incurred in writing this book are many and the chances for repayment slight. The history of the present work includes my debts to able, passionate teachers of Shakespeare: Robert Steele, first of all, then later Karl Zender, René Girard, and finally Richard Fly, to whom my indebtedness is especially great. Professor Fly saw this book in each of its various forms and never tired of offering praise and criticism. Others who have contributed in many ways to the same metamorphoses are Gale Carrithers and Fred See, as well as my colleagues at Boston University, Gerald Fitzgerald, Albert Gilman, and William Carroll. Two other scholars, both from outside the field of Renaissance literary studies, had a profound effect on the inception of this book. Irving Massey's seminars on Romanticism and the image at S.U.N.Y. Buffalo furnished the direct impetus for my thinking about literature as iconoclastic. Less directly but no less importantly, the lectures of Norris K. Smith on Art History at Washington University taught me, along with many other things, that the capacity to love great art is not incompatible with a need to ask hard questions of it. For aid in preparation of the manuscript, I am indebted to the Graduate School of Boston University for a grant that permitted me to employ the typing services of Mrs. E. P. Goodwin.

Acknowledgments

These are some of the people to whom *Shakespearean Iconoclasm* owes much of whatever in it might be good, true, or even well said. That the book exists at all is, however, most especially a tribute to two people. One is named in the dedication; the other is Bill Carroll. Each knows how very much I owe.

· Introduction ·

Methode ist Umweg.
  (Walter Benjamin, *Schriften*)

The fact that the conjunction of "Shakespearean" and "Iconoclasm" creates an oxymoron to modern sensibilities is a tribute not only to the work of those recent scholars and critics who have demonstrated the importance of iconic elements in the plays but also to their forerunners, who championed the plays on the basis of unities unperceived and unperceivable to neoclassical eyes. Even if one is less likely now to encounter the Romantic terminology of "organic unity," that there is unity in spite of appearances of fragmentation and hints of discord remains a ruling assumption in criticism of the plays. So, for example, Bridget Gellert Lyons argues:

> Disease in *Hamlet*, the parts that the hero plays, and the landscape which he inhabits and which includes the other figures in the drama, are all related but varied manifestations of a single image.[1]

Language, characterization, stage setting, even action, according to such a view, cohere as "manifestations of a

Epigraph is from Benjamin, *Schriften*, ed. T. W. Adorno and Gretel Adorno (Frankfurt: Suhrkamp Verlag, 1955), 1:208.

1. *Voices of Melancholy* (1971; rpt. New York: Norton, 1975), 110.

single image," and the singleness of that image lies in a conceptual prototype, the idea of Melancholy, to which its many elements all refer. Thus, what might seem diverse and fragmentary at a surface level is redeemed through its iconicity (*icon* here signifying an image in which conceptual content predominates over the attempt to render perceptual experience).[2]

Yet despite the widespread acceptance enjoyed by such assumptions, the counterarguments have not simply gone away. Although few today would agree with Dennis and Rymer, Tolstoy, or even Eliot concerning the disunity of the plays, there are those—Alfred Harbage and Norman Rabkin are two notable examples—whose work might give one cause to consider the issue more fully.[3] In fact, the existence of conflicting evidence that suggests in the plays an art both encouraging a belief in its own unity and iconicity and also actively frustrating that belief remains puzzling.[4] To venture an analogy that will need supporting, it is as if the dramatist were follow-

2. See A. D. Nuttall, *Two Concepts of Allegory* (London: Routledge and Kegan Paul, 1967), 90.

3. I think here specifically of Harbage's *As They Liked It* (New York: Macmillan, 1947) and Rabkin's *Shakespeare and the Common Understanding* (New York: Free Press, 1967).

4. Besides those critics I mention in the course of my argument, the following are among recent explorers of the disunity in Shakespearean drama: Laurence Michel, *The Thing Contained* (Bloomington: Indiana University Press, 1970); Eugene P. Nasser, *The Rape of Cinderella* (Bloomington: Indiana University Press, 1970); John Bayley's two books *The Characters of Love* (London: Constable, 1960) and *The Uses of Division* (New York: Viking, 1976) are both interesting, as are the remarks of Iris Murdoch in her brief but telling essay "Against Dryness," *Encounter* 88 (1961): 16–20.

ing the impulse that has sometimes made an iconoclast of the artist himself—an artist who, after making an image that might serve as an icon for the divine idea, flaws his creation lest it be mistaken, taken not as a mere limited image, but as truth indeed, as an idol.[5]

The following pages elaborate upon the notion of "Shakespearean iconoclasm." After some remarks about current criticism of the plays, the argument turns to building a historical and theoretical case for adding "iconoclasm" to the critical vocabulary. Thereafter, chapters devoted to specific works take up the iconic/iconoclastic tensions of such works as *Lucrece* and *Henry V* before attempting to deal with the same subject as it finds expression in matters of character, language, and staging in *Caesar*, *Hamlet*, *Lear*, and *The Winter's Tale*.[6]

The arguments of individual chapters may overlap, or at times begin anew, heading in slightly different direc-

---

5. On this problem for the religious artist see Harry L. Berger, Jr., "Theater, Drama, and the Second World: A Prologue to Shakespeare," *Comparative Drama* 2 (1968): 6.

6. I have used the following Arden editions: *The Poems of Shakespeare*, ed. F. T. Prince (London: Methuen, 1969); *Henry V*, ed. J. H. Walter (London: Methuen, 1954); *Julius Caesar*, ed. T. S. Dorsch (London: Methuen, 1955); *King Lear*, ed. Kenneth Muir (London: Methuen, 1952); *The Winter's Tale*, ed. J. H. P. Pafford (London: Methuen, 1963). *Hamlet* is cited from the Variorum edition, ed. H. H. Furness (1877; rpt. New York: Dover, 1963). For the sonnets, I use Stephen Booth's *Shakespeare's Sonnets* (New Haven: Yale University Press, 1977). All other citations from Shakespeare are taken from *The Complete Works of Shakespeare*, ed. David Bevington (Glenview, Ill.: Scott, Foresman, 1980). In quoting from other Renaissance texts, I have silently changed difficult spellings. Where page numbers are lacking for such texts, I have provided signature markings.

tions, qualifying themselves, and resisting completion. This resistance to order and circumscription is as it should be, since *iconoclasm* is an assertion of incongruity itself, while the *Shakespearean* is suggestive—without ends or end.

I

Of necessity, we begin with what criticism has taught us to see and led us to overlook. That one is able to see in the plays unified images where earlier generations saw only collections of fragments is largely a tribute to the work of those modern critics who have followed in the wake of the Romantics. Shakespeare, according to Coleridge, had

> unequivocally proved the indwelling in his mind of imagination, or the power by which one image or feeling is made to modify many others, and by a sort of fusion to force many into one—that which afterwards showed itself in such might and energy in *Lear*, where the deep anguish of a father spreads the feeling of ingratitude and cruelty over the very elements of heaven—and which, combining many circumstances into one moment of consciousness, tends to produce that ultimate end of all human thought and feeling, unity.[7]

From such notions, themselves largely derived from A. W. Schlegel's conception of the plays as unified by a "leading idea," grow such diverse and influential works of early twentieth-century criticism as those of Caroline Spurgeon and G. Wilson Knight.[8] Spurgeon examines

7. *Lectures and Notes on Shakespeare*, ed. T. Ashe (1884, rpt. Freeport, N.Y.: Books for Libraries, 1972), 220.

8. Schlegel's "leading idea" is discussed in the twenty-third lecture on dramatic art and literature, *August Wilhelm von Schlegels Sämmtliche Werke*, ed. Eduard Böcking (Leipzig: Weidmann, 1846), 6: 210.

Shakespeare's verbal images (more specifically, the vehi-
cles of his metaphors) because, she argues, they "reveal
the dominant picture or sensation—and for Shakespeare
the two are identical—in terms of which he sees and feels
the main problem or theme of the play."[9] Knight's *The
Wheel of Fire* takes the whole play itself as an "expanded
metaphor" in which images—visual, verbal, and embodied in characters—serve to reveal a core of unity.[10] Knight
goes beyond Bradley's tentative suggestion that the characters of Shakespeare's late plays might not be so far removed from symbol and allegory, from "personifications
of qualities and abstract ideas," to assert that characters
are symbols of themes: "the Ghost, symbol of the death-
theme in *Hamlet*, or the Weird Sisters, symbols of the evil
in *Macbeth*."[11]

The work of Wolfgang Clemen and Una Ellis-Fermor
expands on these seminal insights, Clemen adding an
awareness of dramatic context to Spurgeon's contextless
examples and Ellis-Fermor emphasizing the idea that
imagery should include elements of stage setting. But

9. "Leading Motives in the Imagery of Shakespeare's Tragedies," The Shakespeare Association Lecture for 1930; rpt. in
Shakespeare: Modern Essays in Criticism, ed. Leonard F. Dean
(London: Oxford University Press, 1967), 72–79. Spurgeon's
most important work is, of course, her *Shakespeare's Imagery and
What It Tells Us* (1935; rpt. Cambridge: Cambridge University
Press, 1958). The most interesting work on Shakespeare's imagery that precedes Spurgeon's is Walter Whiter's *Specimen Commentary on Shakespeare* (London: T. Cadell, 1794). Besides the
works cited below, Kenneth Muir's "Shakespeare's Imagery—
Then and Now," *Shakespeare Survey* 18 (1965): 46–57, furnishes a
good introduction to the topic.

10. Knight, *The Wheel of Fire* (1930; rpt. London: Methuen,
1949), 1–16.

11. Ibid. For Bradley, see *Shakespearean Tragedy*, 2d ed. (1905;
rpt. London: Macmillan, 1915), 265.

always the assumption remains that there is a central thematic unity of which the play's various elements constitute an image. As Clemen puts it, the physical deteriora-
tion of Hamlet's father is an "individual occurrence" that
through iterative imagery "is expanded into a symbol for
the central problem of the play."[12] The idea of Shakespearean drama as "imagery in action" is given greater
currency by Alan S. Downer's emphasis on props, costume, and physical setting, though again the assumptions about the relationship of these "images" to a conceptual core is hardly new. Commenting on the storm
and blinding scenes of *King Lear*, Downer observes, "It is
the dramatization of the image which makes the meaning
of the play evident."[13] Although Downer still cites Coleridge on the imagination as an authority for his assumptions about the relationship of drama to image to concept,
more recent criticism that builds on his understanding of
the plays as primarily visual images is more likely to appeal to a rather different authority.

Instead of depending on a Romantic notion of the
timeless natural genius, modern critics concerned with
the plays as "images" are more likely to view Shakespeare's dramatic practice as an expression of certain
historical attitudes. Maurice Charney, who is widely
credited with making the concept of visual or "presenta-
tional" imagery familiar to critics of Shakespeare, may be

12. Una Ellis-Fermor, *The Frontiers of Drama* (1945; rpt. London:
Methuen, 1964). Clemen's quotation is from *The Development of
Shakespeare's Imagery* (Cambridge, Mass.: Harvard University
Press, 1951), cited in Dean, ed., 233.

13. "The Life of Our Design: The Function of Imagery in the
Poetic Drama," *Hudson Review* 2 (1949): 242–63, especially 252–
53.

taken as a spokesman for these more recent assumptions. Expanding upon the arguments of Lovejoy and Tillyard, Charney maintains in *Shakespeare's Roman Plays* that concentration on the imagery of the plays is appropriate because of a special "image-consciousness," a "figurative view" of reality, that the Elizabethan age had inherited from medieval symbolism. This Elizabethan habit of mind, according to Charney, had the effect of guaranteeing validity to a multitude of "similitudes and correspondences."[14] Among the many who follow Charney's lead, three recent critics may stand as representative. Less likely to acknowledge Lovejoy and Tillyard, members of this group still base their notion of the plays as visual icons upon a belief in continuity between medieval, essentially Neoplatonic, faith in correspondence and Elizabethan modes of art and thought. Dieter Mehl speaks for them all when he asserts that many Elizabethan plays "portray events on the stage in such a manner that they form significant and often emblematic images of the play's meaning."[15] And, in general, the group agrees with Martha Hester Fleischer that Elizabethan plays share so many visual conventions and commonplaces with medieval and Renaissance art, especially the emblem books, that they are "best understood as speaking

14. *Shakespeare's Roman Plays* (Cambridge, Mass.: Harvard University Press, 1961), 197–98. Cf. Rosemond Tuve's recourse to Platonic and Neoplatonic conceptions of reality in order to account for the concern with "patterns" and "concentrated essences" in Elizabethan poetry; see the chapter on "Imitation and Images," in her *Elizabethan and Metaphysical Imagery* (Chicago: University of Chicago Press, 1947).

15. "Emblems in English Renaissance Drama," *Renaissance Drama*, n.s., 2 (1969): 39–57, p. 51.

pictures."[16] Significant effects follow from viewing the plays in such a way. With regard to characterization, John Doebler maintains that Shakespeare's emblematic staging "can draw a character into the role of personification."[17] And beyond this effect upon character, the iconic or emblematic approach to the plays also profoundly modifies perception of dramatic action itself, causing it to appear, in Mehl's terms, as "a kind of visual metaphor," which works "to give wider significance to the action by stylizing the individual event into a timeless situation."[18]

Given their high regard for the image, and for the

16. *The Iconography of the English History Play* (Salzburg: Institut für englische Sprache und Literatur, 1974), 9. The approach to Shakespearean drama as a "speaking picture" is widespread; for a useful bibliography of iconographic approaches see John Doebler, "Bibliography for the Study of Iconography in Renaissance English Literature," *Research Opportunities in Renaissance Drama* 22 (1979): 45–55. On the idea of the "speaking picture" as an aesthetic concept see Jean H. Hagstrum, *The Sister Arts* (Chicago: University of Chicago Press, 1958); Rensselaer W. Lee, *Ut Pictura Poesis* (New York: Norton, 1967); Robert John Clements, *Picta Poesis* (Rome: Edizioni di Storia e Letteratura, 1960); and Mario Praz, *Mnemosyne* (Princeton: Princeton University Press, 1970).

17. *Shakespeare's Speaking Pictures* (Albuquerque: University of New Mexico Press, 1974), 9.

18. "Visual and Rhetorical Imagery in Shakespeare's Plays," *Essays and Studies*, n.s., 25 (1972): 83–100, pp. 88–89. Also in the line of criticism seeing the plays as unified under the dominance of a central meaning are the scholars who work on the relation between Shakespearean drama and the moralities. Among these are Irving Ribner, Edmund Creeth, Jeanne Spencer Kantorowicz, and Alan C. Dessen. Dessen provides a very useful survey of such scholarship and draws attention to the group's shared emphasis on themes or theses that "can readily take precedence over our sense of character or plot" ("Homilies and Anomalies," *Shakespeare Studies* 11 [1978]: 243–58, p. 252).

visual image in particular, as an embodiment of the essential beneath the flux, it is fitting that these critics specifically relate Shakespeare's dramatic practice to Neoplatonic thought. Dieter Mehl argues that Shakespeare's
iconic dramaturgy demonstrates a sympathy with the
Neoplatonic belief that "through the eyes we can perceive
the essence of things which the intrinsically limited and
often clumsy tools of the language cannot express."[19]
With regard to Shakespeare's staging, Doebler asserts,
"When an important detail of blocking, prop, or costume
is combined with surprise . . . we may come very near
Pico della Mirandola's concept of the visual image as offering instant and intuitive recognition of transcendent
reality."[20] Fleischer finds Shakespeare's plays, along with
those of other Elizabethan dramatists, sharing a common
"visual vocabulary" with the artists of the emblem books,
and she claims that "behind the popular language of picture lay a lofty Neoplatonic theory of the nondiscursive
apprehension of knowledge."[21]

To make so near an equation of Shakespeare's dramatic practice and of the Elizabethan world view generally with the tenets of Neoplatonic thought is to beg a
question that is at issue in the plays and under dispute
in Elizabethan society at large. Any account of Shakespeare's plays or of their elements as image, icon, or alle-

19. Mehl, "Visual and Rhetorical Imagery," 87. Of course,
Coleridge himself is heavily indebted to Neoplatonic thought,
as is pointed out by Bishop C. Hunt, Jr., in his "Coleridge and
the Endeavor of Philosophy," *PMLA* 91 (1976): 829–39. Caroline
Spurgeon's own interest in Plotinus is evident in her book *Mys-
ticism in English Literature* (Cambridge: Cambridge University
Press, 1913).

20. Doebler, *Shakespeare's Speaking Pictures*, 13.

21. Fleischer, *Iconography of the English History Play*, 4.

gory must remain very limited indeed if it fails to consider seriously the strains Shakespearean drama puts on its images and the pressures contemporary English thought brought to bear upon likenesses in general and upon visual images in particular. Many of Shakespeare's contemporaries were prepared to see the drama as a "speaking picture," and precisely for that reason were eager to crush it. In certain circles, a remark about the superiority of picture to word, of figure to fact, of the nondiscursive over discourse, of allegorical content to literal text could earn one the label of idolator. Men killed one another over the *dissimilarity* between the "visual image" and "transcendent reality" or over the *difference* between "individual event" and "timeless situation."

II

The search for unity at the level of theme or concept, for the transcendent and essential behind the material and visual image or figure is an understandable response to certain formal features of Shakespeare's plays. There can be no question that Shakespearean drama shares elements and practices with the symbolic modes of emblem and allegory. Anyone familiar with the basics of allegorical exegesis as practiced from the time of Proclus to that of Chapman would be likely to recognize the presence of repetitious verbal imagery, obviously mythopoeic settings, significantly incongruous action, and the like as surface signs of an under sense, or *hyponoia*, at work in the plays, structuring them according to the demands of some meaning or other. However, the uses to which Shakespeare puts these devices are often profoundly at odds with the purposes of that specifically Neoplatonic symbolism with which recent criticism has associated the plays. Since this argument will be pursued at length and in detail in the following chapters, I have thought it fitting to undertake here no more than a brief introductory account of some of the evidence suggesting that in Shakespeare the use of verbal and visual imagery, and the value of the "similitudes and correspondences" upon which such use is presumed to be based, are hardly the simple matters that some have made of them.

Often even the earliest plays handle elements of stage setting in disconcerting ways. In *Titus Andronicus*, for example, a character evokes, in the same scene, two quite opposite versions of the same locale. While attempting to seduce Aaron, Tamora describes their trysting place as a *locus amoenus*:

My lovely Aaron, wherefore look'st thou sad
When everything doth make a gleeful boast?
The birds chant melody on every bush,
The snake lies rolled in the cheerful sun,
The green leaves quiver with the cooling wind,
And make a checker'd shadow on the ground.

(2.3.10–15)

Some seventy-five lines later, she describes the same place, this time intent upon making it appear to her sons as barren and threatening.

A barren detested vale you see it is;
The trees, though summer, yet forlorn and lean,
Overcome with moss and baleful mistletoe;
Here never shines the sun; here nothing breeds,
Unless the nightly owl or fatal raven.

(93–97)

Such a rapid juxtaposition might be troubling, especially in production, but, in this case at least, a simple solution suggests itself: against the backdrop of a bare stage, Tamora's vale is only "there" within her obviously self-interested language. This rhetorical explanation is less successful in accounting for related difficulties in other plays.

In *Julius Caesar* the signs and portents are clearly and objectively there for one to perceive. The question is, and here the discussion of Tamora's vale is telling, what are the great storm and celestial pyrotechnics supposed to *mean*? What is their thematic significance? Characters proclaim the storm to be "like" Caesar or "like" the conspirators, and there has been no lack of critics to follow one or the other of these suggestions, telling us (according to preference) just what the storm reveals about the essence of Tyranny or Treason. In short, both characters and critics alike ignore Cicero's warning:

But men may construe things, after their fashion,
Clean from the purpose of the things themselves.

(1.3.34–35)

This is an appropriate reminder within a play that repeatedly shows characters in the act of "fashioning" events, one another, and even themselves, yet its presence in the storm scene is disturbing, since the portents and signs are so dramatically elaborated that one feels compelled to read them as iconic of something. Thus complication has been added to the problem posed by the conflicting significances of Tamora's description. The dramatist has provided the audience with physical material—"Thunder and lightning" reads the Folio—and added full accounts of its significance, while developing in the remainder of the play a system of physical and verbal imagery that repeats the elements of blood, fire, and unrest. If indeed these portents are, as they seem to be, "images in action" of some thematic content, why then does the dramatist insist upon gratuitously injecting Cicero's skepticism moments before Casca and Cassius exchange highly wrought interpretations of their meaning?

Similar troubles occur in the later dramas. *King Lear* provides the visual emblem of an aged king confronting the violence of a hostile universe. Meanwhile characters draw attention to the underlying significance of this macro-microcosmic confrontation. Yet the fool is also there to suggest, and indeed Lear's own remarks will offer support to this suggestion, that there is another way to see the storm: not the iconic embodiment of universal hostility, the rain is only the rain that falls every day, as Scripture says, on all alike (3.2.77). The implication seems to be that Lear's choice to see the storm as he does is as much a statement about the way *he* sees things as about things themselves; but what a storm it is, and what a multitude of buffetings and contentions there are to repeat its violence in the language and action of the play.

In each of these examples, one sees, at the very least, evidence that the dramatist is concerned—even at cost to the thematic coherence of his work of art—with the part played by subjectivity in the establishment of meaning. Here, as elsewhere, characters are dramatized in the act of recasting nature in an image, making it mean something. Criticism has often been content to follow, selecting one meaning or another as *the* significance to which such images refer and proceeding to erect systems thereon. As Bacon says, the mind is more affected by affirmatives and actives than by negatives and privatives, "Hence also it happens, that whereas there are many things in nature unique and full of dissimilarity, yet the cogitation of man still invents for them relatives, parallels, and conjugates."[22] Instead of following the lead of Bacon's skeptical sailor in resisting the seductions of the figure, criticism of Shakespeare often shows itself all too eager to abandon negative particulars, ignoring some things and turning others into emblems, icons, or images.[23] The plays evidence an acute awareness of this human longing for significance and configuration, but there is also evident in them a desire to allow incongruity just enough voice to trouble an otherwise satisfied sleep.

This argument bears, of course, upon the case of figurative language as well as upon perceptual signs and portents. Poetry itself, Renaissance theorists had argued, could be understood as originating in, and as operating in precisely the same manner as, idolatry; for poetry's purpose, as Bacon puts it, "hath ever been to give some shadow of satisfaction to the mind of man in those points wherein the nature of things doth deny it."[24] Again and again, the plays reveal characters in the act of employing figurative language in order to give order and meaning to things—even at the cost of negative particulars. At the very simplest level, this process occurs when villains seek the appropriate "color" under which to conceal their evil; so the cardinal in *Henry VI*, Part 2, for example, searches

22. *De Augmentis Scientiarum*, 517.

23. Joseph Anthony Mazzeo relates Bacon's emphasis on particulars to the same impulse in Shakespearean drama, *Renaissance and Revolution* (New York: Random House, 1965), esp. 191–92. Howard Felperin explores the relation between Baconian and Shakespearean thinking with considerable insight in *Shakespearean Romance* (Princeton: Princeton University Press, 1972).

24. *The Advancement of Learning*, cited from *Philosophical Works*, ed. Robertson, 88. On poetry and idolatry, see Charles Trinkaus, *In Our Image and Likeness* (Chicago: University of Chicago Press, 1970), 2: 697–98.

for his "color" (3.1.235–36). More ominously, the plays also show us instances of characters entrapped in their own figures—unable to keep their images under control. Northumberland may caution Hotspur about letting his "imagination" get out of control, but he continues his ecstatic rant, making the whole world into the stuff of his figures. The price for such self-serving extravagance is, as Worcester suggests, substantial: "He apprehends a world of figures here, / But not the form of what he should attend" (*Henry IV*, Part 1, 1.3.209–10). The apprehension of images has the power to block attention to fact, even when fact is of vital concern; and, as the rest of the scene dramatizes, satisfaction with images has, paradoxically, a fixating, numbing effect that works to inhibit dialogue. Wrapped (and rapt) in his imagery, Hotspur turns a deaf ear to the practical cautions of his advisors; the mundane reality of such considerations can hardly shake the order and values established with such clarity in his imaginations.[25] Caesar most obviously, but Brutus as well, will suffer from similarly occasioned (and equally disastrous) deafness.

In *Julius Caesar* the search for color and the entrapment of attention in imagery become more complicated matters, and their metadramatic implications correspondingly widen. In the case of Brutus's deliberations about the fate of Caesar, for instance, figurative language—that which makes poetic drama poetic and that which the students of Shakespeare's images believe to be a way to coherence and truth—serves as a means to self-

25. One might think of Macbeth's similarly rapt condition when he yields to the "horrible image" the witches have provided for him, leaving his "function . . . smother'd in surmise" (1.3.140–41).

delusion and murder. No simple villain or mindless pris-
oner of the imagination, Brutus is shown employing
images, specifically such as George Puttenham calls
"icons," in order to bring himself to commit the crime his
judgment abhors:

And since the quarrel
Will bear no colour for the thing he is,
Fashion it thus: that what he is, augmented,
Would run to these and these extremities;
And therefore think him as a serpent's egg,
Which, hatch'd, would, as his kind, grow mischievous,
And kill him in the shell.

(2.1.28–34)

Within the play, the attention accorded the development
of this final icon strongly underlines its inadequacy. In
compounding his images out of half-truths and conjectures about Caesar and out of commonplaces about ser-
pents, Brutus stands as an ominous warning of the dramatist's sensitivity to the potential abuses inherent in his
chosen verbal medium.

This awareness is all the more striking when considered in relation to the way images are employed in earlier
works. In plays such as *Henry VI*, Part 3, Shakespeare
seems quite willing to let massive figures go uncontested.
So, for example, the king sums up his situation:

I, Daedalus; my poor boy, Icarus;
Thy father, Minos, that denied our course;
The sun that sear'd the wings of my sweet boy,
Thy brother Edward; and thyself the sea
Whose envious gulf did swallow up his life.

(5.6.21–25)

And Queen Margaret is permitted an unqualified, fully
elaborated comparison between her own situation and

the ship of state—replete with characters who figure as anchor, mast, tackle, pilot, sea, quicksand, and rocks (5.4.1–36). Surely Clemen is right to describe this sort of extended similitude as an inheritance from medieval allegory, and one may conjecture with G. R. Owst that it was from similarly elaborated exempla that drama first took its shape outside the sermon.[26] But even in the works that precede the major tragedies, the attempt to order action, character, and meaning within such formal figures is seldom allowed such complete success. Lavinia gurgling blood may be said to be "like" a fountain bubbling, but, as is so often the case in *Titus Andronicus*, the hideous incongruity between figure and fact demands attention. The next step is parody.

Early comedies repeatedly show us the discrepancy between characters and their chosen figures or images. Mocking the poetic devices that elsewhere serve him, Shakespeare lets us enjoy the failure of the commedia dell'arte characters of *Love's Labour's Lost* to cast themselves in the images of the nine worthies. Or, in *Two Gentlemen of Verona*, we see Launce's unwitting parody of elaborate figures such as Margaret's ship of state—should Launce's right shoe or his left be likened to his mother at the time of their parting, and who or what should image his dog in the symbolic representation of this dramatic scene? The capacity of the figure to distort the workings of intellect and perception is fully evident in Fluellen's oration on "figures" in *Henry V*, and the beauty of Shakespeare's parody is that, for all its comic qualities, Fluellen's speech accurately reproduces the

26. Clemen, *Development*, 45. G. R. Owst, *Literature and Pulpit in Medieval England* (1933; rpt. New York: Barnes and Noble, 1961), especially chapter eight, "Sermon and Drama."

way in which the figural imagination transforms negative evidence in the interests of order and meaning. Like any good medieval exegete, Fluellen, secure in the conviction that "there is figures in all things," hardly pauses when confronted with a discrepancy between figure and fact:

FLUELLEN: If you mark Alexander's life well, Harry of Monmouth's life is come after it indifferent well; for there is figures in all things. Alexander, God knows, and you know, in his rages, and his furies, and his wraths, and his cholers, and his moods, and his displeasures, and his indignations, and also being a little intoxicates in his prains, did, in his ales and his angers, look you, kill his best friend, Cleitus.

GOWER: Our king is not like him in that: he never killed any of his friends.

FLUELLEN: It is not well done, mark you now, to take the tales out of my mouth, ere it is made and finished. I speak but in the figures and comparison of it: as Alexander killed his friend Cleitus, being in his ales and his cups, so also Harry Monmouth, being in his right wits and his good judgments, turned away the fat knight with the great-belly doublet.

(4.7.33–50)

By his recourse to a time-honored technique of allegorical interpretation, the figure of reversal, Fluellen is able to skirt the problem of the obvious differences between Hal and Alexander.[27] But all is not funny. There is an element even here that points toward problems raised by the trag-

27. Michael Murrin discusses the reversibility of allegory in *The Veil of Allegory* (Chicago: University of Chicago Press, 1969), 59. Cf. Richard Levin's discussion of "fluellenism" in his *New Readings vs. Old Plays* (Chicago: University of Chicago Press, 1979).

edies. Fluellen, after all, mentions the act of murder and does so in a scene that twice calls attention to Hal's murder of his prisoners. Once the figurative mentality takes over, murder is reduced to nothing more than another element in an equation. No longer a particular action, it becomes something with a "meaning" that may be juggled about in relatives, parallels, and conjugates. It has become an image.[28]

III

The idea of approaching the plays as unified images first appears as a response to criticism that had emphasized their discords and discrepancies. For over two centuries, neoclassicists in France and England had disparaged Shakespeare's violations of "the" unities, while expressing fastidious objections to the contradictory behavior of characters or inappropriate uses of language. It is to the great credit of the Romantics that they were able to formulate convincing responses to such longstanding attacks through their various versions of A. W. Schlegel's notion of the "leading idea."[29]

But the issues did not simply go away. With the twentieth century's general loss of faith in the tenets of Romanticism, there came new attention to the problems presented by the plays' discordant elements, thematic

28. For a reading of acts of violence in Renaissance tragedies as "symbolic icons, embodying abstract ideas through conventional images" see Huston Diehl, "The Iconography of Violence in English Renaissance Tragedy," *Renaissance Drama*, n.s. 11 (1980): 27–44.

29. For Schlegel see above, note 8. Goethe's defense of Shakespeare on the basis of unity of idea is in accord with Schlegel; see Arthur M. Eastman, *A Short History of Shakespeare Criticism* (1968; rpt. New York: Norton, 1974), 84–85.

contradictions, and seeming uneasiness about the very power of likening upon which poetic drama depends. By far the majority of those recent critics who have emphasized these matters that present problems for the imagery critics have followed the lead of T. S. Eliot. Eliot located the problem in a general failure of Elizabethan art to separate the pursuit of "complete realism" from the imitation of "unrealistic conventions." This failure of discrimination results, according to Eliot, in an "impure" art that thoughtlessly mixes elements conventionally iconic of concepts with other elements that are only likenesses for phenomenal experience—i.e., without any intended or generally accepted *meaning* (complete realism).[30] Few who have accepted Eliot's account of the origin of Elizabethan discords have been so disparaging of the resultant drama. In fact, several have found cause to praise where Eliot damns. S. L. Bethell, for one, values precisely the naive expression of the "plasticity of unselfconscious art," which he finds typically English. Bethell finds profundity, albeit unconscious profundity, in Elizabethan paradoxes, since similar paradoxes are endemic to "any profound reading of experience."[31]

More recently, critics such as Bernard Spivack, Alvin B. Kernan, and Nicholas Brooke have pushed Eliot's insights in slightly different directions, without sharing Bethell's belief that the Shakespearean discords are unconscious. In each case, however, whether discussing the plays as stratified by layers of inherited metaphoric

30. Eliot, *Selected Essays* (1932; rpt. New York: Harcourt, Brace, 1950), 97, 115.

31. *Shakespeare and the Popular Dramatic Tradition* (London: Staples Press, 1944), 26–29.

drama and newer naturalism (Spivack), as exhibiting Shakespeare's intention to dramatize the encounter of these modes (Kernan), or as embodying the conflict between a consciousness of men as mere men and a language that is by inheritance emblematic (Brooke), the work of these three assumes Eliot's opposition between "complete realism" and convention.[32] Useful and important as this opposition is as a historically grounded counter to Neoplatonic readings, it cannot adequately account for the range of discord in the plays.

Here the analysis of Schlegel himself is suggestive. While arguing that the redeeming quality of Shakespearean drama lies in its ability to image abstract unities, Schlegel is astute enough to realize that the plays also go to some trouble to disappoint the very expectations they have aroused. Schlegel draws attention to the presence of certain maneuvers in the plays signaling that the playwright, like some Romantic ironist *avant la lettre*, has the ability to annihilate his creation.[33] That is, beyond any conflict between iconic and mimetic elements, the plays also exhibit the compounded complexity of willful conflict among iconic elements themselves.

This position is interestingly developed by Alfred

32. Bernard Spivack, *Shakespeare and the Allegory of Evil* (New York: Columbia University Press, 1958); Alvin B. Kernan, "Formalism and Realism in Elizabethan Drama: The Miracles in *King Lear*," *Renaissance Drama* 9 (1966): 59–66; Nicholas Brooke, *Shakespeare's Early Tragedies* (London: Methuen, 1968). The argument over conventions and "realism" is placed in relation to developments in Elizabethan poetry by W. B. C. Watkins in his article "The Two Techniques in *King Lear*," *Review of English Studies* 18 (1942): 1–26.

33. Schlegel, 6: 198–99.

Harbage, who, in his remarkable *As They Liked It*, maintains at great length and with much originality of analysis
that "On every point that is in the least degree debatable,
[Shakespeare's] plays argue both sides."[34] The means by
which the plays accomplish this purpose, furthermore,
include deliberate inconsistencies in their meaningful
elements; and, more radically, Harbage maintains that
the intention behind such incongruity is not, as Robert
Bridges had claimed, gratification of the audience's demand for surprise, but rather the *exercise* of our moral and
intellectual faculties.[35] Despite the richness of his examples and the skill of his analysis, however, Harbage ends
up claiming that the flux of incongruity and discord that
he finds is itself merely a "surface" phenomenon, which
rests on a bedrock of moral stability and "inner tranquility."[36]

No such inner stability is assumed in the arguments
of Norman Rabkin concerning the use of "polar opposites" in the plays:

> Reason and passion in *Hamlet*, for instance, or reason
> and faith, reason and love, reason and imagination;
> *Realpolitik* and the traditional political order, *Realpol-
> itik* and political idealism; hedonism and responsibil-
> ity, the world and the transcendent, life and death,
> justice and mercy. . . . Always the dramatic struc-
> ture sets up the opposed elements as equally valid,
> equally desirable, and equally destructive, so that

34. Harbage, 47.

35. Ibid., 71. Robert Bridges, *On the Influence of the Audience*
(1907; rpt. New York: Haskell House, 1966).

36. Harbage, 113. This movement through incongruity to
deeper levels of certainty suggests the features of Neoplatonic
allegorical criticism; see James A. Coulter, *The Literary Microcosm*
(Leiden: E. J. Brill, 1976).

the choice that the play forces the reader to make becomes impossible.[37]

The problem with this recourse to the principle of "complementarity" is that although Tudor drama generally suggests just such a form modeled upon debate, Shakespeare's plays are rather more tricky.[38] As the work of

37. Rabkin, *Shakepeare and the Common Understanding*, 12.

38. Rabkin's more recent work, *Shakespeare and the Problem of Meaning* (Chicago: University of Chicago Press, 1981), although explicitly taking note of the loss of "life" suffered in reducing a play to a statement of complementarities (61), still recurs to such formulations in practice; see his remarks on "rival gestalts" (61–62). And, in principle, he seems to remain committed to the idea that in the plays "radically opposed and equally total commitments to the meaning of life coexist in a single harmonious vision" (113). Robert Grudin's argument concerning the plays develops the notion of orderliness and clarity within contrariety: "Experience born of oppositions is neither chaotic nor inscrutable, it is merely contrary, obeying particular rules and revealing its secrets to those who are aware of its basic structure" (*Mighty Opposites* [Berkeley and Los Angeles: University of California Press, 1980], 2). On the debate form in Tudor drama see Joel B. Altman's excellent *The Tudor Play of Mind* (Berkeley and Los Angeles: University of California Press, 1978). Altman emphasizes the discontinuities of Tudor drama in order to show how the plays are structured as arguments on both sides of any question, but I would have to agree with Angus Fletcher that debate is, in the final analysis, another way to control and order what might otherwise break through as disorder; see Fletcher's *Allegory* (Ithaca, N.Y.: Cornell University Press, 1964), 344. The concept of the "problem play" is also important to this line of criticism, insofar as the qualities of the problem play—that is, in A. P. Rossiter's phrase, the throwing of "opposed or contrary views into the mind: only to leave the resulting equations without any settled or soothing solutions"—have been seen (by Ernest Schanzer and others) at work in plays other than those in the traditional list of problem plays: see Schanzer's discussion of

Mark Rose has demonstrated, there is little in Rabkin's formulation to prevent the adaptation of polar opposition to the uses of "speaking picture" criticism, but René Girard has advanced the terms of the discussion in an interesting direction.[39] According to Girard, the plays simultaneously support such Hegelian or Lévi-Straussian bipolar schematization and resist it by violating the oppositions upon which such formal organization depends.[40] *Hamlet* is no more an allegory of reason opposing passion than it is a realistic biography of a Danish prince; for, as in the Sonnets, so in the plays, scarcely an identity escapes invasion by difference, a difference that does not include similarity, a deference that is not simultaneously a conflict. As Stephen Booth has maintained, the Sonnets evidence "Shakespeare's delight in words and phrases that support a particular position or evoke a particular response and simultaneously confound it."[41] This confounding delight is apparent in Sonnet 105, "Let not my love be called idolatry," a sonnet in which iconicity and its delusions are matters of explicit concern.

The speaker of Sonnet 105 claims that the proper relationship between his work of art and the abstract themes it images is repetition—and more. In truth, his

Rossiter's *Angel with Horns* (New York: Theatre Arts, 1974) in *The Problem Plays of Shakespeare* (New York: Schocken, 1963). What Rabkin's "complementarity" does is to expand the problematic component of Shakespeare until it includes the canon. Rabkin uses "always" where Rossiter speaks of "these plays."

39. Mark Rose, *Shakespearean Design* (Cambridge, Mass.: Harvard University Press, 1972), especially 65–66.

40. "Lévi-Strauss, Frye, Derrida and Shakespearean Criticism," *Diacritics* 3 (1973): 34–38.

41. *Shakespeare's Sonnets*, 209.

verses should be seen, if he were to have his way, as iconic embodiment. Because his love is constant, his work of art should be a series of varied, but related, images of that unchanging constancy. The poem itself is hardly such a verbal icon:

Let not my love be called idolatry,
Nor my belovèd as an idol show,
Since all alike my songs and praises be
To one, of one, still such, and ever so.
Kind is my love today, tomorrow kind,
Still constant in a wondrous excellence;
Therefore my verse to constancy confined,
One thing expressing, leaves out difference.
Fair, kind, and true, is all my argument,
Fair, kind, and true, varying to other words;
And in this change is my invention spent—
Three themes in one, which wondrous scope affords.
Fair, kind, and true, have often lived alone,
Which three, till now, never kept seat in one.[42]

Not merely constant but also extravagant, not just kind but unkind as well, not only the same but different, the poem—like much of Shakespearean drama and unlike the speaker's ideal iconic art—exposes and undermines the very ideals and assumptions upon which it exists.

The difficulties begin even in the poem's initial assertion of difference in the face of a threatened likening. The speaker, confident in his ability to discriminate, defends his love from verbal denomination as "idolatry" even as he protects his beloved from being seen "as an idol." Neither his emotion nor its object, in other words, should be taken as an image, or at least not as *such* images. When it

42. On this sonnet see also n. 29 in chapter 1, below.

comes to reading the characteristics of his own verses, however, the speaker confidently assumes them to testify as images, as iconic signs for the true nature of his love and his beloved. No mere metaphor, the likeness that is the poem itself offers an extended map of the qualities of both. Since his songs and praises exhibit uniformity, "all alike" in being "To one, of one, still such, and ever so," therefore, he reasons, constancy is the defining quality of both his purpose and his beloved.

Of course, in making this argument, he betrays an obvious privileging of one very restricted meaning for "idolatry" and "idol"—i.e., an Elizabethan usage equating idolatry with polytheism—at the cost of other more obvious and more damning definitions.[43] But even as he speaks, the more traditional meaning of the term, to offer honor to anyone or anything in likeness of the reverence due God alone, rises into view, betraying the oppositions of his "argument." His very proclamation of monotheism—"To one, of one, still such, and ever so"—represents a perverted image of the *Gloria Patri* ("As it was in the beginning, is now, and ever shall be"), while his expression of joy at finding the three themes that keep seat in one manages to mutilate the Trinitarian theology of multiple unity that it simulates. Rebelliously and simultaneously, the speaker's verses signify similarity between his devotion and idolatry, between his beloved and an idol, even as he asserts their difference. Manner is incongruous with matter.

Or, more radically, his very matter itself is already out of congruity with itself, betraying what the speaker intends and believes; for, complementing its exposure of

43. On idolatry as polytheism see Booth, *Shakespeare's Sonnets*, 336.

the speaker's false differences, the poem also assaults a claim of likeness:

Kind is my love today, tomorrow kind,
Still constant in a wondrous excellence;
Therefore my verse to constancy confined,
One thing expressing, leaves out difference.

As today and tomorrow, as his beloved, so his love, so his verse "One thing expressing, leaves out difference." So one reads. However, instead of injecting a misleading and tangential difference, and despite their disarming appearance of honest confession, these lines omit crucial differences: condensing the person of the beloved, the love of the speaker, and the poem itself into one substance; confusing the speaker's intention with what the poem itself says; compressing time and history, today and tomorrow, under one timeless, conceptual "kind." Read with the caution born of our encounters with the speaker's other lapses, these lines open a play of conflicting significances. Is the speaker a narcissist more in love with his love and *its* own "wondrous excellence" than with his beloved object? Is he one who, in Hector's phrase, is precisely an idolator for making the service greater than the god (*Troilus and Cressida*, 2.2.57)? Might there have been a time past, a yesterday, when his beloved or his love was different from what they are today and from what he assumes they will be tomorrow? Is the speaker, however dimly and hopelessly, supposed to be aware of, and uncomfortable about, the fact that his words are at war with the constraints imposed upon them by the predominance of his preconceived meaning for them, the "one thing" or theme that they are supposed to image without "difference"?

Introduction

Despite the poem's assertion that its material elements constitute an iconic repetition of the qualities of fairness, kindness, and truth, which are shared by both the beloved and his love, these three do not dominate the verses except in the form of ruins, mutilated by the poem itself—neither fair, nor kind, nor true. Where are the vitality, confusion, disorder, and dissimulation, the riotous subversion and effrontery of the sonnet in the psychomachia of contradiction among reified abstractions described by Rabkin? Polar oppositions lead to unity, after all, even if that unity is called "complementarity."

Similar / different, simultaneous / deferred—oppositions crucial to the poetic drama—but how are we to talk about a poetic drama that will not abide these schemata, that seems to want things, not both ways, but every sort of way: in characterization, action, timing, setting, verbal imagery, and even in its themes? How are we to name a species of difference that undercuts the verbal simile and discredits the visual similitude of symbolic staging while the play itself is using them in ways to suggest their relation to conceptual content? Faced with the problem of literally coming to terms for an art that arouses expectations of allegorical or realistic unities while remaining uncommitted to the values, intentions, and limitations demanded by either; for an art that insistently surprises and frustrates by its incongruity of elements and violation of premises; for an art that means and refuses to mean; that moves to tears and then douses with cold water, one can envision a turn to various modern critical vocabularies. Terms like *ambiguity* and *ambivalence* have been useful in the past, and one can anticipate a full-scale exploration of Russian formalism's concept of *ostrennie*, or defamiliarization, proposed by V. B. Shklovsky. Yet Shklovsky's term is so very broad—applying, he claims, to any work of art—that one might wonder how it can shed light on the particular difficulties of Shakespearean drama.[44]

There are signs that some critics, alert to the issues we have been discussing, have been visiting the *couloirs* of Derridean post-structuralism. "De-construction," because capable of talking about the play of difference and deferral, would be welcomed by many, the thin air of *differance* bracing for those grown weary of trying to invent a vocabulary to deal with the inevitable discrepancies between systematic interpretations of "meaning" and the nuanced play of meanings within the plays themselves. Still, as Girard has argued, the post-structuralists' "semio-clastic" critique of presence should be viewed in relation to its general limitations and in relation to the particular difficulties it encounters in the texts of Shakespeare.

In the case of Shakespearean drama, the de-constructive enterprise encounters texts that have often already done themselves inside out before the critic arrives to expose them. There is little likelihood of exposing absence and self-deception masquerading as presence and certainty in texts that are so adept at violating themselves: "Shakespeare has already done it to himself. . . . Where does that leave the rest of us?"[45] Girard himself has

44. The notion of "ambivalence" is well-developed in Rossiter's *Angel with Horns*, especially in the chapter "Ambivalence: The Dialectic of the Histories." Shklovsky's claims for defamiliarization lead him to argue that it is found "almost everwhere an image is found"; see R. H. Stacy, *Defamiliarization in Language and Literature* (Syracuse, N.Y.: Syracuse University Press, 1977), 18.

45. Girard, "Lévi-Strauss, Frye, Derrida and Shakespearean Criticism," 38.

suggested an answer from the other side of cognitive nihilism.

By invading the temple and attacking reigning idols such as the dominance of meaning over the signifier, the de-constructionists have, it is true, generated a certain uneasiness. But, on the other hand, their endeavor may yet have a liberating effect upon speculation. Newer, more hypothetical courses of enquiry may yet grow into being where absolutism has failed to establish itself completely. Girard's theories about sacrifice and scapegoating within the plays constitute one venture into hypothesis.[46] This book suggests another: certain features of Shakespearean drama can be profitably understood as refracting the struggles over imagery and likeness that vexed post-Reformation England and found their most obvious expression in the various phenomena of iconoclasm. If this be to interpret the war against images as an image, so be it; that sort of discomfiting paradox would be alien neither to those who thought seriously about the act of iconoclasm nor to the poet who wrote the sonnet that begins "Let not my love be called idolatry."

IV

In modern times, several critics have spoken of idolatry and iconoclasm in discussing Shakespeare. Frances Yates, for instance, conjectures a possible relationship between religious iconoclasm and Shakespearean drama by posing a question that suggests a complex interaction between that drama, the destruction of religious images, the "inner iconoclasm" of Ramist method, and the exten-

46. On cognitive nihilism and hypothesis, see Girard's remarks in "Interview," *Diacritics* 8 (1978): 31–54.

sion of medieval symbolism represented by Giordano
Bruno's Neoplatonism:

> Either the inner images are to be totally removed by
> the Ramist method or they are to be magically devel-
> oped into the sole instruments for the grasp of real-
> ity. Either the corporeal similitudes of medieval piety
> are to be smashed or they are to be transposed into
> vast figures formed by Zeuxis and Phidias, the Re-
> naissance artists of the fantasy. May not the urgency
> and the agony of this conflict have helped to precip-
> itate the emergence of Shakespeare?[47]

Yates has other concerns, however, and leaves this ave-
nue unexplored. Philip Edwards's discussion of Shakespeare as an artist who both "had faith in his art and
scoffed at it too" leads into an examination of drama as
icon and simulacrum, but Edwards does not explore the
full implications of this vocabulary.[48] Others, such as

47. *The Art of Memory* (Chicago: University of Chicago Press,
1966), 286. Shakespeare's own relation to religion and particularly to the matter of images and iconoclasm presents a history
of ambiguous clues. John Shakespeare seems to have had a role
in defacing Catholic emblems and mutilating pictures, cruci-
fixes, and the like in Stratford's Guild Chapel; see T. Carter,
Shakespeare: Puritan and Recusant (1897; rpt. New York: AMS,
1970), 25–27. Shakespeare himself seems to have done some
work as a visual artist, making an impresa for James I in 1613;
see William S. Heckscher, "Shakespeare in His Relationship to
the Visual Arts: A Study in Paradox," *Research Opportunities in
Renaissance Drama* 13–14 (1970–71): 5–71. See also note 55, below.
For a recent examination of Shakespeare's religious leanings, see
Peter J. Milward, *Shakespeare's Religious Background* (Bloomington: Indiana University Press, 1973).

48. *Shakespeare and the Confines of Art* (London: Methuen, 1968),
especially 3–5.

Introduction

Preston Thomas Roberts, Jr., and J. Leeds Barroll have
made more extensive cases for using the term *idolatry* in
the discussion of the plays, and Barroll's sense of the
meaning of *idol* and of the image in Renaissance psychology is especially informed and useful.[49]

Despite Barroll's ample documentation, "idolatry"
may seem like no more than a convenient analogy in a
discussion of the visual, verbal, and conceptual discords
of Shakespearean drama. In fact, however, there is ample
historical warrant in the polemic and aesthetic literature
of the Elizabethan period for our employment of such
language to describe these diverse phenomena. Furthermore, the plays were written and performed in the middle of an era, lasting more than two centuries, during
which an entire society, not just its theological or academic components, was convulsed by a series of violent
disputes about likeness generally and about imagery in
particular—disputes that recurred again and again to arguments about the nature and value of simile, icon, allegory, and drama.

The identification of dramatic representation with
idolatry dates back to Patristic writings. "If you come to
the make-believe of the theatres," writes Tertullian, "I
very much doubt whether it is pleasing to God. God forbids the making of any similitude. How much more does
He forbid the making of a similitude of His own image,
man! The author of truth loves not falsehood: everything
fictitious is in His eyes adultery."[50] A humorous echo of

49. Preston T. Roberts, Jr., "Theology and Imaginative Literature" (diss., University of Chicago, 1950). J. Leeds Barroll, *Artificial Persons* (Columbia, S.C.: University of South Carolina
Press, 1974).
50. *De Spectaculis* 18, cited in E. R. Bevan, *Holy Images* (London:
George Allen and Unwin, 1940), 88. References to the theatre as

this charge recurs in Mistress Quickly's reference to "harlotry players" (*Henry IV*, Part 1, 2.4.395), but the scope of the serious concern and sensitivities that inform the war over imagery is not widely appreciated.[51]

---

idolatrous abound; see, for example, Henry Crosse, *Vertues Common-wealth* (London, 1603), and Stephen Gosson, *Plays Confuted in Five Actions* (London, 1582). Arthur Freeman's multivolume series of reprints is an invaluable source of polemic texts: *The English Stage: Attack and Defense, 1577–1730* (New York: Garland, 1972–74). On the war against theatre generally, see Jonas Barish, *The Antitheatrical Prejudice* (Berkeley and Los Angeles: University of California Press, 1981).

51. For a general history of the iconoclastic disputes in England, see John Phillips, *The Reformation of Images* (Berkeley and Los Angeles: University of California Press, 1973); on the iconoclasm of the periods 1534 and 1547–49, see Leonard J. Trinterud, *Elizabethan Puritanism* (New York: Oxford University Press, 1971), especially 268ff. The effects of English iconoclasm are described in Lawrence Stone's introduction to *Sculpture in Britain: The Middle Ages* (Harmondsworth: Penguin Books, 1972). See also A. Caiger-Smith's chapter "The Destruction of Images" in his *English Medieval Mural Paintings* (Oxford: Clarendon Press, 1963). On European iconoclasm see David Freedberg's article, "The Structure of Byzantine and European Iconoclasm," in *Iconoclasm*, ed. Anthony Bryer and Judith Herrin (Birmingham: Center for Byzantine Studies, 1977); also Martin Warnke, ed., *Bildersturm* (Munich: Carl Hanser, 1973); and Charles Garside, Jr., *Zwingli and the Arts* (New Haven: Yale University Press, 1966). For an understanding of the intellectual issues involved in iconoclasm, certain works remain essential: Gerhart B. Ladner's "Origin and Significance of the Byzantine Iconoclastic Controversy," in *Medieval Studies*, 2 (New York and London, 1940): 127–50, and "The Concept of the Image in the Greek Fathers and the Byzantine Iconoclastic Controversy," *Dumbarton Oaks Papers*, no. 7 (Cambridge, Mass., 1953), 1–34; also Ernst Kitzinger's "The Cult of Images in the Age before Iconoclasm," *Dumbarton Oaks Papers*, no. 8 (Cambridge, Mass., 1954), 83–150. Roy C. Strong follows an interesting line of argument when he argues

Introduction

That the reformers could not abide religious statuary in the church is common knowledge; but it is less generally understood how there could be, as Roy C. Strong points out, a hostility toward visual images of any sort—sacred or not.[52] It may even be understandable to us that Queen Elizabeth could denounce woodcuts in a prayer book as "idolatry," but it is hard to conceive why Thomas Hoccleve would be nervous about appending a portrait of Chaucer to his edition of *The Regiment of Princes*, or why the reformer Rudolf Gualter would refuse to send a portrait of himself to Christopher Hales "lest a door shall hereafter be opened to idolatry." We fail to realize how deeply some portions of the English public had internalized a complex of attitudes related to Calvin's quarrel with Rome concerning the visibility of the Church.[53]

Shakespeare, like his contemporary John Marston, occasionally plays upon the association of the visual image with the sin of idolatry. So Venus denounces Adonis in language taken from religious polemic:

---

that what happens to English art during the period of Protestant iconoclasm can be compared with similar developments in Byzantine art during the iconoclastic controversies; see *The English Icon* (New Haven: Yale University Press, 1969).

52. Strong, *English Icon*, 3.

53. Elizabeth's reaction to the woodcut is recorded in Glynne Wickham, *Early English Stages* (London: Routledge and Kegan Paul, 1959–63), 2, pt. 1: 349n. Strong discusses Gualter and Hales in *English Icon*, 3. On Calvin, see Jonas Barish, "Exhibitionism and Antitheatrical Prejudice," *ELH*, 36 (1969): 4–9. On Calvinism's pervasive presence in Elizabethan England see H. R. McAdoo, *The Spirit of Anglicanism* (New York: Charles Scribner's Sons, 1965), especially 5. For Hoccleve see *Hoccleve's Works*, ed. Frederick J. Furnivall (London: Kegan Paul, for the Early English Text Society, 1897), 180–81.

Fie, lifeless picture, cold and senseless stone,
Well-painted idol, image dull and dead,
Statue contenting but the eye alone,
Thing like a man, but of no woman bred![54]

(211–16)

More seriously, the comedies, as William G. Madsen has argued, parallel Protestant prejudice in their consistent relegation of the eye and its satisfactions to a position below that occupied by the ear.[55] Bassanio, for example, is warned that fancy, not love, is bred in the eyes (*The Merchant of Venice*, 3.2.63–72); Claudio proves worthy of Hero only when he agrees to accept her unseen (*Much Ado About Nothing*, 5.4).

54. Compare Marston's "Metamorphosis of Pygmalion's Image":

Looke how the peevish Papists crouch, and kneels
To some dum Idoll with their offering,
As if a senceless carved stone could feele
The ardor of his bootles chattering,
So fond he was, and earnest in his sute
To his remorseless Image, dum and mute.

> Arnold Davenport, ed., *The Poems of John Marston*, (Liverpool University Press, 1961).

55. *From Shadowy Types to Truth* (New Haven: Yale University Press, 1968), 161. Compare the treatment of the eye in Sonnet 137. Rosalie Colie suggests the extent to which the sonnet inverts Neoplatonic love doctrine, *Shakespeare's Living Art* (Princeton: Princeton University Press, 1974), 119–20. As D. J. Gordon has argued, there is nothing in Shakespeare's use of terms such as *image* or *imagination* to evidence any of that respect for the sacred character of the visual that Gombrich has described in his seminal essay on the role of the image in Neoplatonic thought, "Icones Symbolicae," *Journal of the Warburg and Courtauld Institutes* 11 (1948): 163–92. See D. J. Gordon, *The Renaissance Imagination* (Berkeley and Los Angeles: University of California Press, 1975), 20.

But a concern about idolatry was important to Shakespeare's contemporaries in their consideration of areas of experience quite removed from the merely visual. Besides its application to discussion of drama itself or of various forms of visual experience, the vocabulary of idol and icon proved useful to the Elizabethans in considering such important components of poetic drama as figurative language and characterization.

Long before Bacon discussed linguistic phenomena among his various "idols," the terms *icon* and *idol* had served others in considerations of language. *Icon*, though originally referring to an actual statue of a fixed, conventional type, is widely employed by classical and Renaissance rhetoricians as a term in their own discipline.[56] During the Elizabethan period, one sense of the word denotes vivid verbal description, what George Puttenham calls "Hypotyposis" or the "kindly counterfeit" of "things, in such sort as it should appear they were truly before our eyes though they were not present."[57] But when E. K. calls attention to an instance of its appearance in Spenser's *The Shepheardes Calendar*, his example is the far from naturalistically representational Aesopian fable of the Oak and the Briere, which, he maintains, constitutes an "Icon or Hypotyposis of disdainfull younkers."[58] Thus the iconic is plainly akin to the allegorical or em-

56. For a history of usage for *icon*, see S. Clark Hulse, " 'A Piece of Skillful Painting' in Shakespeare's *Lucrece*," *Shakespeare Survey* 31 (1978): 13–22.

57. *The Arte of English Poesie*, ed. Gladys Doidge Willcock and Alice Walker (Cambridge: Cambridge University Press, 1970), 238.

58. *The Works of Edmund Spenser*, ed. Edwin Greenlaw et al. (Baltimore: Johns Hopkins University Press, 1932–57), vol. 1, *The Minor Poems*, 27.

blematic—i.e., an image dominated, as indeed is Elizabethan portraiture itself, by conceptual content or idea, by the pursuit of the essential and typical, the "kindly" rather than the psychologically individual or the perceptually particular.[59] And, elsewhere, Puttenham's own examples support this sense of the word by suggesting that the iconic is characterized by the poet's use of physical objects and beings to stand in for, to make present, the qualities or ideas to which they bear some "proportion of similitude."[60]

Something of the continuity between medieval and Renaissance thought about language is suggested by the echo of Aquinas in such phrasing. When Puttenham discusses the poet's use of gold for yellowness, the stone for hardness, the lion for courage, or the angel for beauty, the implication is that, as in the case of the poem he cites, "our soveraigne lady" is not possessed of lips of stone or hair of gold but of the qualities to which such *things* naturally refer. Similarly Aquinas argues that references in Scripture to the arm of God are to be read as proportional similitudes for the idea of "active power" they signify.[61] Something of the differences between medieval sacramentalism and Elizabethan skepticism in approaching language is conveyed by Puttenham's choice of terms when he goes on to ascribe such conjoining of thing and

59. On the iconic, even Byzantine, quality of Elizabethan portraiture, see Strong, *English Icon*. See also Strong's chapter "Theory" in his *Portraits of Queen Elizabeth I* (Oxford: Clarendon Press, 1963).

60. Puttenham, *Arte of English Poesie*, 244.

61. *Summa Theologica*, part 1, question 1, article 10, in *Aquinas On Nature and Grace*, ed. A. M. Fairweather (Philadelphia: Westminster Press, 1954), 49.

idea to "common usurpation" rather than to divine ordination.[62]

In England the word *idol* never enjoys the nonpejorative use that develops in Italian Renaissance aesthetics. No Englishman takes up the line that runs from classical Greece to Jacopo Mazzoni, culminating in the latter's wide-ranging discussion of Dante's similitudes, as well as of his words themselves, as "idols."[63] In fact, when Bacon denounces as "most troublesome" the Idols of the Marketplace, "which have crept into the understanding through the tacit agreement of men concerning the imposition of words and names," or when he describes the frenzy of Pygmalion as manifested in his contemporaries, maintaining that "to fall in love with [words] is all one as to fall in love with a picture," he only articulates a longstanding English uneasiness about the idolatrous potentials of language.[64]

William Perkins, for one instance, writes in response to contemporary English suspicions of "set prayer" as an "abominable Idol."[65] Such attacks on set prayer reflect a generalized distrust of established forms, a distrust that grows from the primary demands of Protestantism for an authentically interior and individual religious experience rather than an external and objective observation. But

62. Puttenham, *Arte of English Poesie*, 243.

63. Jacopo Mazzoni, *Della difesa della comedia di Dante* (Cesena, 1587).

64. Bacon, *De Augmentis Scientiarum*, 518; *Advancement of Learning*, 54.

65. *The Workes of the Famous and Worthie Minister of Christ in the Universitie of Cambridge, M. William Perkins* (Cambridge, 1612–13), 3, 119–20.

Elizabethan suspicion of language is not directed solely toward aspects of formal liturgical usage. Throughout the sixteenth century, there are consistent and repeated attacks on the use of rhetorical ornamentation in general, which is likened to idolatry in that it substitutes a shadow for genuine substance.[66] As Bishop John Jewel writes, "idle men have fashioned all these things for themselves, and they become much more conversant with this arsenal than with the subject itself and with truth."[67] The fear is that figurative language, like carved stone, may lead men to be satisfied with the representation, the substitute that they themselves have fashioned, valuing it more highly than they value truth. John Bradford associates those who value "the vaine sound, number, and order of words" over "matter" with those who come to hear God's word "with the Idols of mens imaginations in their hartes."[68] And Holinshed is determined to write in the plain style of truth, "rather then with vaine affectation of eloquence to paint out a rotten sepulchre."[69]

Of course, the rejection of figurative language and the suspicion of words themselves is no more new to the sixteenth century than is the attack on religious im-

66. See R. F. Jones, "The Moral Sense of Simplicity," *Studies in Honor of Frederick W. Shipley*, Washington University Studies, No. 14 (St. Louis, 1942), 284. For a contemporary instance of equating idolatry with the use of "golden sentences and silver shining eloquence," see "Against Perill of Idolatrie" in *Certain Sermons or Homilies* (London, 1623), 70.

67. Hoyt H. Hudson, "Jewel's Oration Against Rhetoric," *The Quarterly Journal of Speech* 14 (1928): 374–92, p. 384.

68. Jones, "Moral Sense of Simplicity," 283.

69. Raphael Holinshed, *The Chronicles of England, Scotland, and Ireland* (London, 1577), 1, preface.

agery.[70] What *is* new is the way this suspicion spills over until it is no longer merely a concern of the learned but a truly popular worry. It is as if the struggle for independence from an inherited Catholicism had made a large portion of the English public dimly aware of the fact that the forms in which they felt themselves to have been imprisoned were ultimately derived from figures of language (the treasury of merit, transubstantiation) gone rigid; and that, since this was the case, no statement in any area of experience was above (or beneath) scrutiny for its idols. Within this climate of suspicion, poetic drama appears trebly dangerous. Based on fictions, plays not only present visible images of men assuming the likenesses of other men—or, worse still, of women or animals—but also compound these offenses by employing what Henry Crosse calls "fluent terms, and imbossed words to varnish theyr lyes and fables."[71] The chapters that follow will argue that the plays of Shakespeare often dramatize a suspicion of their own figures. When Brutus searches for a "color" under which to condemn Caesar and finally settles on his icon, then Bishop Jewel's charges should echo in the air: "What do they want with tropes and *schemata* and what they call 'colors' (to me they seem rather *shades*)."[72]

Finally, in the matter of characterization, the vocabulary of idolatry is historically validated. Outside the

70. Suspicions of rhetoric and praise for plain style are recurrent in classical and medieval writings; see C. S. Baldwin, *Medieval Rhetoric and Poetic* (New York: Macmillan, 1928), 2.

71. *Vertues Common-wealth*, sigs. o². On the poison of figurative language in plays see Stephen Gosson, *Playes Confuted in Five Actions* (London, 1582), second motion.

72. Hudson, "Jewel's Oration," 383.

theatre, people are said to take on the form or "idol" of another when they disguise themselves.[73] Inside the theatre, the same language is used in relation to iconic characterization. For example, near the close of George Chapman's *Bussy D'Ambois*, the enraged Montsurrey and his adulterous wife, Tamyra, have the following exchange:

TAMYRA: How are you turn'd to stone; with my heart
    blood
    Dissolve yourself again, or you will grow
    Into the image of all Tyranny.
MONTSURREY: As thou art of Adultery, I will still
    Prove thee my like in ill, being most a monster:
    Thus I express thee yet. [*Stabs her again*]
TAMYRA: And yet I live.
MONTSURREY: Ay, for thy monstrous idol is not done yet:
    This tool hath wrought enough.[74]
                                              (5.1.125–36)

To Tamyra, Montsurrey's actions render him the hardened image of "all Tyranny." To Montsurrey, Tamyra's wounded appearance images all "Adultery." In this exchange, their characters are not historical, psychological selves but the embodiment of ideas. Each wound of hers and each cruel act of his merely figures those concepts more clearly, until they approach utter congruence with the timeless patterns of which they are the icons or idols. Even if Chapman's drama does not, the plays of Shakespeare will provide ample opportunity to explore the con-

73. For this usage see Reginald Scot, *Discouerie of Witchcraft* (1584), ed. Brinsley Nicholson (London: E. Stock, 1886), bk. 15, ch. 2, p. 325.

74. Chapman, *Bussy D'Ambois*, ed. Nicholas Brooke (London: Methuen), 1964.

notations of sham and delusion that haunt this nomen-clature. When Lear determines to prove himself in action "the pattern of all patience" (3.2.37), or when the Ghost designates Gertrude as incarnate "Lust" (1.5.55), one should remember that for the Elizabethans such usage may rightly be termed idolatrous.

1

Iconoclasm:

SOME ISSUES
AND IMPLICATIONS

Rit forsothe, as the lyknesse of myraclis we clepen myraclis, rigt so the golden calfe the children of Israel clepiden it God; in the whiche thei hadden mynde of the olde miraclis of God beforn, and for that licness thei worschipiden and prayseden, as thei worshippiden and presiden God in the dede of his myraclis to hem, and therefore thei diden expresse maumetrye. So sythen now on daies myche of the puple worschipith and preysithe onely the licness of the myraclis of God.

(*Tretise of Miraclis Playinge*)

Who those characteristicall Ideas
Conceives, which science of the Godhead be?
But in their stead we raise and mould Tropheas,
Formes of Opinion, Wit, and Vanity,
Which we call Arts; and fall in love with these,
As did Pygmalion with his carved tree;
For which men, all the life they here enjoy,
Still fight, as for the Helens of their Troy.

(Fulke Greville, *Of Humane Learning*)

With occasions for idolatry appearing wherever they looked and in whatever they read or thought, and disputants occupying every conceivable point in a spectrum

Epigraphs are from T. Wright, *Reliquae Antiquae* (London, 1843), 2: 42–57; p. 55, and from *The Poems and Dramas of Fulke Greville*, ed. Geoffrey Bullough (New York: Oxford University Press, 1945), 1: 160.

that stretched from "idolatrous" to "iconoclastic" positions, Englishmen of the Renaissance lived amid a chaos of contention. The struggle was pervasive enough to touch the lives of all and bitter enough to end careers, close théatres, demolish works of art, sunder families, and lead, on occasion, to bloodshed.[1] Even if the plays did not expressly raise questions about their own visual and verbal imagery, there is strong reason to suspect that the issues that vexed society at large would have been of concern to the audience of Shakespeare, and this would be cause enough to justify a fuller consideration of the controversy.

I

The points at issue are many and various, but beneath the staccato of charge and countercharge runs a ground bass of dispute about the relation between image and prototype and of concern about freedom and bondage. To the party of reform, the honoring of images seems a diversion of the honor due God alone, the attention expended upon figurative language costly at the expense of truth, and the effort spent in the exercise of the allegorical imagination a slighting of literal, historical fact. But in each of these cases, "idolatry" is something more—an attempt to bind transcendent reality to the demands of human desire and the limits of human imagining. Paradoxically, this hubristic exercise of freedom, or rather, license, leads ultimately to a kind of bondage for its audacious promul-

1. For one account of a family literally divided by the difficulties arising from the attempt to distinguish idols from images see the "Narrative of William Maldon of Newington," in *Records of the English Bible*, ed., Alfred W. Pollard (London: Oxford University Press, 1911), 268–71.

gators. The iconoclast William Perkins speaks for a host of followers when he denounces the use of images in worship because "we may not binde the presence of God, the operation of his Spirit, and his hearing of us to anything, to which God hath not bound himselfe. . . . Now God hath not bound himself by any word to be present at images."[2] Perkins does not limit his definition of imagery to statues in churches, either. "So soone as the minde frames unto itselfe any forme of God (as when he is popishly conceived to be like an old man sitting in heaven in a throne with a sceptre in his hand)," Perkins warns, "an idol is set up in the minde."[3] In fact, he would brand *any* use of the imagination to form *any* image with the stigma of idolatry: "A thing fained in the mind by imagination is an idoll."[4]

The form-giving power of the imagination is thus in

2. William Perkins, "A Warning Against the Idolatrie of the Last Times," in *The Workes of the Famous and Worthie Minister of Christ in the Universitie of Cambridge, M. William Perkins* (Cambridge, 1612–13), 1: 676. Even Laud expresses nervousness about "binding" God; see Charles H. and Katherine George, *The Protestant Mind of the English Reformation* (Princeton: Princeton University Press, 1961), 349.

3. Ibid., 686.

4. Ibid., 695. Compare Frances Yates's discussion of Perkins's attitudes toward the imagination in *The Art of Memory* (Chicago: University of Chicago Press, 1966), 277–78; also on Perkins, see U. Milo Kaufmann, *"The Pilgrim's Progress" and Traditions of Puritan Meditation* (New Haven: Yale University Press, 1966), 153. The refusal to discriminate between idol and image is frequent during the period, cf. William Fulke's *Reioynder to John Martials Reply*, in Richard Gibbings, ed., *Stapleton's Fortress Overthrown* (Cambridge: Cambridge University Press, 1848), 123. The homily "Against Perill of Idolatrie" makes essentially the same point, *Certain Sermons or Homilies* (London, 1623), 12–13.

itself suspect for its part in the idolatrous attempt to bind reality in representation. The act of imagining that produces the idol is, however, neither the first moment nor the end of idolatry. Wiliam Tyndale follows Paul in asserting that the true origin of idolatry is human "covetousness"—a desire for satisfaction that includes the love of wealth and the world's goods but also includes virtually every inordinate demand for satisfaction this side of heaven.[5] Nicholas Ridley (among many others) cites the following account from the Book of Wisdom as the "first invention of images, and occasion of idolatry":

> Thus some parent mourning bitterly for a son who hath been taken from him, makes an image of his child; and him who before had been to his family as a dead man they now begin to worship as a god; rites and sacrifices being instituted to be observed by his dependents.[6]

The same account is cited by Coluccio Salutati in his conjectures concerning the twofold origins of poetry. Because they seem "most similar," poetry and idolatry, he argues, share a common origin—either in the manner described in Wisdom or in the parallel instance of the "figurative words" used by the Hebrews for their mysterious, hidden God.[7] In any case, the desire to turn an absence into a present object, a silence into a metaphor,

5. William Tyndale, "The Obedience of a Christian Man," in *Doctrinal Treatises and Introductions*, ed. Henry Walter (1848; rpt. Cambridge: Cambridge University Press, 1968), 161.

6. Nicholas Ridley, "A Treatise on the Worship of Images," in *The Works of Nicholas Ridley*, ed. Henry Christmas (Cambridge: Cambridge University Press, 1843).

7. Salutati is discussed in Charles Trinkaus, *In Our Image and Likeness* (Chicago: University of Chicago Press, 1970), 2: 697–98.

is found to prompt these attempts to find satisfaction through a substitute. As Christopher Giarda says approvingly, the image "functions, as it were, vicariously and we tacitly accept it instead of what is absent."[8]

This same process of substitution is seen by Luther as lying at the origin of allegorical interpretation. Here, too, the imagination answers the longings of covetousness with a deceptive substitute:

> For allegory is like a beautiful harlot who fondles men in such a way that it is impossible for her not to be loved, especially by idle men who are free from a trial. Men of this kind think that they are in the middle of Paradise and on God's lap whenever they indulge in such speculations. At first allegories originated from stupid and idle monks. Finally they spread so widely that some men turned Ovid's *Metamorphoses* into allegories. They made a laurel tree Mary, and Apollo they made Christ. Although this is absurd, nevertheless, when it is set forth to youths who lack experience but are lovers and students of literature, it is so pleasing to them at the onset that they devote themselves completely to those interpretations. Consequently, I hate allegories, but if anyone wants to make use of them, let him see to it that he handles them with discretion.[9]

From the perch they believe to be the lap of God, the allegorists may be able to avoid any too close encounter with the strenuous demands of the historical reading Luther champions, but they also fail to notice that the harlot

8. Giarda is cited by E. H. Gombrich in *Symbolic Images* (London: Phaidon, 1972), 146.

9. Quotation from D. C. Allen, *Mysteriously Meant* (Baltimore: Johns Hopkins University Press, 1970), 240.

to which they "devote themselves completely" carries chains.[10] The pursuit of such imaginary satisfaction from what William Tyndale calls "false similitudes and likenesses" results not in the plenitude of presence and fulfilled desire but in a bondage to rites, observances, methods—a dependence on special times, places, dress, ritual, and "an hundred thousand like things."[11] In fact, Tyndale maintains, the "greatest cause" of Christianity's captivity under the Pope actually "sprang first of allegories," and the party of reform find similar processes at work wherever they look.[12] Desire, attempting to capture its transcendent object (God, the beloved, truth, and so forth), incites the imagination to a representation of that object, but ultimately the idolator only succeeds in entangling himself in his own illusions. Taken historically, such idolatry is found informing the development of the Catholic church; more personally, it is seen (among other places) in the pursuits of the learned, the methods of the courtly lover, and the self-indulgence of the proud.[13]

10. See ibid. on Luther's attitude to history and allegory.

11. Tyndale, "Obedience," 160. Calvin writes to the same effect concerning the "bondage" of observations in *Theological Treatises* (Philadelphia: Westminster Press, 1954), 192.

12. Tyndale, 307–8; see also 308–14 for further development of the connection between allegorical interpretation and "idolatry."

13. For learning, see the epigraph to this chapter from Fulke Greville. One can imagine what the reformers' reactions would have been to Castiglione's account of the courtier's love in action: "Hence, to escape the torment of this absence and to enjoy beauty without suffering, the Courtier, aided by reason, must turn his desire entirely away from the body and to beauty alone, contemplate it in its simple and pure self, in so far as he is able, and in his imagination give it a shape distinct from all matter;

Given the widespread anxiety about idolatry, the sense of its operation, and the diverse forms in which it might occur, one can understand how it could be detected in secular literature, portraiture, and drama. But the accusations did not go unanswered, and the terms of defense are revealing, for they show to what an extent thought about drama *was* thought about images. At the same time, they serve to underline the central position of allegorism in such thought.

The honor paid to an image passes to its prototype, so goes one mainline defense of religious images.[14] The attention paid to religious drama is justified by the parallel argument that this form of "honor" passes to the conceptual truths that serve it as prototypes. In the orthodox defenses, images and drama are actually visual "books," which by virtue of their visual corporeality surpass the written or merely spoken word in their power to shape the memory of, and quicken emotional response to, their referents. As Thomas Aquinas on images—

---

and thus make it loving and dear to his soul, and there enjoy it" (*The Book of the Courtier* [New York: Doubleday, 1959], 351). Here is love of an icon. The image of "beauty" is to be sundered as far as possible from the actual "absent" beloved in order for the lover to possess it with greater satisfaction. J. Leeds Barroll's *Artificial Persons* (Columbia, S.C.: University of South Carolina Press, 1974) is particularly useful on the idolatry of platonic love. For an instance of the sin of pride considered as idolatry see the fifteenth-century "La Fleur des commandemens de Dieu," discussed in C. R. Frankish, "The Theme of Idolatry in Garnier's *Les Jeufves*," *Bibliothèque d'Humanisme et Renaissance* 30 (1968): 65–84.

14. The argument goes back through John of Damascus to a passage in Saint Basil. For a Renaissance example, see the dialogue of *Dives and Pauper* (London, 1536), 11–14.

There was a threefold reason for the institution of images in the church. Firstly, for the instruction of the simple who are taught by them as though by books; secondly, in order that the mystery of the Incarnation and the examples of the saints may be more firmly in our memory when they are daily made present to the sight; thirdly, to excite the feeling of devotion, which is more effectually excited by what is seen than by what is heard—

so an unnamed apologist for miracle plays—

Also, sithen it is leveful to han the myraclis of God payntid, why is not as wel leveful to han the myraclis of God pleyed, sythen men mowen bettere reden the wille of God and his mervelous werkis in the pleyinge of hem than in the peyntynge, and betere thei ben holden in mennus mynde, and oftere rehersid by the pleyinge of hem than by the peyntynge, for this is a deed bok, the tother a quick.[15]

Variants on these defenses can be found virtually anywhere that images or drama is under attack: whether in second-century arguments in defense of Neoplatonic cult statues, in fourteenth-century responses to Lollard attacks on drama, or in sixteenth-century religious polemic. In a remarkable instance of continuity across barriers of time, space, and culture, arguments and attitudes persist from Plotinus on images of Greek gods through Aquinas on images of Christ, reappear under attack from

15. Both quotes are taken from Rosemary Woolf's *The English Mystery Plays* (Berkeley and Los Angeles: University of California Press, 1972), 366 and 86. My argument is deeply indebted to Woolf's consideration of imagery and drama.

the Lollards, and emerge in Marsilio Ficino's reflections on emblems or in the marshaled arguments of the Counter-Reformation.[16]

Furthermore, as a reply to the story from the Book of Wisdom, the pro-image party could avail itself of another account of visual commemoration that carried far different implications. Maximus of Tyre emphasizes the positive role of imagery in the development of religious devotion:

> in a whole nation you will not find one who recollects divinity and who is not in want of this kind of assistance, which resembles that devised by writing-masters for boys who give them dim marks as copies, by writing over which, their hand being guided by that of their masters, they become, through memory, accustomed to the art. It appears to me, therefore, that legislators devised these statues for men, as if for a certain kind of boys, as tokens of the honour which should be paid to divinity, and a certain manuduction as it were and path to reminiscence.

It is easy to see how the terms of Maximus's Platonism could be translated into Christian didactic and contemplative uses, and they were.[17]

When the reformers denounce images in favor of the pure, unadorned word, the orthodox could counter with

16. See ibid., ch. 5, "Attitudes to Drama and Dramatic Theory"; also N. H. Baynes, "Idolatry and the Early Church," in *Byzantine Studies and Other Essays* (London: University of London Press, 1960), 116–43.

17. Cited in Baynes from Maximus's *Dissertations* (no. 38), 132.

the claim that images are not only capable of doing what words do, but that they perform the same tasks better than words. In fact, far from being instances of frivolous amusement or vain "eye-service," images are said to be capable of being so filled with the power and presence of their prototypes that they are virtually irresistible, as Saint Gregory of Nyssa, for one, found out when he first saw a painting of Isaac's sacrifice, the account of which he had read unmoved numerous times.[18]

Rather than hindrances to truth, images are living books wherein the truth may best be "read," as Stephen Gardiner maintains, "in that fashion of contract writing, wherein is wrapped up a great many of sentences, suddenly opened with one sudden sight, to him that hath been experienced in reading of them."[19]And in response to the attacks upon such essentially allegorical interpretation, a favorite source was Paul's remark in Rom. 1:20, which points to an underlying significance in creation itself.[20] Furthermore, Augustine's development of the notion of a world filled with vestigial images, each thing witnessing something of its divine prototype, found many echoes.[21] If all nature were such a book testifying to invisible qualities by visible signs, then how could it be wrong to read the elements of Scripture, or of secular literature—even Ovid—in the same way? And what of the book of history? Such an attention to the underlying

18. Woolf, *English Mystery Plays*, 88.

19. Cited in John Foxe, *Acts and Monuments*, ed. George Townsend (New York: AMS, 1965), 6: 60.

20. Ficino's response to Paul is discussed in Trinkaus, *In Our Image and Likeness*, 2: 746–47.

21. On *vestigia Trinitatis* in Augustine's *De Trinitate* see Johan Chydenius, *The Theory of Medieval Symbolism* (Helsinki: Societas Scientiarum Fennica, 1960), 9–10, 19.

sense is, after all, another way of directing honor through an image to a prototypal principle, idea, or conception of divinity.[22]

It is true that despite their repeated attacks on just such allegorical interpretation, on visual imagery, figurative language, and drama, the major reformers made use of them all.[23] Luther on occasion writes or reads allegorically, recommends painting, and praises academic drama.[24] Tyndale admits that allegorical interpretation can have its uses "to express a text or an open conclusion of the scripture, and as it were to paint it before thine eyes, that thou mayest feel the meaning and the power of scripture in thine heart."[25] But it would be a mistake simply to dismiss the whole controversy as an exercise in goring the opponent's ox while protecting your own.[26]

What appeared to the reformers as a chief defect in the opposing position was something inherited from the arguments of Neoplatonism—the substantial relation of

22. Peter Haidu explores these matters in his "Repetition: Modern Reflections on Medieval Aesthetics," *MLN* 92 (1977): 875–87.

23. As David Freedberg points out, the lesser reformers were much more absolute in their denunciations. See "The Structure of Byzantine and European Iconoclasm," in Anthony Bryer and Judith Herrin, eds., *Iconoclasm* (Birmingham: Center for Byzantine Studies, 1977), 166.

24. On his allegorizing see Allen, *Mysteriously Meant*, 293–94. Luther's recommendation of drama is recorded by Johannes Janssen, *History of the German People at the Close of the Middle Ages* (New York: AMS, 1966), 12: 17. The positive side of metaphor for the Protestants is discussed by Barbara Kiefer Lewalski in *Protestant Poetics* (Princeton: Princeton University Press, 1979).

25. *Doctrinal Treatises and Introductions*, 343.

26. Russell Fraser suggests dismissing many points of contention between the parties in *The War Against Poetry* (Princeton: Princeton University Press, 1970), 128.

image to prototype. While early Neoplatonism was of several minds concerning this relationship, later developments bequeathed a certain tendency to the church.[27] True, to some, images might be only images, mere signifying elements as dependent on arbitrary convention as the letters Maximus had imagined students struggling to repeat, as dependent on memory and custom for their meaning as Stephen Gardiner's reference to the "exercise" of reading suggests. To others, however, images could be something more, and it is this something more, which is already suggested in the Platonic resonances of Maximus's "recollection" and by the more mysterious accounts of imagery's ability to communicate nondiscursively the highest truths of doctrine to the truly *un*exercised, that arouses the suspicions of the reformers and in their eyes undercuts the attempts of orthodoxy to differentiate its worship using sacramental symbols from the pagan idolatry that seems its likeness.

This main issue of contention is jokingly suggested in Shakespeare's Sonnet 105. "Let not my love be called idolatry," the speaker asks,

Nor my belovèd as an idol show,
Since all alike my songs and praises be
To one, of one, still such, and ever so.

What is to be the force of "Since"? For all his humble protests of sincere devotion, the speaker has imagined for himself something of a godlike power. Since his songs are such, the beloved must be so, the qualities of the represented bound to the representation by some sort of essential connection. It is as a response to similar assumptions

27. On this development toward theurgy, see Baynes, "Idolatry and the Early Church," 128–34.

about the unity of image and prototype that Tyndale insists one cannot *prove* anything about the truth itself from the imaginary figures of allegorical interpretation.[28]

There is evidence to suggest that a belief in substantial unity between image and prototype was indeed tenable for the contemporaries of Shakespeare. If Luther and Melanchthon went so far as to exercise allegorical techniques in reading the features of deformed calves as comments on the Papacy, there were others who went further. Luther never recommends cutting off the ears of the *Mönchskalb* as a means of ending the tyranny of auricular confession, but repeated attempts to stab, burn, hang, or even secretly poison images of Queen Elizabeth indicate an intention to destroy not only her, but the principles and qualities such schematic likenesses represent.[29] Among the learned, a similar dream of unity between image and the imaged idea or concept seems to have haunted those who indulged the hieroglyphic craze and

28. *Doctrinal Treatises,* 306. So my reading of "since" reverses the image-prototype relation assumed in Sonnet 105 by J. W. Lever, who argues, "Because the friend's kindness is unchanging, the poet's verse forms an unalterable liturgy" (*The Elizabethan Love Sonnet* [London: Methuen, 1966], 259). My reading is in fundamental agreement with Jane Roessner's assertion that this sonnet is about the work of creating an image of constancy *in place of* the friend who is false; see her "Double Exposure: Shakespeare's Sonnets 100–114," *ELH* 46 (1979): 357–78.

29. Gombrich discusses the *Mönchskalb* in *Symbolic Images,* 178, as part of a consideration of "natural symbols." The attacks on portraits of Elizabeth are mentioned in Roy C. Strong's *Portraits of Queen Elizabeth I* (Oxford: Clarendon Press, 1963), 33–41, esp. 39–40. See Strong on the conceptual nature of Elizabethan painting. Webster's Duchess mentions the wasting effect attributed to having one's effigy "Stuck with a magical needle" (*The Duchess of Malfi,* 4.1.62–64).

the emblematic fashion that grew out of it. Marsilio Ficino, for example, cites Plotinus's remark on Egyptian image writing, "Thus each picture was a kind of understanding and wisdom and substance and given all at once, and not discursive reasoning and deliberation," and adds his own explanatory gloss:

> The Egyptian Priests did not use individual letters to signify mysteries, but whole images of plants, trees and animals; because God has knowledge of things *not* through a multiplicity of thought processes but rather as a simple and firm form of the thing.[30]

And, in general, as Rudolph Wittkower puts it, "in Ficino's exposition the image does not simply represent the concept—it embodies it."[31] It is an icon.

Is it any wonder that behind such beliefs the reformers could detect the hiss of the serpent's temptation—"ye shall be as gods"—that makes the imagination so dangerous? In light of the fact that the King James Bible consistently renders references to thoughts that oppose God's truth as variants on the phrase "the imagination of men's hearts," the license given the imagination by Neoplatonism is clearly a threat.[32] In Ficino's language the disturb-

30. Cited in Rudolph Wittkower, *Allegory and the Migration of Symbols* (Boulder, Colo.: Westview Press, 1977), 116.

31. Ibid.

32. On the King James version, see Kenneth Hamilton, *To Turn from Idols* (Grand Rapids, Mich.: Eerdmans, 1973), 29. Of course the sensitivity to danger from the imagination has a long history in England; so, for example, the vice figure in the early sixteenth-century play *Hickscorner* is called "Imagination" before his conversion and after being converted is known as "Good Remembrance." In the fourteenth century legislation forbade the imagining of the death of the King, and no thought was given to the difference between mere thinking and actual plotting; see

ing possibility suggests itself that man might look upon images and find them good—good enough—that he might in his delusions infringe upon God's claim to solitary eminence as absolute subject.[33] There was, after all, precedent for such worries in the case of the alchemists, who, following their own debased version of Neoplatonism, believed themselves capable of acting in some semblance to the creator.[34] If reformers and iconoclasts, as well as those merely affected by the ideas of reform and iconoclasm, produced images, similes, emblems, allegories, and dramas, they did so in the context of attitudes strongly opposed to a belief in the unity of likeness and the likened.

II

Because the Christian's conception of the sacraments may have an important effect in setting limits on his understanding of likeness, there is no better index to the uneasy status of likeness during the post-Reformation period than the debates over the nature of the Eucharist.[35] The debate centers on the precise nature of the relation-

---

Stephen Greenblatt, *Renaissance Self-fashioning* (Chicago: University of Chicago Press, 1980), 277.

33. Dominique Barthélemy, *God and His Image* (New York: Sheed and Ward, 1966).

34. Edgar Wind argues that alchemy is fallen Neoplatonism in his *Pagan Mysteries in the Renaissance* (London: Faber and Faber, 1967), 214–15.

35. This point is made by William G. Madsen in *From Shadowy Types to Truth* (New Haven: Yale University Press, 1968), 69. Michael Baxandall relates Zwingli's rejection of images to his rejection of the real presence in *The Limewood Sculptors of Renaissance Germany* (New Haven: Yale University Press, 1980), 74.

ship of the material means to the body and blood of Christ, but its complexity is suggested by the fact that in 1577 a book could be written that contained more than two hundred meanings for the words of institution, "This is my body."[36]

Henry Cornelius Agrippa does rough justice to the main lines of disagreement when he remarks that, for the "Bohemians" and the "Waldenses" and their sympathizers, "this worde, is, which they would have only be spoken *Symbolically*, and *significatively*, and that there is a figure in the wordes, the Romische Churche expound[s] it essentially."[37] According to Agrippa, the two groups differ in that one insists upon the distance between symbol and referent, while the other sees them as essentially unified. The dispute raged for hundreds of years, of course, but the fact that the issues involved were raised not merely in the confines of theological debate, but popularly and generally has profound implications for our discussion of Elizabethan drama. After all, the arguments in this dispute question the very core of the world order that Charney and his followers in the study of imagery have assumed Shakespeare to share with the Middle Ages.[38] If

36. Christopher Rasperger, *Ducentae . . . interpretations* (Ingolstadt, 1577).

37. Henry Cornelius Agrippa, *Of the Vanitie and Uncertaintie of Artes and Sciences* (London, 1569), 9. See also Calvin, *Tracts and Treatises* (Grand Rapids, Mich.: Eerdmans, 1958), 2: 219.

38. Johan Huizinga explains the centrality of the Eucharist in later medieval symbolism: "Eventually all symbols group themselves about the central mystery of the Eucharist; here there is more than symbolic similitude, there is identity: the Host is Christ and the priest in eating it becomes truly the sepulchre of the Lord" (*The Waning of the Middle Ages* [1924; rpt. Garden City, N.Y.: Doubleday, 1954], 206).

the leading assumptions of Neoplatonic symbolism were under attack long before Bacon turned against correspondences, if the same miracle plays could be seen in popular Catholic tradition as sacramental means to indulgence *and* be denounced by Lollards for providing only "licness" rather than the substance of truth, what guarantee is there that Shakespeare inhabited a world where "similitudes and correspondences" had some kind of inherent and unquestionable validity?[39]

It is a historical commonplace to describe the Reformation as demanding an interiorization of religion while effecting a withdrawal of validity from the outer, or material, means of Christian ritual. Charles and Katherine George document Protestantism's shift of emphasis from the objective efficacy of the sacramental means toward the "spiritual state of the recipient."[40] Hooker speaks of the Anglican position when he writes, "The real presence of Christ's most blessed body and blood is not . . . to be sought in the sacrament," but, "in the worthy receiver of the sacrament."[41] There are, of course, a whole series of positions leftward of the Anglican, culminating perhaps in the Zwinglian reduction of the Eucharist to merely memorial significance, but the important point is that the reformers insisted upon the active role of human consciousness in determining the significance of object or event.[42] Without an active consciousness of the histori-

39. E. K. Chambers documents the indulgence tradition in *The Medieval Stage* (London: Oxford University Press, 1903), 2: 348–51.

40. George and George, *Protestant Mind*, 348. This position is echoed in Henry V's denunciation of "Idol ceremony" as mere hollow form.

41. George and George, *Protestant Mind*.

42. Ibid.

cally instituted meaning of a ritual, it became worse than indifferent; it became an idol.[43] It is crucial, furthermore, that the believer realize that the meaning he is personally keeping alive is not a simple fact of ontology validated by likeness but a *historical* truth. So Tyndale writes of the sacraments:

> Even so Christ wrote the covenant of his body and blood in bread and wine; giving them that name, that ought to keep the covenant in remembrance.
>
> And hereof ye see, that our sacraments are bodies of stories only; and that there is none other virtue in them, than to testify, and exhibit to the senses and understanding, the covenants and promises made in Christ's blood. And here ye see, that where the sacraments or ceremonies are not understood, there they be clean unprofitable.[44]

The sacraments are bodies of stories *only*. So the Eucharist reminds one of the unique historical event—Christ's sacrifice of body and blood—and its elements are bread and wine only because Christ has named them as representations. Without that act of naming, of inscribing a likeness between the elements and his flesh, there would be no relationship between this symbol and that referent. Without the historically occasioned writing of God, without His chosen establishment of meaning, and without the believer's subjective consciousness of the particular story in which that meaning originated, the arbitrary

43. The anonymous author of *The Originall of Idolatries* (London, 1630), calls transubstantiation "a grosser kind of Idolatrie, then ever was invented by any Pagane" (4).

44. *Doctrinal Treatises*, 357–58.

physical element is without value.[45] It is of the utmost importance, then, that one get that history right and be as clear as is humanly possible about exactly what happened in that past which the Scriptures record. Assuming such values, any imaginary additions to the stories are, at best, dangerous. For Tyndale, and for many others in sixteenth-century England, such elaborations are idolatrous "fleshly imaginations."[46] These views offer the strongest contrast to the general emphases of the medieval and Renaissance strains of Neoplatonism from which Charney and others derive their assumptions about Shakespeare's "figurative" view of the world.[47]

H. O. Taylor has described how the medieval period "exalted the symbolical principle into an ultimate explanation of the universe," and C. S. Lewis provides a description of the way this Neoplatonic principle worked in the thought of Hugh of St. Victor:

45. This attitude is in marked contrast to that of thirteenth- and fourteenth-century mystics who considered mere visual contemplation of the elements as a means of union with Christ. See C. W. Dugmore, *The Mass and the English Reformers* (London: Macmillan, 1958), 65–72; cf. Jonas A. Barish, "Exhibitionism and Antitheatrical Prejudice," *ELH* 36 (1969): 1–29, esp. 4–9. Barish indicates that the reformers viewed ecclesiastical observances as dangerous insofar as they "had come to replace, rather than merely signify invisible realities" (5). One might contrast the position of those who followed Pseudo-Dionysius in making the believer unimportant and the elements themselves all important; see M.-D. Chenu, *Nature, Man, and Society in the Twelfth Century* (Chicago: University of Chicago Press, 1968), 126.

46. *An Answer to Sir Thomas More's Dialogue*, ed. Henry Walter (Cambridge: Cambridge University Press, 1850), 81.

47. On the near identity of Renaissance and medieval strains of Neoplatonism see Jean Seznec, *The Survival of the Pagan Gods* (Princeton: Princeton University Press, 1972), 103–4.

For Hugo, the material element in the Christian ritual is no mere concession to our sensuous weakness and has nothing arbitrary about it. On the contrary, there are three conditions necessary for any sacrament, and of these three the positive ordinance of God is only the second. The first is the pre-existing *similitudo* between the material element and the spiritual reality. Water, *ex naturali qualitate*, was an image of the grace of the Holy Ghost even before the sacrament of baptism was ordained. *Quod videtur in imagine sacramentum est*. On the literary side the chief monuments of the symbolical idea, in the Middle Ages, are the Bestiaries.[48]

In this view, God's ordinance follows from (the reformers might say "is bound to") the timeless unity of physical element and spiritual reality. In such a world, there are truly figures in all things and truth in all figures, quite independent of historical fact. But at what cost?

Huizinga's comments on late medieval thought suggest both the power and the limitations of such a consciousness:

The tendency to symbolize and personify was so spontaneous that nearly every thought, of itself, took a figurative shape. Every idea being considered as an entity, and every quality as an essence, they were at once invested by the imagination with a personal form.[49]

Huizinga has in mind instances such as that detailed in Denis the Carthusian's vision of the reformed church as

48. H. O. Taylor, *The Medieval Mind* (Cambridge, Mass.: Harvard University Press, 1949), 2: 86–101; C. S. Lewis, *The Allegory of Love* (London: Oxford University Press, 1959), 46.
49. Huizinga, *Waning of the Middle Ages*, 209.

a splendid garment, but one might also cite the *Nemo* sermons of the late thirteenth century as a further example of this propensity to think in images.[50] In these sermons, the homilist collects every scriptural reference containing the word *Nemo* (no-man), and, treating the word as though it were a proper noun, imagines a character in whom all these varied but related instances might be unified. Thus the imagination is granted license for its most exuberant activity, both the world and Scripture, as in Bernard's reading of Canticles, offering opportunity, seemingly without limit, for imaginary embellishment.[51]

Failings are closely bound to such strengths. In Denis's vision of the purified church, for example, the attention lavished on the depiction of the marvelous garment, which is the image of the church, overwhelms any notice of practical measures of reform. These, being largely matters of prosaic political process, offer no convenient outline for inclusion in a timeless image. And, in fact, the proclivity to think in images presents a serious obstacle to the development of specifically causal and genetic modes of thought, since the relationships which are the subject of such thought "must needs look insignificant by the side of symbolic connections."[52] As an example of the stranglehold that symbolic thought processes could exercise, Huizinga cites the sacred symbolism of the Papacy

50. On Denis, see ibid., 210. The Nemo sermons are discussed in G. R. Owst, *Literature and Pulpit in Medieval England* (1933; rpt. New York: Harper and Row, 1962), 63–64.

51. On Bernard see Kaufmann, *Traditions of Puritan Meditation*, 33.

52. Huizinga, *Waning of the Middle Ages*, 213. Cf. Chenu, *Nature, Man, and Society*, 124, on the tendency of meaning to dominate explanation in Neoplatonism.

and the Empire—a network of images that for a long time prevented historical and juridical scrutiny of papal authorities and institutions.

> For the symbolizing of Papacy and Empire as the Sun and the Moon, or as the two swords brought by the Disciples, was to the medieval mind far more than a striking comparison; it revealed the mystic foundation of the two powers, and established directly the precedence of Saint Peter. Dante, in order to investigate the historical foundation of the Pope's primacy, had first to deny the appropriateness of the symbolism.[53]

However exuberantly metaphorical at birth, the image in this system seems almost inevitably to tend toward hardening into a principle, a mechanism.[54]

As an example of the way this process could work, the case of the treasury of merit is particularly interesting. Beginning as a metaphor, which originally pointed to an ill-defined similarity between the superabundant merit of Christ and a financial institution, the treasury of merit becomes altogether literalized by Clement VI's bull *Unigenitus* of 1343. The mysterious reality of the divine atonement had originally needed an image in order to make it humanly comprehensible, but once the metaphor has been accepted, something of the mysteriousness of the idea is lost. Furthermore, all the ways in which the atonement is *unlike* the commonplace notions of an abundant

53. Huizinga, *Waning of the Middle Ages*, 213.

54. As Huizinga argues, "Symbolism at all times shows a tendency to become mechanical. Once accepted as a principle, it becomes a product, not of poetical enthusiasm only, but of subtle reasoning as well, and as such it grows to be a parasite clinging to thought, causing it to degenerate" (ibid., 207).

treasury are relegated to the background. Negative particulars have little chance against the schema which the
image imposes on its referent. A good metaphor thus
functions like an icon in ordering one's notion of its prototype. And, in addition, the employment of metaphor,
as this case illustrates, may have the additional effect of
activating the attitudes that might accrue to thought
about the vehicle.[55] So one finds indulgences awarded as
lottery prizes, put up for bid, and dispensed as payment
for necessary services—all this complete with the most
minutely worked out legal regulation. In sum, a figure of
speech imposes the alien form of contractual obligation
upon a transcendent relationship.[56]

What has become of the character and works of the
saints and of Christ? What of those historical persons and
their acts the merits of which have been deposited in the
treasury? All particular beauties and virtues are lost, individual pathos and pain forgotten as attention shifts
from history to their meaning as counters in the larger

55. On the way this process operates see Max Black, "Metaphor," *Proceedings of the Aristotelian Society* 55 (1954–55): 273–94.

56. Similar processes may be observed elsewhere during the
Renaissance. For example, when Raymond Sebonde sets out to
describe the number and condition of the angels in his *Natural
Theology*, a metaphor of correspondence robs the angelic reality
of any sort of mysteriousness. Sebonde's reasoning allows the
vehicle or symbol to order its tenor or referent completely; because there is a certain order in the state and the Church, there
must be a similar marshaling among the angels. See the selec-
tions from Sebonde in E. M. W. Tillyard, *Shakespeare's History
Plays* (1944; rpt. New York: Macmillan, 1962), 24–25. Paul de
Man makes some penetrating remarks on this sort of use of metaphor in "The Timid God: A Reading of Rousseau's 'Profession
de foi du vicaire savoyard,' " *Georgia Review* 29 (1975): 551.

total schema. The general formulation—deeds of merit— has subsumed their particular realities; or, to put it another way, theme has overridden dramatic action.[57] One of the most exciting things about the Elizabethan period is the way attention to the particulars of the self and its actions—social, historical, and psychological elements— begins seriously to challenge the predominant tendency of medieval thought, which made these dimensions of reality subservient to timeless, universal principles.[58] This shift of attention is not a uniform development, of course, but its presence in the late sixteenth century makes for a particularly powerful tension between various forms of Neoplatonic idealism and newer, essentially iconoclastic ways of approaching history and character.

III

Sidney's *Apology* argues for the superiority of the poet over the historian on the basis of the poet's license to be "liberal" of a "perfect pattern," while the historian is "bound to tell things as things were."[59] So the poet is,

57. The point is precisely that argued by Gregory of Tours, who maintains that it is more proper to speak of the life of the saints than of their individual lives; see David L. Jeffrey, "English Saints' Plays," in *Medieval Drama*, ed. Neville Denny (London: Edward Arnold, 1973), 72. Compare Alan C. Dessen's treatment of violence in *King Lear* in his "The Logic of Elizabethan Stage Violence," *Renaissance Drama* 9 (1978): 60.

58. See Joseph Anthony Mazzeo, *Renaissance and Revolution* (New York: Random House, 1965), 38. F. J. Levy discusses the adoption of historical techniques to the uses of theological polemic during the English Reformation in his *Tudor Historical Thought* (San Marino, Calif.: Huntington Library, 1967), esp. 95.

59. *An Apology for Poetry*, ed. Forrest G. Robinson (New York: Bobbs-Merrill, 1970), 32.

according to Sidney, both free to teach the ways of virtue and the pitfalls of vice and able, as the historian is not, to pattern the actions he records in accordance with his purposes. Sidney's notion of the historian's limitations appears rather remarkable when one considers the claims contemporary historians could make for their discipline. If one examines the prefaces of works such as John Brand's translations of *Quintus Curtius* (1553), or Henry North's *Plutarch* (1579), or the title page of Henry Bynneman's translation of Appian on the Roman Wars (1578), one finds evidence to support the contention of F. P. Wilson that these sixteenth-century writers of history believed the virtue of history lay in its providing examples that enabled the reader "to compare things past with things present and gather easily what is to be followed and what to be eschewed."[60] Despite the evidence that suggests a sense of purpose shared with Sidney's ideal poet, however, there is a particular sense in which Sidney's contrast is useful. During this period, the idea of history is undergoing the first steps of a subtle evolution of emphasis—an evolution with profound implication for the study of attitudes toward likeness.

Trevisa's translation of Higden's *Polychronicon* (1482) contains a "Prohyme" that differentiates history from the fables of poets; but, as Lily B. Campbell points out, it also parallels history of a secular kind with the Golden Legend and its exemplary stories of holy saints.[61] Within the work itself, one finds admissions that some of the accounts recorded might be untrue as records of fact, but

60. F. P. Wilson, *Shakespearian and Other Studies*, ed. Helen Gardner (Oxford: Clarendon Press, 1969), 5.

61. Lily B. Campbell, *Shakespeare's Histories* (San Marino, Calif.: Huntington Library, 1947), 55–80.

their inclusion is justified because they provide lively examples of virtue and vice.[62] If not truly factual, such episodes are true in their reflection of the *pattern* of divine Providence. Between the time of the *Polychronicon* and that of Sidney's *Apology*, several histories are written that, while still looking to history as a source of examples, challenge such an attitude to historical fact.

In part the challenge to previous modes of history writing is spurred by the Protestant attempt to undermine papal legend, but the challenge is too pervasive to be characterized wholly as so narrowly partisan in intention.[63] Melchior Cano, a Catholic bishop, also challenges prevailing opinion, for example. In Book 2 of his *De Locis Theologicis* (1550), Cano insists that theology itself cannot be separated from considerations of historical fact. Despite their congruence to pattern, even ecclesiastical traditions must come in for critical scrutiny. He points out errors of fact in Philo, Sozomenus, and Eusebius, and goes on to generalize: "Among ecclesiastics, there is not one who can be taken as a thoroughly trustworthy [*probabilis*] historian."[64] If theology and ecclesiastical tradition were not above the demand for historical verity, it is not surprising to find attacks on venerable national myths being written in the same period. Polydore Vergil's *Anglia Historica* (1534) occasioned a great outcry when it exposed as fraudulent such popular fables as the descent of the

62. See the Preface to *Polychronicon Ranulphi Higden*, ed. Churchill Babington (London: Longman, Green, 1865), 17, 19.

63. Cf. Campbell on the Reformation's special pleading.

64. Cano is quoted in G. G. Coulton, *Art and Reformation* (Oxford: Basil Blackwell, 1928), 399.

British from Trojan Brutus, the prowess of Arthur, and the prophecies of Merlin.[65]

The kind of truth these historians demand in their accounts is markedly different from that which other chroniclers had set out to provide. Ideally, Cano and Polydore Vergil would not sacrifice the evidence of negative particulars or the qualifications that might arise from historical context in pursuit of some larger, timeless formulation. Not that they would deny the exemplary nature of a recorded event, but they would make matters of factuality and context primary, quite contrary to the practice of many who valued emblematic pattern over all.[66]

Joseph Mazzeo claims that "for the medieval scholar, the works of the past lived in an eternal present and, whenever the text seemed remote, the solution to difficulties of interpretation did not lie in historical or philological data but in an act of allegorical exegesis."[67] So, for example, Aquinas approaches Aristotle's *Politics* as a "statement of essentially timeless propositions," but Mazzeo's ideal Renaissance scholar comes to the same

65. On the lengthy battle that raged over Vergil until well into the seventeenth century see Glynne Wickham, *Early English Stages* (London: Routledge and Kegan Paul, 1959–63), 2, pt. 1: 26–28. As F. Smith Fussner observes, "In science, in religion, in politics, as well as in history and philosophy, all kinds of authorities were coming under attack in the sixteenth century" (*The Historical Revolution* [New York: Columbia University Press, 1962], 239).

66. All through the seventeenth century, emblem writers like Pere Menestier were capable of arguing that "Les figures de l'histoire prophane et de la fable même peuvent servir à faire des emblèmes sacrez." See Seznec, *Survival of the Pagan Gods*, 274.

67. Mazzeo, *Renaissance and Revolution*, 38.

work with a concern for the particulars of historical context and political experience that inform it.[68] In effect, what had seemed to the medieval thinker mere distracting contingency began, during the Renaissance, to acquire an importance, a voice of its own. For many, truth is in time, and accounts of that truth must therefore face new questions. Not just timeless propositions, or meaning, but the actual circumstances of an occurrence become primary matters of concern.

Something of this same historical attitude seems to have been shared by the author of one of the very earliest surviving English attacks on drama. In this particular case, it is not the fact of "licness" per se that offends the polemicist, but the specifically unhistorical nature of the dramatic image:

First thai gabben on God that alle men may se
When thai hangen him on hegh on a grene tre,
With leves and wit blossemes that bright are of ble,
That was never Goddes Son by my leute.[69]

Seemingly unable to concentrate his attention on the transcendent referent, the universal meaning the event might be said to symbolize, the observer focuses on the features of the enactment and finds them wanting. Instead of representing a Christ hung on a cross in some realistically convincing manner, the crucifixion scene appears to have been intended symbolically. Perhaps the green tree and the "wit blossemes" were intended as iconic embodiments of the new life to come as a result of the crucifixion, but the polemicist, unlike a medieval ex-

68. Ibid.
69. Cited in Jeffrey, "English Saints' Plays," 71, where the polemicist's "historical" attitude is also discussed.

egete, shows no attraction to this easily available atemporal meaning because he cannot overlook the scene's violation of temporal fact, the mere "was."[70]

Similar tensions between pattern or meaning and factual particulars are also alive in the consideration of character during the sixteenth century. The neoclassical *Directions for Speech and Style* of John Hoskins exemplifies the majority position. Under the heading, "Illustration," Hoskins prescribes the proper method of depicting a character:

> He that will truly set down a man in a figured story must first learn truly to set down a humor, a passion, a virtue, a vice, and therein keeping decent proportion add but names and knit together the accidents and encounters.[71]

Hoskins praises Sidney for having followed this course, which he attributes to Aristotle's *Rhetoric* and Theophrastus's *Imagines*, and he is quite specific about the virtues of Sidney's *Arcadia*:

> But to our purpose—what personages and affections are set forth in *Arcadia*. For man: pleasant idle retiredness in King Basilius, and the dangerous end of it; unfortunate valor in Plangus; courteous valor in Anaxius; hospitality in Kalander.[72]

From this point of view, then, Sidney's characters are, at

70. The symbolic meaning of the flower-decked cross seems to be indicated in such references as the mention in the fifteenth-century morality play *The Castle of Perseverance* of "a rose that on rode was rent" (line 2,220).

71. John Hoskins, *Directions for Speech and Style*, ed. H. H. Hudson (Princeton: Princeton University Press, 1935), 41.

72. Ibid., 42.

best, figures in a figured story, consistent icons that conform decorously to the ideas they embody.

It is just such iconic characterization that Montaigne rejects in his essays. Allowing those who have chosen to depict the self as a "lively image" of an idea to have their say, he uncovers manifold contradictions:

> Those which exercise themselves in controuling humane actions, finde no such let in any one part, as to peece them together, and bring them to one same lustre: For, they commonly contradict one another so strangely, as it seemeth impossible they should be parcels of one Warehouse. Young *Marius* is sometimes found to be the sonne of *Mars*, and other times the childe of *Venus*. Pope Boniface the Eight, is reported to have entred into his charge, as a Fox; to have carried himselfe therein, as a Lion; and to have died like a dog. And who would thinke it was *Nero*, that lively image of cruelty, who being required to signe (as the custome was) the sentence of a criminall offendor, that had beene condemned to die, that ever he should answer Oh would to God I could never have written! So neare was his heart grieved to doome a man to death. The world is so full of such examples, that every man may store himselfe; and I wonder to see men of understanding trouble themselves with sorting these parcels: Sithence (me seemeth) irresolution is the most apparent and common vice of our nature.[73]

Instead of considering a man aptly characterized by assimilating him to any one pattern—Marius embodying qualities of Mars or Venus, Boniface the human icon of

73. *The Essays of Montaigne* (New York: Modern Library, 1933), 292.

various bestialities, Nero the incarnation of cruelty—
Montaigne would have one view the self as "shapeless
and diverse."[74]

The self for Montaigne, in other words, is a transcendent reality that, like the God of the iconoclasts, cannot
be bound to an image. And the procedure he uses as a
means to break the hold of iconic modes of thought about
the self follows a course familiar to historical and religious
iconoclasts in their own wars against idols. Montaigne
writes of a young woman who wounded herself in order
to escape the attacks of a rapist. By "her earnest speeches,
resolute countenance, and gored blood (a true testimony
of her chaste vertue) she might appeare to be the lively
patterne of another *Lucrece*," but appearances were de-
ceiving. "Both before that time, and afterward," he
writes, "she had beene enjoyed of others upon easier
composition."[75] And in the case of a courageous young
warrior, Montaigne cautions:

> He whom you saw yesterday so boldly-venturous,
> wonder not if you see him a dastardly meacocke to
> morrow next: for either anger or necessitie, company
> or wine, a sudden fury or the clang of a trumpet,
> might rowze-up his heart, and stir up his courage.

In both instances, the lesson is that no sudden moment is
revelatory of the essential character of the actor, or even
meaningful apart from the particular circumstances that
form its full context. "Circumstances," Montaigne insists, guide actions, and, "Therefore it is no marvell if by
other contrary circumstances" the warrior or virgin were

74. Ibid., 298.   75. Ibid., 294.

to become "a craven or change copy."[76] Montaigne couples his emphases on temporal and circumstantial contexts when he observes that, in order to judge a person properly, "We must a long time follow, and very curiously marke his steps."[77] This conception of character, unlike Sidney's, does not arise in an aesthetic context, but any account of character in Shakespearean drama ignores it only with peril.

Shakespeare's plays are informed by the tensions that vex considerations of history and character during the Elizabethan period. Critics such as Fleischer and Rose are correct when they point out moments when the plays appear to order their dramatic action into tableaux or to treat their characters as images of some universal, timeless significance. And critics like Brooke are correct when they point to naturalistic elements alongside the iconic. But most interesting to me is the way the iconic elements of the play are used seemingly to offer the audience likenesses for some theme (the storm, Cassius tells us, is like Caesar's tyranny) and then are so consistently complicated (the storm is also like the violence of civil uprising, Cassius adds) or even rejected (the storm, Cicero cautions, may be interpreted as men wish) that one is forced to wonder what is going on. Perhaps such likenesses are

76. Ibid., 295. For a parallel concern with circumstances in post-Reformation historiography, compare Arthur B. Ferguson, "Circumstances and the Sense of History in Tudor England," in *Medieval and Renaissance Studies*, ed. John M. Headley (Chapel Hill: University of North Carolina Press, 1968). It is true that Shakespeare has Warwick speak of a history in a man's life (*Henry IV*, Part 2, 3.1.83–89) that will serve to predict the future, but this argument is contradicted by the antics of Hal himself, who is not what he was.

77. Ibid., 297.

offered as enticing bait. Once one has been swallowed, another is proffered, and it takes time to realize that the taste is not as satisfying as one had thought it would be. Given enough such disappointed expectations, one may not be so quick to overlook the particulars of the offering or the temporal context in which it is offered. In time, one might even come to agree with Bacon that whatever the mind "seizes and dwells upon with peculiar satisfaction is to be held in suspicion"—an observation that anyone of iconoclastic sympathies would find compelling.[78]

78. *The Works of Francis Bacon*, ed. James Spedding, Robert Leslie Ellis, and Douglas Denon Heath (1860; rpt. Stuttgart: Frommann Verlag, 1962), 4: 60. Stanley E. Fish discusses the Baconian therapeutic in his *Self-Consuming Artifacts* (Berkeley and Los Angeles: University of California Press, 1972).

2

The "image bound":

ICON AND ICONOCLASM
IN *Lucrece* AND *Henry V*

The notion of Shakespearean art as a series of varied, but related, "images" of internal conceptual unities would seem easiest to demonstrate in such works as the narrative poem *The Rape of Lucrece* or in the partially narrated history play *Henry V*. Both poem and play are patterned by obvious controlling metaphors: in *Lucrece* the visual image of Troy's betrayal and violation repeats the tragedy of the protagonist, while in *Henry V* the verbal image of the bee's commonwealth clearly images the play's history of contrary wills brought to one purpose.[1] Besides their use of narrative commentary and their obvious patterning, features both works share with standard allegory, the two also employ emblematic staging—whether physical or, in the case of the poem, imagined—to establish abstract meanings for characters and their actions.[2] Fur-

1. On the fallen city image as a form of love's castle see D. C. Allen, "Some Observations on *The Rape of Lucrece*," *Shakespeare Survey* 15 (1962): 89–98; on the hive in *Henry V* see Andrew Gurr, "*Henry V* and the Bee's Commonwealth," *Shakespeare Survey* 30 (1977): 61–72.

2. On "ritual form" in *Henry V* see O. B. Hardison's remarks in *Christian Rite and Christian Drama in the Middle Ages* (Baltimore:

thermore, since the integrity of this underlying meaning depends on the poet's modification of preexisting story or history, the two works offer useful examples of those imaginative techniques for the making of many into one that Coleridge found so Shakespearean, and that his disciples, the imagery critics, have continued to find important.

At the same time, however, the two works also exhibit incongruities in their very manifestations of unity, and they thereby suggest troubles to come in the later works. In *Lucrece* disunity is more suggested than realized, appearing as lines of stress in an otherwise dominant coherence. In *Henry V* the flaws are more insistent, like the wretches in Henry's prison managing to make their existence felt even as the play seems bent on directing attention to the "Mirror of all Christian Kings" and, through him, to the noble virtues for which he is the "pattern" or living icon. Coming when it does, in the period just preceding the composition of the great tragedies, *Henry V* serves as a warning far more troubling than the confusions and difficulties of earlier plays such as *Titus Andronicus*; for in the case of *Henry V*, we encounter a

---

Johns Hopkins University Press, 1965), 290–91. Angus Fletcher finds Shakespeare's histories generally "most monumental"; certainly, *Henry V*'s rigidity, isolation, and hypersymmetry bring it close to the formal qualities of allegory (see Fletcher, *Allegory* [Ithaca: Cornell University Press, 1964], 362). Geoffrey Bullough's remarks on *Lucrece* in his *Narrative and Dramatic Sources of Shakespeare* (New York: Columbia University Press, 1957–73) describe the poem as a "ritualistic stylization," enforcing the oppositions of "virtue and vice, innocence and lust, hospitality and betrayal" (1:180).

drama that seems conscious, even deliberate in its employment of incongruity and dissonance.

I

From the poem's first mention of "Lust-breathed Tarquin" (3) and "Lucrece, the chaste" (7), the "devil" and the "earthly saint" seem to be firmly fixed in a tightly patterned allegorical image of "Drunken desire" (703) violating "the picture of pure piety" (542).[3] This fact appears to be confirmed by a number of the poem's features. Its language, for example, often suggests morality play figures; so Tarquin:

My part is youth, and beats these from the stage.
Desire my pilot is, beauty my prize.

(278–79)

Its events frequently serve as obvious emblems for spiritual or psychological realities: Lucrece's tokens warn Tarquin away from her (304–22), while the desire in his "hot heart" ignites the torch that lights his way to her (313–15). In fact, the whole poem consists of a series of patterned repetitions: the betrayal and fall of Lucrece's personal Troy (1,547); the fall of the city of Troy itself in the painted account of Sinon's treachery; the violation of Tarquin's own reason by the rude lust of his "rebel will" (625); and the fall of Tarquin's Roman rule. Nevertheless, for all its abstract characterization, allegorical language, emblematic action, and structuring parallels between different orders of reality, the poem still threatens to violate its own unities.

The chief device by which the unity of the poem is

3. Even Lucrece's groom becomes a figure—"this pattern of the worn-out age" (line 1,350).

made manifest is the visual representation of Troy and its fall. In the painting, the various actions, themes, and characters of Lucrece's story find their images. Like some painted version of the Shakespearean subplot, the image of Troy's betrayal presents an elaborate reflection of the main plot, giving the poet a chance to add emphasis and universality and providing the protagonist with an opportunity to find clarification for her own experience.

Lucrece turns to the visual image, we are told, because she seeks in it "means to mourn some new way" (1,365), but her quest represents more than a search for novelty—either on her part or on the part of the poet. She approaches the painting in desperation, hoping to find in its features an escape from the inadequacies of words. Words have failed her, the poem tells us, first, because they are only "helpless smoke," unprofitable, arbitrary abstractions unable to embody immediately the things to which they refer.[4] This weakness is expressed by their fitness for the lowly work of "mediators" for "trembling clients" (1,020)—i.e., those who fear to express their desires or fears directly and immediately. Second, because language is a temporal medium, it is said to be subject to certain weaknesses: both the demands of syntax and the pressures of stylistic usage preclude saying *one thing* clearly, leading one instead into delay and confusion as words themselves prove insubordinate.

Conceit and grief an eager combat fight,
What wit sets down is blotted straight with will:
This is too curious-good, this blunt and ill.

4. Groans are only "wasting monuments" of the true "lasting moans" to which they refer (798). On the weakness of words see also lines 1,040–43.

Much like a press of people at a door,
Throng her inventions, which shall go before.
(1,298–1,302)

Finally, words are said to provide inferior means to arouse sympathy because they cannot convey the *totality* of a feeling or experience:

'Tis but a part of sorrow that we hear:
Deep sounds make lesser noise than shallow fords,
And sorrow ebbs, being blown with wind of words.
(1,328–30)

By contrast with its repeated references to the weaknesses of words, the poem acclaims the power of the visual image, citing (even before the encounter with the artistic representation of Troy) two major Christian defenses.[5] Using the ancient argument based on the idea of the visual image as the *liber laicorum*, the universal book accessible to all regardless of inexperience or ignorance, Lucrece makes a high claim for the image of perceptual experience:

Yea, the illiterate that know not how
To cipher what is writ in learned books,
Will quote my loathsome trespass in my looks.
(810–12)

Furthermore, again echoing Christian apologetics, the narrator argues that the image can move more profoundly than words:

To see sad sights moves more than hear them told.
(1,324)

5. For a fuller account of the orthodox defense, see chapter 1 above.

The "image bound"

The church had based its use of this argument on an Aristotelian hierarchy of the senses, but the poem rests its claim instead on a particular conception of the image itself. In direct contrast to the unruliness and insubordination associated with the ineffectuality of verbal communication, the visual image is said to be supremely capable of unity, of subordinating every part of itself to a single underlying purpose:

> For then the eye interprets to the ear
> The heavy motion that it doth behold
> When every part a part of woe doth bear.
>
> (1,325–27)

Every "part" bears its part of the theme of woe—each element serving as a related, but varied, image for the same thing. Thus, the poem emphasizes the potential of the visual image to correct the mediacy, temporality, and confusions inherent in merely verbal communication. However, the extent to which the poem privileges the visual over the verbal is only fully illustrated in Lucrece's experience with the painting of Troy. Her response to this visual image enacts the final and most crucial tenet of the orthodox Christian defense, but it also lapses momentarily into a significant violation of it.

In the image of Troy, Lucrece's desire to mourn finds the satisfaction denied by mere words. In contrast to the discursiveness and mediacy of language, the visual image of Troy is in every way "so compact, so kind" (1,423). Both illusionistic and schematic, the "conceit deceitful" does everything—and does it at once. *Temporally*, this image, like any number of Elizabethan narrative paintings, contains an entire chronicle history.[6] In defiance of modern ideas of aesthetic limitation, effects are already present with their causes—"here Priam dies," while elsewhere he appears listening to the first deceptive words that are the remote cause of that doleful end (1,548). *Thematically*, the image is unified by the one sad truth of mutability to which its "thousand lamentable objects" (1,373) refer. So, for example, against all naturalistic probability, even the disembodied eyes visible through the chinks in Troy's walls convey sadness (1,383), while the joy of the Trojan mothers watching their warrior sons go forth to battle betrays through an "odd action" their "heavy fear" (1,435). Even landscape repeats the theme of sad destruction as it battles with itself (1,438). Finally, in its *characterization*, the visual image of Troy compactly renders the essential natures of its various figures by presenting "signs" (1,419) of their characters. "Physiognomy" tells all in the cases of Ajax and Ulysses—"the face of either cipher'd either's heart" (1,396)—the one blunt rage and rigor, the other deep regard and government. For Nestor one "sober action," a flourish of the hand, conveys his significance as the embodiment of grave oratory (1,403); while in the case of Achilles, a single attribute, the spear, stands for his unseen warlike essence (1,424–28).[7]

6. R. M. Frye's article, "Ways of Seeing in Shakespearean Drama and Elizabethan Painting," *Shakespeare Quarterly* 31 (1980): 323–42, discusses the genre of Elizabethan narrative painting.

7. Here my reading differs from that of S. Clark Hulse in "'A Piece of Skillful Painting' in Shakespeare's *Lucrece*," *Shakespeare Survey* 31 (1978): 13–22. Hulse sees the painting as related to a passage in Philostratus's *Eikones* concerned with an illusionistic rendering of a battle scene. I see the painting of Achilles, for

Ultimately, however, the image has more to offer Lucrece than a way to circumvent the inadequacies of the verbal because, as the poem suggests, the power of the image lies in a capacity of a far higher order—a capacity illustrated through the figure of Hecuba. The image of Hecuba, unlike that of Achilles or Priam, is not merely expressive of her own limited role in the history of Troy, for in her "all distress is stell'ed" (1,444). Every one of the figures exhibits some aspect of Troy's lamentable sorrows, but Hecuba, in turn, carries it "all" within her— "Time's ruin, beauty's wreck, and grim care's reign" (1,451). More than an image of a human victim of a single historical concurrence of events, the painting of Hecuba is the icon wherein this broadly abstract essence—the sorrow of mutability—is fixed and "stell'd"; in its totality "anatomiz'd." Thus, it is fitting that Lucrece should choose to shape her own individual sorrows to the pattern of the beldam's universal Woe. Yet the relationship between such an icon or pattern and its spiritual content and the further relationship of the audience to them gives rise to problems for the poem, as indeed similar issues had once created problems for the Church.

When Lucrece submits herself to Hecuba's pattern of sorrow, she is responding to something that she had come looking for in the first place; coming to find, she finds the satisfaction she seeks.[8] However, her encounter

---

instance, not as "anti-Platonic" illusionism, but as self-consciously iconic. The spear stands not just for the presence of any soldier, but for Achilles; by its presence the unseen warlike essence of Achilles is made recognizable.

8. The self-validating nature of this encounter is explicit at 1,493–98. Cf. Theseus on imagination and emotion in *A*

with the image of Sinon is more complex. True, Sinon is like Hecuba in existing outside the painting as a conventional figure for an idea—in his case, deceit. Yet this particular painting apparently belies Sinon's conventional significance. Unlike the other figures in the painting, Sinon's image does not seem to convey immediately what he is and means. The appearance of "Patience," suffering, and humility, the "signs of truth" that he exhibits, contradict the nature of the "mind so ill" (1,530) that he should, according to tradition, possess:

Such signs of truth in his plain face she spied,
That she concludes the picture was belied.
(1,532–33)

Momentarily deceived by these signs, Lucrece soon is brought to a recognition of the truth by an awakening of her memory:

"It cannot be," quoth she, "that so much guile,"—
She would have said,—"can lurk in such a look."
But Tarquin's shape came in her mind the while,
And from her tongue "can lurk" from "cannot" took:
"It cannot be" she in that sense forsook,
And turn'd it thus: "It cannot be, I find,
But such a face should bear a wicked mind."
(1,534–40)

That the visual image has special power to awaken memory is an assertion current from the time of Maximus of

---

Midsummer Night's Dream, 5.1.18–22; also Anthony Munday's remarks on the sins of spectators at plays in *A Second and Third Blast* (London, 1580), 96.

84

Tyre to that of the Renaissance writers on the art of memory.[9] But beyond simple recollection—Sinon's facial features recalling those of Tarquin—the visual image is here depicted as leading to a higher, more universal level of insight: "It cannot be," Lucrece discovers, "But such a face should bear a wicked mind." This universal principle resolves the problem posed by the seeming incongruity between Sinon's conventional meaning as an "image bound" to the essence of deceit and the plain "signs of truth" that his figure exhibits in the painting. Despite appearances, the painter has not in fact chosen to portray Sinon as an individual momentarily in the throes of self-division; rather than signs of a self-contradictory character momentarily penetrated by sympathy for the remorse and suffering of his victims, Sinon's signs of truth may be subsumed under the treachery he conventionally embodies.

In taking the image of Sinon for the icon of deceit and in assuming that *all* such faces must inevitably mean that a "wicked mind" lurks beneath them, Lucrece has performed well as an audience for the painting. As the orthodox defenses had long maintained, the supreme value that finally makes the visual image worth preserving, in spite of its accompanying risks, lies not in its clarity of expression, emotive power, or recollective utility, but rather in its capacity to communicate universal insights.[10] In her actions immediately subsequent to this moment, Lucrece demonstrates, however, just the sort of confusion that this allegorical defense of the image had been designed to counter:

9. See chapter 1 above.   10. See chapter 1 above.

She tears the senseless Sinon with her nails,
Comparing him to that unhappy guest
Whose deed hath made herself herself detest.
                    (1,563–66)

The visual image carries with it the dangerous suggestion of a real physical connection, an aura of real presence that threatens to override any precise intellectual differentiation between the material symbol and the conceptual signified. Within the church, no amount of insistence upon the image-prototype distinction, no repeated insistence on allegorical interpretation rather than physical veneration, no amount of reliance on schematic abstraction in the actual production of images ever quite eradicated the potential for error such as Lucrece here exhibits. Outside the church, the various attacks on the painted likenesses of Elizabeth suggest a similar confusion about the relationship of image to prototype. Despite the fact that surviving images of Elizabeth seem to our eyes merely schematic figures illustrative of abstract principles, the accounts of their being attacked with poisoned implements illustrate just how deep such confusions about the relation of image and prototype could run. A similar set of mind would seem to underlie the phenomena of celebrating the presence of royal images and setting banquets for them.[11] Lucrece's fit of passion passes, of course, giving way to smiles at this mistaken attack and occasioning condescension from the narrator (1,567–82). Yet this momentary confusion intersects strikingly with the treatment of images elsewhere in the poem.

11. Roy C. Strong's chapter on the theory of images in his *Portraits of Queen Elizabeth I* (Oxford: Clarendon Press, 1963) is useful on this topic. For use of images to inflict pain see Reginald Scot, *Discouerie of Witchcraft* (London, 1584), 257–59.

Of the poem's several examples of violence directed at imagery, the two most important instances occur at the time of Lucrece's suicide. The act of self-destruction, in which Lucrece shatters the "glass" of her father's own image (1,753–64), paradoxically effects her own assumption into the realm of the symbolic, allowing her blood to be revealed as the physical embodiment of a timeless pattern: "And ever since, as pitying Lucrece' woes, / Corrupted blood some watery token shows" (1,747–48).[12] Nevertheless, despite the fact that the elaborate behavior of her blood objectifies the imagery of pollution running throughout the poem and thereby affirms her suicide as the only means to release her soul from its "polluted prison" (1,726), herein there arises a dilemma. Scarcely has this iconic revelation been completed when Brutus intrudes with an utterly demythologizing reinterpretation of it. Denying the logic of allegory by which Lucrece must die—as Troy, her image, so she, her own Troy, must perish once bereft of her original identity—Brutus passes harsh judgment:

Thy wretched wife mistook the matter so,
To slay herself that should have slain her foe.
(1,826–27)

In providing this rapid alteration of perspectives on its own images, the poem creates a larger analogue for the quick reversal in Lucrece's own reactions to the image of

12. Walter Benjamin offers the following remarks on the corpse and allegory: "Die Allegorisierung der Physis kann nur an der Leiche sich energisch durchsetzen. Und die Personen des Trauerspiels sterben, weil sie nur so, als Leichen in die allegorische Heimat eingehen" (*Ursprung des deutschen Trauerspiels* [Frankfurt: Suhrkamp Verlag, 1963], 246).

Sinon. The narrator may condescend to Lucrece, but what is one to make a poem that at one moment takes its images literally, going so far as to give the verbal symbolism of stain and pollution objective presence in Lucrece's blood, and then quickly turns a chilling skepticism upon its own values? Such a conflict implies the kind of double vision that Nicholas Brooke has described in his discussions of the emblematic and naturalistic modes of the early tragedies; yet the circumstances of this particular instance make it especially problematic.[13] Brutus's refusal to acknowledge the icon before him and his suggestion that Lucrece's suicide is "childish humor" rather than an objective necessity toward which everything within the poem has been pointing represent just the kind of abuse of the image that Tarquin exhibits in his villainy. It is Tarquin, after all, who is the poem's most obvious violator of iconicity.

Although demonstrably capable of perceiving the images that surround him (see 176–82), Tarquin expresses a general rejection of accepted meanings and restrictions—whether conveyed through verbal or visual means:

Who fears a sentence or an old man's saw
Shall by a painted cloth be kept in awe.

(244–45)

13. Nicholas Brooke, *Shakespeare's Early Tragedies* (London: Methuen, 1968). For further relation of *Lucrece* to the tragedies see Harold R. Walley, "*The Rape of Lucrece* and Shakespearean Tragedy," *PMLA* 73 (1961): 480–87; Robert Y. Turner, *Shakespeare's Apprenticeship* (Chicago: University of Chicago Press, 1974), esp. 108–12; and R. Thomas Simone, *Shakespeare and "Lucrece"* (Salzburg: Institut für englische Sprache und Literatur, 1974).

Thus, it is not surprising that the nature of his villainy finds expression—even before his violent attack on the "true type" of the loyal wife (1,048–50)—in the lesser, but still related, blasphemy of his devaluation of the poem's own significant images:

But all these poor forbiddings could not stay him;
He in the worst sense consters their denial.
The doors, the wind, the glove, that did delay him,
He takes for accidental things of trial;
Or as those bars which stop the hourly dial,
Who with a ling'ring stay his course doth let,
Till every minute pays the hour his debt.

(323–29)

Denying these iconic signs their validity as images bound to their prototype, chaste Lucrece, Tarquin takes them as merely arbitrary signifiers—"accidental things" as fit for his own rhetorical figures as for any other significance. From substantial icons, they have been reduced to the status of mere words, weak mediators pliantly adaptable to any sort of self-serving "saw" for which he might wish to use them:

"So, so," quoth he, "these lets attend the time,
Like little frosts that sometime threat the spring,
To add a more rejoicing to the prime,
And give the sneaped birds more cause to sing.
Pain pays the income of each precious thing:
Huge rocks, high winds, strong pirates, shelves and
    sands
The merchant fears ere rich at home he lands."

(330–36)

Now this blatant abuse of the poem's givens could fit within the narrator's larger purposes easily enough: Tarquin's subversive misinterpretations could be seen as exhibiting an instance of the general collapse of hierarchy and order that attends upon the overthrow of reason's sovereignty by the "rebel will." As surely as the outer social order depends upon the inner order obtaining among the individual's faculties, so, too, it had traditionally been thought also to rest upon proper respect for the image and its public significance—this respect being demonstrated in a reverent deference to fixed, universally apprehensible meanings.[14] But in such a context, what is one to make of the similarities between the anti-iconic readings of Brutus and Tarquin? Nor is this all. The poem sets up related difficulties that prove equally resistant to easy solution.

Although generally consistent in observing the formal dictates of allegory, in two instances the poem gives one pause. First of all, there are the lines describing Tarquin's remorse. The description begins appropriately enough, with animated abstractions—"Pure Chastity" rifled and "Lust, the thief" dispirited—and it manages to maintain a series of animal images for the rapist (694–

14. The stars above Troy need its image of them in order to preserve their own stable order (1,525–26). Bishop Stephen Gardiner declares in his letter to Captain Edward Vaughan: "the destruction of images containeth an enterprise to subvert religion and the state of the world with it, and especially the nobility, who by images, set forth and spread abroad, to be read of all people, their lineage and parentage, with remembrance of their state and acts" (*The Letters of Stephen Gardiner*, ed. J. A. Muller [Cambridge: Cambridge University Press, 1933], 272). One thinks of Lady Macbeth, who sees in Duncan's death not Macduff's "great doom's image," but only "the sleeping and the dead," who are "but as pictures. 'Tis the eye of childhood / That fears a painted devil" (2.2.52–53).

700), all good examples of Puttenham's idea of the verbal figure of icon.[15] But amid this thoroughly predictable machinery, there intrude some surprising lines:

O, deeper sin than bottomless conceit
Can comprehand in still imagination!
Drunken desire must vomit his receipt,
Ere he can see his own abomination.
While lust is in his pride no exclamation
Can curb his heat or rein his rash desire,
Till, like a jade, self-will himself doth tire.

And then with lank and lean discolour'd cheek,
With heavy eye, knit brow, and strengthless pace,
Feeble desire, all recreant, poor and meek,
Like to a bankrout beggar wails his case.
The flesh being proud, desire doth fight with grace;
For there it revels; and when that decays,
The guilty rebel for remission prays.

So fares it with this faultful lord of Rome,
Who this accomplishment so hotly chased;
For now against himself he sounds this doom,
That through the length of times he stands disgraced.
Besides, his soul's fair temple is defaced,
To whose weak ruins muster troops of cares,
To ask the spotted princess how she fares.

She says her subjects with foul insurrection
Have batter'd down her consecrated wall,
And by their mortal fault brought in subjection
Her immortality, and made her thrall
To living death and pain perpetual:

15. *The Arte of English Poesie*, ed. Gladys Doidge Willcock and Alice Walker (Cambridge: Cambridge University Press, 1970), 243–44.

Which in her prescience she controlled still,
But her foresight could not forestall their will.

(701–28)

Who would have thought? In following the logic of allegory, the poem has violated some of its own iconic principles. First, there is the claim that some aspects of reality
cannot be caught even in the capacious comprehension
of the "conceit" or image—whether considered as verbal
(1,298) or as visual (1,423)—but can only be fathomed
through temporal experience itself. Oddly enough, the
poem, which elsewhere represents its heroine as being
capable of reaching her moment of insight only through
the painted "conceit deceitful," here claims that conceit,
no matter how "bottomless," cannot comprehend the full
content of experience. The nature of the something that
escapes capture in the image is suggested in the lines that
constitute the rest of this passage.

By recurring to the abstractions of allegorical characterization while making explicit reference to the atempor-
ality of such typing ("through the length of times he
stands disgraced"), the narrator's account seems to be
proclaiming the power of the "still imagination." Tarquin
is clearly being fixed, or re-fixed, as the icon of deceitful
lust, but this capture of the temporal and particular
within the patterning of the eternal and typical quickly
gives rise to strange inversion and oxymoron. Of course
the idea of Tarquin's soul as a "spotted princess," violated
by rebellious "subjects" due to the failure of her foresight, her conceit, does represent an image that fits the
larger patterns of the poem—as one more instance of deceived Virtue's downfall at the hands of ambitious Desire.
Yet the proliferation of oxymora in the lines that follow

indicate the effort with which the poem is struggling to suggest an experience that might lie beyond its own patterns of logic and language. And with the image of the rapist "Bearing away the wound that nothing healeth" (731), the poem threatens to push the paradoxical idea of interpenetration between victim and violator farther than the "still imagination" can comfortably follow:

Ev'n in this thought through the dark night he stealeth,
A captive victor that hath lost in gain,
Bearing away the wound that nothing healeth,
The scar that will despite of cure remain;
Leaving his spoil perplexed in greater pain:
She bears the load of lust he left behind,
And he the burden of a guilty mind.

(729–35)

This image of a captive, violated, and vaginate Tarquin and of a Lucrece burdened with lust, reminiscent of a metaphysical conceit in its audacity, is problematic not because the ideas are difficult intellectually but because the poem has elsewhere been so consistent in rendering Tarquin as the icon of active, ambitious, and deceitful lust, while reserving for Lucrece the image of invaded, violated Virtue. It is the fact that these two clusters of meanings are kept so distinctly separate in their respective iconic agents, without any hint that those agents might be more humanly naturalistic characters, in whom traits might be mixed and mingled, that makes this sudden interpenetration so troubling. This interchange is not at all like the case of the fusion of the two birds in "The Phoenix and the Turtle," because the loving merger of the two agents in that poem remains under the control of conventional formulae—as the title of the collection in which the poem was first published puts it, "Allegorically shadowing the truth of Love." By contrast, *Lucrece*, momentarily and from within its own heavily allegorical structure, seems to be reaching toward something else, a something else suggested in the striking difference between the poem's treatment of Tarquin and Lucrece's treatment of Sinon.

The deceit for which Sinon is an eternal icon, outside any particular representation of Trojan history, momentarily conflicts with the "signs of truth" that Lucrece perceives in his image. However, Lucrece quickly realizes that these signs are completely conformable, in fact essential, to the pattern of deceit, all deceit. Tautology finally rules: deceit is a deceiver, equally itself even in the moments when it looks like its opposite. When, however, the deceitful lust for which Tarquin functions as a timeless icon momentarily conflicts with the signs of passivity and violation the poem shows us, these signs, instead of being easily reduced to elements in a single, unified pattern of lust, open the notion of lustfulness to different perspectives. Rather than being itself and only itself—lust being lustful, always and everywhere—lust is shown to be a moment in a temporal history that concludes in captive suffering, guilt, wounds, and remorse. Furthermore, the public, legal, conventional schematization of the crime as an aggressive violation of the innocent is not totally adequate to the matter. In truth, the criminal rapist is wounded in his transgressions and violated for his iniquity. Thus lust is revealed as an act that gives way—in time—to its own opposite, and so does its agent. Paradoxically and contrary to the iconic mode of the poem, lust and its image turn out to have a history fraught with difference and division.

The difference between Shakespeare's quasi-historical treatment of Tarquin and Lucrece's tautological treatment of Sinon suggests something of the difference between an art that values the image as an icon or pure fixation of some prototypal meaning and an art that takes temporal existence more seriously, immersing its characters and elements in the demands of time. Still, a further distinction needs to be made, a distinction that emerges from the poem's treatment of Lucrece. Shakespeare's treatment of the elements of Lucrece's physiognomy betrays a disunity within the poem, a disunity that will help to mark off the iconoclasm of Shakespearean drama from the sometimes contrary harmonies of allegory itself.

The flexibility of allegory allows for differing perspectives on its content and may provide a home for paradox and temporal development.[16] Historically, however, it has been a fundamental tenet of allegorical exegesis to search for underlying unities of value or concept wherever surface incongruities appear.[17] The allegorical interpreter should discover, as does Lucrece with the painting of Sinon, an underlying sense in which the seeming difficulties can be reconciled. Instead of finding multiple Sinons—patient, humble, remorseful—within Sinon, as might be possible in a historically or naturalistically conceived figure, Lucrece, quite properly, finds only various aspects of one essential deceit. Similarly, in the case of Tarquin, even though the icon of lustful deceit has been expanded into a figure whose emotions and actions do elicit a wider range of interpretations, those actions and emotions are ultimately reconcilable with the idea of

16. I think especially of Spenser.

17. On incongruity and higher unity see Michael Murrin, *The Veil of Allegory* (Chicago: University of Chicago Press, 1969).

lust's progress from inception to negation. Tarquin remains understandable, even though more complex than Sinon, as the embodiment of a unifying concept. Yet in its treatment of its own image of virtue, the poem threatens violence in a way that warns one of the difficulties the plays will add to the minor problems created by the poem's treatment of Tarquin.

The initial, highly abstract description of the virtuous Lucrece is notoriously difficult to follow:

When at Collatium this false lord arrived,
Well was he welcom'd by the Roman dame,
Within whose face beauty and virtue strived
Which of them both should underprop her fame.
When virtue bragg'd, beauty would blush for shame;
When beauty boasted blushes, in despite
Virtue would stain that o'er with silver white.

But beauty in that white entituled
From Venus' doves, doth challenge that fair field;
Then virtue claims from beauty beauty's red,
Which virtue gave the golden age to gild
Their silver cheeks, and call'd it then their shield;
Teaching them thus to use it in the fight,
When shame assail'd, the red should fence the white.

This heraldry in Lucrece' face was seen,
Argu'd by beauty's red and virtue's white;
Of either's colour was the other queen,
Proving from world's minority their right.
Yet their ambition makes them still to fight;
The sov'reignty of either being so great,
That oft they interchange each other's seat.
                                                    (50–70)

It is scarcely a matter of what she *looks* like; one learns nothing of her hair, eyes, or other features, nor can one be certain whether the colors that traverse her face are actually momentary blushes or her usual complexion. The poem provides heraldic signs—beauty's red and virtue's white—instead of naturalistic features, but their interaction with each other renders these signs very difficult to interpret.[18] The conventional connections between signifier and signified have been made confusing: beauty, it turns out, is at times in white "entituled," while virtue sometimes "claims" beauty's red for its own—"oft they interchange each other's seat."

This uncharacteristic behavior becomes truly disconcerting when seen in relation to the poem's dominant patterns. The usurpation of each other's power and dominion, born, the poem claims, of their "ambition," connects the red and white to the poem's underlying allegorical sense in a disturbing way, for it is Tarquin's rape of Lucrece, after all, that constitutes the poem's dominant image of ambitious usurpation. The sight of Lucrece

in Tarquin new ambition bred;
Who like a foul usurper went about,
From this fair throne to heave the owner out.
(411–13)

The problem is somewhat like that posed for us by Tarquin's momentary inclusion in the pattern of violated passivity, yet it remains far more resistant to resolution.

One can imagine the intention to cast Tarquin's lust as a violation of his soul's inherent nobility, but one balks at the idea that Lucrece ought to be characterized as con-

18. The difficulties of this passage have been pointed out by Coppélia Kahn in her "The Rape of Shakespeare's *Lucrece*," *Shakespeare Studies* 9 (1976): 45–72.

taminated by self-division related in any way to the sinful dissension in Tarquin. To consider her features as truly signifying the pride, ambition, and anarchic contention they iconically enact would be to implicate Lucrece in her own violation. And that would mean that the poem itself plays the role of Tarquin—denying the obvious signifiers of the poem their accepted signification (Lucrece = purity, chastity, and wifely honor), and, in the face of the narrator's own pronouncements, awarding them entirely new meanings. Such suspicions about the poem are not unprecedented; and following the pattern suggested by the identification of her story with the plight of Troy might lead one to legitimate suspicions about a possible Helen within her "walls."[19] After all, the poem itself rather oddly chooses to follow the Dictys manuscript in treating the fall of Troy as a result of its sovereign's own lack of control over his subjects: "Had doting Priam check'd his son's desire, / Troy had been bright with fame and not with fire" (1,490–91).[20]

Such a rude violation of its own given meanings and explicit values would make the poem neither paradoxical nor polysemous in a manner acceptable to traditional notions of allegory; rather, it would be iconoclastic, since it would both have created a sense of coherence and signif-

19. Roy W. Battenhouse's chapter on *Lucrece* in *Shakespearean Tragedy: Its Art and Christian Premises* (Bloomington: Indiana University Press, 1969) sees Lucrece's sweaty palms as a dangerous sign. The problem occurs elsewhere in the poem; e.g., Hecuba's "blue blood changed to black" (1,454) shares with Lucrece's own blood the color of moral stain (1,743–50).

20. On the Dictys manuscript see Robert Kimbrough, *Shakespeare's "Troilus and Cressida" and its Setting* (Cambridge, Mass.: Harvard University Press, 1964), 31.

icance and willfully violated it. That the evidence has not been compelling enough to initiate much critical questioning of Lucrece's status as a "virtuous monument" does not lessen the poem's usefulness as an introduction to the difficulties of the plays. Neither the poem nor the plays are finally like the painting of Troy. Where the "conceit deceitful" of painted Troy is represented to us as an icon "so compact, so kind," clearly unified in theme, consistent in characterization, and emblematic in action, the poet's own work relies on an *admittedly* untrustworthy, mediate discourse to present an action capable of diverse interpretations, performed by characters who are themselves subject to change and reinterpretation. And yet all this does not go without saying, for the poem does seem in large part to suggest, to aspire to the contrary virtues of an iconic, visual aesthetic: unity, subordination, emotive power, and universality of meaning. To this point, the poem's echoes of the commonplace apologetics for the visual image and its extensive evocation of the image of Troy speak most forcefully. In the light of the obvious gap between what the poem suggests and its practice, it should be noted that the poem provides instances of the four major modes of iconoclasm. In Lucrece's attack on the image of Sinon there is simple destruction. In the poem's own treatment of Tarquin, the image of lust, we find a partial reinscription of an icon into the matrix of history. Brutus's response to Lucrece's death and transfiguration and Tarquin's reading of the poem's emblems illustrate the desacralizing and designifying naturalization of the iconic. And in the poem's treatment of Lucrece's features, there is suggested the ironic clash of signifiers characteristic of acts of mutilation.

The source from which these assaults spring is indicated in the narrator's reflections on the limitations of the imagination and its images:

O, deeper sin than bottomless conceit
Can comprehend in still imagination!
Drunken desire must vomit his receipt,
Ere he can see his own abomination.

(701–4)

Much of Shakespeare's art is suggested in the tension between the limited "conceit" and the open-ended "receipt" here made to rhyme. Whether "conceit" be taken in any one of the ways the poem uses it—as a fore-conception that preforms the verbal before it is uttered (1,298), as the visual image of art (1,423), or as the everyday, nonaesthetic imagination (701)—these lines suggest that, contrary to Platonizing aesthetics, the tautologies "so compact, so kind" of the self-fulfilling imagination need the important corrective that temporal experience with its "bias and thwart" is alone capable of providing. Taking these lines seriously might lead one to reinterpret Lucrece's experience with the painting of Troy: her discovery of a timeless, universal meaning underlying the image of Sinon depends, after all, upon her own particular experience of violation and displacement from her "true type."

Perhaps thought about the poetic drama and the inevitable disjunctions between its pre-formative and per-formative aspects would lead naturally to a consideration of such tensions. Whatever their origins, the lines of stress detectable in *Lucrece* reappear in *Henry V* as obvious fissures between the play's predominant conceits and their dramatic representations.

II

Henry V comes close to realizing the values of Lucrece's painting in the medium of poetic drama. There are moments when the play forms iconic tableaux that seem quite as significant as does the painting of Troy to the work in which it occurs. Yet the meaningful stasis into which the play often appears to settle is repeatedly disrupted by an iconoclastic counterforce which demands that one notice the particulars—the how, why, by whom, and of what substance—such moments are made.

The play comes closest to being iconic in its treatment of Henry himself. Repeatedly the "mirror of all Christian kings" (a model as essentially defined as is Hecuba for "all" sorrow) is caught in appropriately stylized postures—in council, at wooing, in the field, and so forth. A procession of such ideal images is clearly what the Prologue envisions for proper tribute to Henry:

Then should the warlike Harry, like himself,
Assume the port of Mars; and at his heels,
Leash'd in like hounds, should famine, sword, and fire
Crouch for employment.

(5–8)

And to the end of rendering Henry both as this icon of Mars and as the mirror of martial kingship, the play takes certain definite steps in its attempt to make him appear as much "like himself" as possible.[21]

One of these iconizing strategies is the play's violent abbreviation of historical time. Action that took place during the six-year period from Lent of 1414 to May 1420

---

21. This is the emblem of war in the *Mirrour for Magistrates*.

is greatly compressed, while the various French dauphins of the period are condensed into the single figure
of "the Dauphin." Beyond these condensations of time
and character, certain cause and effect relationships are
radically altered as well. So, for example, all references to
the battles fought after Henry's return to France in 1417
are eliminated, creating the impression that the English
victory at Agincourt was the direct cause of the French
readiness to make peace. Furthermore, certain specific
actions are strategically altered in order to draw attention
away from their true origins and direct it instead to a focus on the present moment.

These strategies—abbreviating time, condensing
character, and diverting attention from causal and genetic relationships—play their part in rendering Henry
as an icon. The shortening of historical time frees Henry's
image from a welter of distracting (if not unflattering) detail. The condensation of dauphins heightens the sense
of simple opposition suggested by the chorus's vision of
"two mighty monarchies" confronting one another. And
the elision of cause and genesis works to create strong
impressions of Henry's virtuous effectiveness. From
these processes there might well emerge an image of
Christian kingship as compelling as that of Hecuba as a
model of hopeless sorrow; but unlike the painted icon of
all grief, the dramatic icon of militant English Christianity
is seriously challenged by the work of art in which it is
set. For every moment in which the play seems to be providing clear graphic embodiment of praiseworthy virtues, there are problems. In fact, the dramatic world of
Henry V is haunted by the archbishop of Canterbury's
pronouncement of the Protestant doctrine of the cessation of miracles:

miracles are ceas'd;
And therefore we must needs admit the means
How things are perfected.

(1.1.67–69)

The difference between this "means" of things and what they may be said to "mean" in themselves is crucial to an understanding of the play's complex operations. For one example of this difference, in the case of Henry's act of forgiving the drunken railer, the action (which is Shakespeare's invention from first to last) signifies his royal Christian magnanimity—if, that is, the moment is considered by itself, quite apart from the larger context in which it arises. The dramatic sight of Henry iconically embodying this quality tempts one to forget the role otherwise played by this moment as part of Henry's ongoing conflict with the rebels, and it is precisely this restricted interpretation that Laurence Olivier gives to the incident in his film of the play. With strategic editing, Olivier manages to represent Henry's act of forgiveness as an image signifying *only* magnanimity. Such a use of the image precisely parallels that analyzed by Roland Barthes in his discussion of a magazine photo of an African in French uniform saluting the French flag. As Barthes says, the powerful clarity of the image encourages the viewer to forget both the complicated history surrounding its origins and the designs implicit in its ends, suggesting instead that one simply accept its meaning as given, or "natural."[22] As the "natural" position of the African is supposed to be obeisance to the self-evident glories of European civilization, so the English who reject Henry are meant to be thought unnatural "monsters" (2.2.85),

22. *Mythologies* (New York: Hill and Wang, 1972), 116–17.

whose actions are "inhuman" (95), cruel beyond all "natural cause" (107). After all, Henry's natural generosity has just been demonstrated, and it is to this very quality in him that the conspirators themselves will appeal when revealed in their deceit.

To take this incident as it seems to be asking to be taken obviously calls for ignorance both of its genesis in Henry's own schemes against the rebels and of the historical sequence lying behind their rebellion. Surprisingly, however, this very scene reminds one of both, recalling the struggles of Henry's father and mentioning Henry's plots to apprehend the traitors in public view. One is pointedly reminded of the means, the why and how behind the scene, even when such spurs to consciousness severely complicate its import through their contradiction of an otherwise clear-cut meaning. Thus the play breaks out of the circumscribed limits of allegory (Henry's actions = magnanimity) and pushes instead into something resembling the realm of history, where, at each moment, disorder and discrepancy force one to take up the burden of interpretation, to consider before and after, origin and end, purpose and conclusion, without any promise of satisfying certainty to come.[23] In sum, *Henry V* seems to want things in the way both of Lucrece and of Tarquin. All those pleas from the chorus, beseeching the audience to work thoughts or grapple minds to the story, to follow, bless, and believe in Henry, are asking for a Lucretian reaction to the image; while time and

23. On history and the burden of interpretation see Herbert N. Schneidau, *Sacred Discontent* (Berkeley and Los Angeles: University of California Press, 1976), and the chapter on *Julius Caesar* below.

again the play provides disturbing details, odd resonances, that seem to call out for a Tarquinian reaction
instead.[24]

Examples are everywhere. On one hand, there is
Henry in the first act, the very image of long-suffering
righteousness provoked to wrath, raising his "rightful
hand in a well-hallowed cause" (1.2.293). But, on the
other hand, the play demonstrates that the king's clerical
advisers are anything but disinterested in their detailing
of his infringed "right." Their testimony is explicitly
shown to originate in a desire for political protection and
so cannot but appear as a calculated attempt to tell Henry
what he wants to hear.[25] The evidence of underlying po-
litical/historical means by which Henry's claim arises severely undercuts the meaning conveyed by his posture of
righteous indignation. It may be true, as Bullough has
pointed out, that there is no source for Shakespeare's portrayal of the "dignity of Henry's answer, his insistence on
his kingly state . . . his majesty, and his appeal to the will

24. Among those who most recently have explored these factors is Norman Rabkin, whose book *Shakespeare and the Problem
of Meaning* (Chicago: University of Chicago Press, 1981) contains
an extended analysis of *Henry V*'s "inscrutability" as the "inscrutability of history" (62). Rabkin's work supports my own
sense of numerous incidents in the play; my only reservations
about his fine reading are expressed in the introduction above.
For a survey of critical positions on the play see Gordon Ross
Smith, "Shakespeare's *Henry V*: Another Part of the Critical Forest," *Journal of the History of Ideas* 37 (1976): 3–26.

25. Shakespeare even goes so far as to suggest, surely ironically, the many quite proper and Christian uses, both civil and
military, to which this wealth might otherwise be put (1.1.11–
19). In the *Famous Victories of Henry V* (London, 1598) the whole
speech detailing Henry's right consists of four lines.

of God."[26] And it is undeniable that the playwright has carefully and unhistorically placed the incident of the tennis balls so that Henry's kingly rage might have some appearance of justification in heated blood.[27] Yet, as the chorus has suggested, the value of a cipher is inseparable from its position in the series that extends before and after it; and the same rule holds true for this compromised image of kingly resolution. Preceded by Henry's decision to bend France to his will or "break it all to pieces" (1.2.225) and followed by the troubling disproportionality between the dauphin's "mock" and Henry's threat to mock widows, mothers, cities, and generations yet unborn out of life and limb (282–96), the stance of righteousness appears as hollow as an empty cipher.

As another example of the conflict between iconic and iconoclastic impulses in the play, the siege of Harfleur is striking. In preparing the audience to witness the siege, the chorus promises a scene of truly epic martial achievement. Like mighty cannon, the puissant English "cavaliers" will bear down "all before them." And Henry's two lengthy speeches do, in fact, create the impression that he commands great powers—both literally in the form of troops and figuratively in the rhetorical facility that wins the French surrender. In these scenes, the play would seem to be presenting in compact, emblematic form Henry's powers of leadership and oratory. But this image does not fit so well when seen in the contexts that the play provides.

Henry's fiery exhortation, which urges the English peers to live up to their noble ancestry and the yeomen to

26. See Bullough, *Narrative and Dramatic Sources*, 4: 357.
27. Contrast Holinshed's chronology.

make good on the equally noble promise glowing in their own eyes (3.1.17–30), although it certainly creates a compelling image of properly regal oratory, rings hollow when followed by a view of the men in the field. Instead of noble luster, one finds the lesser lights of Macmorris's blind fury ("I would have blowed up the town, so Chrish save me, la! in an hour") and of Bardolph, Nym, and Pistol's cowardice. Indeed, it is not the force of oratory but of blows that sends these last as close as they come to doing battle, as Fluellen drives them toward the action. This crew scarcely bear all before them, and, by the same token, Harfleur does not exactly fling wide its gates in response to Henry's just argument and in full confidence of his mercy. Through the juxtaposition of his speech with the surrender of the town (3.3), it might seem that the speech is the cause of the surrender. But the governor reveals that, in fact, his capitulation is rather a response to the dauphin's decision to abandon the town:

Our expectation hath this day an end.
The Dauphin, whom of succors we entreated,
Returns us that his powers are yet not ready
To raise so great a siege. Therefore, great king,
We yield our town and lives to thy soft mercy.
                    (3.3.44–48)

Still, all this is not to say that Henry's speech is uninteresting; on the contrary, whatever its relationship to the surrender of Harfleur, it does occasion some interesting problems.

For instance, how ought one take the language of Henry's threats?

Your naked infants spitted upon pikes,
Whiles the mad mothers with their howls confus'd

Do break the clouds, as did the wives of Jewry
At Herod's bloody-hunting slaughtermen.

(3.3.38–41)

With these lines, the positive image, which seems to be
the purpose of this episode as a whole, suffers grotesque
disfigurement. It is not the threat of cruelty that makes
these lines so troubling either. After all, cruel words may
serve in the present situation as substitutes for crueler
deeds undone. The problem is instead the way Henry's
speech has suddenly recast the virtue of *kingly oratory* that
is otherwise exemplified by this scene into its negative
form as *tyrannical rant*. Henry the Christian orator and
king has become, in his own figures, Herod the ranting
tyrant. This, of course, is exactly what happens in the
very first act, when Canterbury, speaking for Henry's
French claims, unfortunately echoes the biblical responses of the crowd to Pilate: "The sin upon my head"
(1.2.97).[28] If the same acts may be *interpreted* as exemplary
for Christian counselors or Christian kings and worthy of
the frenzied mob or of Herod, then they may rightly be
considered to *be* neither in essence.

Coupling the idea of Herod's rant with the idea of
Henry's Christian oratory breaks the necessary connection that would otherwise link an important signifier—
the staged scene of Henry's oration—and its signified—
the exemplary forensic ability and ethical restraint Henry
embodies as model king. In this instance, then, the play
handles an obviously iconic moment somewhat as Tar-

28. On Herod as "rant" see Hamlet's speech to the players.
Shakespeare makes pointed use of the echoes from the account
of Christ before Pilate in order to compromise Bolingbroke in
Richard II.

quin treats the symbolic events that offer to warn him away from Lucrece. And there is a more general sense in which the various iconoclastic elements of *Henry V* are related to the character of Tarquin. Tarquin's experience of remorse suggests that some truths can only be gathered along the strands of experience in time; thus, it is fitting that the iconoclastic elements of *Henry V* lead one to look before and after, to ask why and how, and for whom things are done. Instead of providing one with the tautological answers of icon, emblem, and allegory, the play prods one with questions, the very sorts of questions that had begun to haunt Tudor historical enquiry.

It is true that the general outline of historical biography during the English Renaissance usually kept close to the traditional forms of sacred hagiography. And it is also true that history plays like *Henry V* or *Henry IV* do seem to follow the schemata of saints' lives and related forms: in the one case reproducing those aspects of sacred literature that O. B. Hardison terms "ritual form," and in the other duplicating some of the features of the prodigal son stories. Furthermore, both Tudor history play and Tudor history do often resemble traditional hagiography in their readiness to treat matters of fact as secondary to didactic purpose and symbolic pageant. But, as Arthur B. Ferguson argues, Tudor history is marked by the emergence of an intense concern for details of cause and effect, particularities of historical context, and evidence of origins.[29] It would be surprising indeed if this new impetus did not make itself felt in the works of a

29. "Circumstances and the Sense of History in Tudor England: The Coming of the Historical Revolution," in *Medieval and Renaissance Studies*, ed. John M. Headley (Chapel Hill: University of North Carolina Press, 1967–68), 170–205; esp. 178–81.

writer as well versed in historical study as was Shake-speare, since the general European current of which it is a part makes itself felt even in such unlikely places as Catholic hagiography and Calvinist aesthetics.

Rejecting the imaginary accretions of popular ha-giography, which had substituted typical, idealized, per-sonified abstractions for the historical individuality of the saints, the Bollandist scholars pursued the rigors of "his-torical method" even within the Church of Rome. While their forerunners had been content to represent iconic figures frozen into the stillness of "attitudes" dictated by attributes—their very beings imaginatively reconstituted from metaphors of conventional representation, as Jo-seph, forever virginal because he happens in paintings of the Holy Family to hold the lily symbolic of the Virgin Birth—the Bollandists sought instead the actions of the living individual, in a time, in a place.[30] Such concerns created genuine tensions in the intellectual life of the six-teenth and seventeenth centuries—and in its art.

In fact, the relative merits of moment and move-ment, meaning and means, allegory and history consti-tute a major source of debate between Catholic and Cal-vinist positions on the visual arts. In the *Institutes* Calvin carefully discriminates between visual representations of "histories and events," which he allows as useful, and the portrayal of "images and forms of bodies without any de-picting of past events," which he damns as debased prod-

---

30. On the Bollandists see Hippolyte Delehaye, *The Legends of the Saints* (New York: Fordham University Press, 1962). On the tendency of hagiography, Charles W. Jones observes that in many cases "a halo or some other iconographic symbol was enough for a biography" (*Saints Lives and Chronicles in Early En-gland* [Ithaca, N.Y.: Cornell University Press, 1947], 63).

ucts of human "craving."[31] The mainline Catholic response to this distinction as expressed in the *Dictionnaire de théologie catholique* is interesting and worth quoting in full:

> Calvin accepte bien que l'on représente des scènes historiques qui relatent les actions vertueuses des saints, mais il ne veut point que l'on fasse des images de personnages isolés. D'abord, quel inconvénient y a-t-il? Ensuite, s'il est utile de nous remettre sous les yeux des actions vertueuses, il est pareillement utile de nous rappeler les saints qui les ont accomplies, indépendamment de telle ou telle action déterminée, et seulement avec la pensée générale de leur héroïsme sur la terre et de leur triomphe dans le ciel. Si ce souvenir est utile, pourquoi ne pas l'aider par l'image du saint, même représenté isolément? Du reste, assez souvent, les saints sont représentés dans une attitude ou avec un attribut qui rappelle un souvenir plus précis. Le lis de saint Joseph nous parle de sa virginité et le gril de saint Laurent nous fait penser à son martyre.[32]

31. Jean Calvin, *Institutes of the Christian Religion* (Philadelphia: Westminster Press, 1960), 112.

32. "Calvin accepts that one may represent historical scenes which report the virtuous acts of the saints, but he does not at all wish that one fashion images of isolated figures. First, what objection is there? Then, if it is useful to set virtuous acts before our eyes, it is similarly useful to remind ourselves of the saints who accomplished them, independently of this or that definite action, solely with the general idea of their heroism on this earth and their triumph in heaven. If such recollection is useful, why not aid it with the image of the saint, even if represented in isolation? Moreover, often enough, the saints are represented in an attitude or with an attribute that recalls a more precise memory. The lily of Saint Joseph tells us of his virginity and the grill of

Rejecting the Calvinist emphasis on "such and such a determinate action" in a certain and ascertainable historical context, the Catholic response acknowledges no important difference between such a highly particularized "historical" image and an image "generally" signifying some abstract quality through the presentation of a stylized "attitude" or "attribute."

Within *Henry V* these values are in conflict: the one confident that truth can be rendered in the iconic, the other insistent upon context and qualification. On the one hand, the play seems conceived as something like the bee's commonwealth, in that it seems to assume that many varied but related images may all find their place in a unified hierarchy of intended meanings:

> many things, having full reference
> To one consent, may work contrariously;
> As many arrows, loosed several ways,
> Come to one mark.
>
> (1.2.205–9)

And Henry's English warrior's Christian virtue is clearly their mark. On the other hand, there is the ironic enactment, best summed up in Fluellen's somewhat lower expression of the same idea:

FLUELLEN: What call you the town's name where Alexander the Pig was born?
GOWER: Alexander the Great.
FLUELLEN: Why, I pray you, is not pig great? the pig, or the great, or the mighty, or the huge, or the magnan-

---

Saint Lawrence makes us think of his martyrdom" (A. Vacant and E. Mangenot, *Dictionnaire de théologie catholique* [Paris: Letouzey et Ané, 1922], 7: 807). Translation is my own.

imous, are all one reckonings, save the phrase is a little variations.

(4.7.14–19)

A little various the phrase, the element, the particular image may be from its prototypal concept! What a difference the difference between general fore-conceit and particular receipt makes. The breach between signifier and signified may be opened, as it is in this case, so far that the effect is not at all that of Lucrece's blood flowing into larger circles of significance and order, but rather that of an invasion whereby the citadel of significance is made vulnerable to violation. Even Henry's Aristotelian quality of true princely magnanimity is opened to reinterpretation in Fluellen's association of swinishness with power.

The fall of Lucrece's "sweet city" differs from the fall of Harfleur to the extent that the poetic dramatist has come to strengthen the force of Fluellen's second critical truism—"There is occasions and causes why and wherefore in all things" (5.1.3)—against his first—"there is figures in all things" (4.7.35). In *Julius Caesar* these modes of understanding grapple with each other with such near equality of strength that "oft they interchange each other's seat."

· 3 ·

"Every like is not the same":

FIGURATION AND THE "KNOT OF US" IN *Julius Caesar*

SOCRATES: *And he who gives all gives a perfect picture or figure, and he who takes away or adds also gives a picture or figure, but not a good one.*

CRATYLUS: *Yes.*

SOCRATES: *In like manner, he who by syllables and letters imitates the nature of things, if he gives all that is appropriate will produce a good image, or in other words a name, but if he subtracts or perhaps adds a little, he will make an image but not a good one; whence I infer that some names are well and others ill made.*

(Plato, *Cratylus*)

The foremost work of Elizabethan literary theory, Sir Philip Sidney's *Apology*, shares with its chief classical precursor, Aristotle's *Poetics*, a high appraisal of poetry and a corresponding devaluation of history.[1] Both works are certain that history has little to offer the artist. This judg-

Epigraph is from Plato's *Cratylus*, trans. Benjamin Jowett, in *Plato: The Collected Dialogues*, ed. Edith Hamilton and Huntington Cairns (Princeton: Princeton University Press, 1961), 431c–d.

1. On the Aristotelian preference see C. A. Patrides, *The Grand Design of God* (London: Routledge and Kegan Paul, 1972), 2, and the *Poetics*, ch. 9, 1,451b. For Sidney's preference see *An Apology for Poetry*, ed. Forrest G. Robinson (New York: Bobbs-Merrill, 1970), 32–33.

ment makes sense for Aristotle, since classical Greek drama, upon which the *Poetics* draws so heavily, had abandoned the use of historical source material, choosing instead to work upon the stories of myth.[2] In Sidney's day, however, the value of history as a source for drama is less easily dismissed. Nowhere is this fact more obvious than in the works of Shakespeare, and nowhere is the debt of Shakespearean drama to historical sources more pronounced than in *Julius Caesar*. Character, incident, imagery, even entire speeches are taken, sometimes verbatim, from North's Plutarch and incorporated into the play.[3] More interesting than the mere fact of this borrowing, however, is the way Shakespeare's play and Plutarch's history demonstrate a shared concern not only for their subject but for the interpretation of it. This concern, moreover, combines with certain special features of the play to make it important to an account of Shakespearean iconoclasm.

Scenically, *Julius Caesar* has a peculiarly static, even iconic quality. As R. J. Kaufmann and Clifford J. Ronan have observed:

> Again and again scenes are organized like painters' compositions or sculptors' groupings. When the action moves it is as if it were formally choreographed. The principal characters come on (or are revealed) in studied postures; they strike attitudes; they classify themselves; they await their individual fates.[4]

2. Consult Bruno Snell, *The Discovery of Mind: The Greek Origins of European Thought*, trans. T. G. Rosenmeyer (New York: Harper and Row, 1960), 133.

3. As always Geoffrey Bullough's analysis is useful; see *Narrative and Dramatic Sources of Shakespeare* (New York: Columbia University Press, 1964), vol. 5.

4. "Shakespeare's *Julius Caesar*: An Apollonian and Comparative Reading," *Comparative Drama* 4 (1970–71): 18–51, p. 20.

This formal, sculptural quality suggests, in other words, a series of visual realizations of commonplace *topoi*. Verbally, this self-consciously significant staging is complemented by the way in which the play's limited use of metaphor, its "Roman" spareness of diction puts its use of figurative language into especially high relief, isolating metaphors and drawing our attention perforce to both the origin of such figures and the circumstances of their application.[5] In the process, I would argue, the play reveals its usages as highly suspect and alerts us to the elements of figuration at work even in simpler uses of language as basic as naming itself.

I

The force of a similitude not being to prove anything to a contrary disputer, but only to explain to a willing hearer.
(Sidney, *An Apology for Poetry*)

Whatever the differences otherwise separating descendant from original, Sidney and Aristotle find history deficient in one vital way. Unlike the poet's art, the historian's task—rendering the "bare was" of things—demands that one give up the satisfactions provided by "Perfect Pattern."[6] Given this high regard for formal pattern, a regard reinforced by frequent recourse to analogies derived from visual experience occurring in both the *Poetics* and the *Apology*, it is not surprising that Aristotle would see the ideal source for the tragic drama in the highly pat-

5. On the diction of *Julius Caesar*, see esp. Roman Jakobson, "Linguistics and Poetics," in *Style in Language*, ed. Thos. A. Sebeok (Cambridge, Mass.: MIT Press, 1960), 375–76; and Reuben A. Brower, *Hero and Saint* (Oxford: Oxford University Press, 1971), esp. 218.

6. *Apology*, ed. Robinson, 32–33; *Poetics* 1,451b.

terned realm of myth.[7] One is surprised, however, to find Sidney rejecting history as a basis for art when one considers the sort of texts that passed for "history" in the Elizabethan period. To modern eyes, these saints' lives, chronicles, and mirrors often display the simple binary oppositions, embodied metaphors, cosmic continuities, and recurrent patterns—the various signs of totalizing structure—typical of myth.[8] The wheel of Fortune may revolve vertically instead of within the horizontal plane of vegetation cycles, but its course seems equally inevitable. But perhaps Sidney had in mind such histories as Plutarch's recently translated *Lives*, for in them there may be detected at least something of a historical quality to which Sidney would likely have objected.[9]

7. On the highly visual language of Sidney see Forrest G. Robinson, *The Shape of Things Known* (Cambridge, Mass.: Harvard University Press, 1972).

8. On myth and totalization see Herbert N. Schneidau, *Sacred Discontent* (Berkeley and Los Angeles: University of California Press, 1976). My argument in this chapter has been strongly influenced by Schneidau. On pattern in Elizabethan histories see Patrides on Edward Hall's treatment of Agincourt in *The Grand Design of God*, 73. Even Machiavelli is attracted to the patterned account and is by no means above rearranging events to satisfy the desire to make history illustrative of maxim. On Machiavellian history see Alice-Lyle Scoufos, *Shakespeare's Typological Satire* (Athens, Ohio: Ohio University Press, 1979), 11; see also 15. As Bacon puts it, the virtue of poetry is to provide some "shadow of satisfaction" where "the acts or events of true history have not that magnitude which satisfieth the mind of man" (*The Advancement of Learning*, in *The Philosophical Works of Francis Bacon*, ed. John M. Robertson [London: Routledge and Kegan Paul, 1905]).

9. On the *Apology* as Sidney's response to Amyot's translation of Plutarch with its high opinion of history as "la nue vérité" see William Nelson, *Fact or Fiction* (Cambridge, Mass.: Harvard University Press, 1973), 51–52. On the further relation of the *Apology*

It is not so much a matter of stated intentions; the *Lives* claim a right of selectivity not far removed from the privilege Sidney reserves for the art of poetry.[10] Yet, in point of fact, Plutarch's text reads more like history than such disclaimers would suggest. Reuben Brower points out the presence of numerous accounts of battlefield detail of the sort Plutarch specifically disavows.[11] But more importantly, the *Lives* create the *effect* of history by the way in which the text repeatedly interrupts its progress and violates its nascent patterns with reminders of discrepant, and even contradictory, reports among various sources. While one authority maintains one thing, "others are of the opinion," or even "doe denie" that the case was such, arguing in fact for quite different accounts.[12] True, in Plutarch's account similarities and differences between characters are noted, moral judgments passed, simple oppositions established, and details doubtless omitted.[13] Nevertheless, an emphasis on factuality repeatedly tempers emerging patterns with qualifications. Caesar may once manifest "plain tyranny," yet his "Clemency" is also recorded.[14] Instead of being an exer-

---

to Gosson see Jacob Bronowski, *The Poet's Defence* (Cambridge: Cambridge University Press, 1939).

10. Compare the passage concerning the historian's right of abbreviation and portraiture that asks leave "to seeke out the signes and tokens of the minde only" in Thomas North's translation of Plutarch's *Lives of the Noble Grecians and Romans* (1579; Stratford: Shakespeare Head Press, 1928), 5: 165, with Sidney's remarks in the *Apology*.

11. Brower, *Hero and Saint*, 207.

12. *Lives*, 5: 342–43.

13. See above, n. 10.

14. *Lives*, 5: 333–34. Plutarch's attention to the implications of style is strongly evident in his reply to Herodotus, "The Malice

cise in cultural confirmation for the reader, a reencounter with subject matter already subsumed under the cognitive and social fixities of myth, Plutarch's text constantly reminds one of gaps and discrepancies, discord and disagreement, confronting one with the necessary burden of interpretation.[15] Neither event nor person nor thing comes to one securely fixed into one and only one pattern. Instead, the text urges sifting and evaluation in a way and to a degree quite foreign to the mythic.[16] Such demands, of course, are not unrelated to certain demands potential within the form of poetic drama.

Formal potentials, however, are not necessarily pursued and developed. Instead of critical distance, dramatists of Sidney's day, even when they did make use of historical material—for example, Marlowe's *Tamburlaine*—would seem to have been after enraptured response, a

---

of Herodotus" (Plutarch's *Moralia*, trans. Lionel Pearson and F. H. Sandbach [Cambridge, Mass.: Harvard University Press, 1965], 11: 854ff.). He produces a general outline of the signs to be watched for as evidence of "disingenuous and hostile narrative." He does specifically warn against the historian who mixes praise with blame, but again, principle is not practice, cf. n. 10 above.

15. This need for the reader's "discretion" is precisely what Sidney objects to in the *Apology*, 33.

16. Lévi-Strauss objects to this view of history by insisting, quite rightly, on the necessary selectivity of any historical account; see the chapter entitled "History and Dialectic" in *The Savage Mind* (Chicago: University of Chicago Press, 1966). My point is not to deny history's selectiveness, but to emphasize that such historical texts as Plutarch's manifest an awareness of discrepancy and opinion that is alien to the self-assurance of accepted myth.

surrender of critical faculties in a swoon of assent.[17] The Prologue to *Henry V* thus dreams of an ideal drama that would recast history into myth, representation into ritual reenactment:

A kingdom for a stage, princes to act
And monarchs to behold the swelling scene!
Then should the warlike Harry, like himself,
Assume the port of Mars; and at his heels,
Leash'd in like hounds, should famine, sword, and fire
Crouch for employment.[18]

Were wishes acts and dreams scenes, the Prologue would not need to deploy arbitrarily designated actors in the arbitrarily representative spaces of the common stage, before randomly collected and disparate audiences. Rather, in some Renaissance heroic equivalent of the medieval Mass, the play would ritually reenact the original action upon which it is based.[19] As a result of using such nonarbitrary *natural* symbols—kingdoms for kingdoms, royalty for royalty—the Prologue envisions an apotheosis of

17. C. F. Tucker Brooke has argued that *Tamburlaine* is "more than any other drama the source and original of the Elizabethan history play" (*The Tudor Drama* [Boston: Houghton Mifflin, 1911], 302). Irving Ribner's argument that Marlowe used Polybius for the idea of human beings as unchangeable "natural forces" in their essential characteristics is related to this point; cf. "The Idea of History in Marlowe's *Tamburlaine*," *ELH* 20 (1953): 251–66, p. 258. It should be noted, in the light of what we shall have to say about Brutus, that Plutarch claims Brutus to have been a great reader of Polybius.

18. See chapter 2 above.

19. On the medieval Mass as reenactment see O. B. Hardison's comments in *Christian Rite and Christian Drama in the Middle Ages* (Baltimore: Johns Hopkins University Press, 1965).

real presence.[20] King Henry would appear not only "like himself" but would furthermore assume the frozen posture of an iconic figure representative of the mythic original upon which his self-likeness is grounded. In the Prologue's ideal theater, the replacement of mere hollow "ciphers"—those contingent counters with which dramatic representation is forced to trade once it has left ritual behind—by natural symbols, which partake essentially of the reality they symbolize, would convert the vagaries of dramatic action with its change, its motion and resistance, its necessary making *unlike* themselves of things, to the scenic certainties of iconic stasis and significance.

However, since, in a fallen world, "every like is not the same"—cannot be the same substantially, but only, at best, somewhat *like* its referent in limited matters of form or appearance—the Prologue is forced to turn some other way with its dream.[21] Imagination, pure imaginative assent, is suggested as the only way to redeem the theater's merely conventional, man-made "ciphers" for the "great accompt" in place of which they stand. If the audience would only submit its thoughts to the Prologue's mea-

20. The problem of distinction between arbitrary and natural symbols has been important since Plato's *Cratylus*, and is treated by, among others, Addison, Du Bos, Burke, Lessing, Gombrich, and Derrida. The problem is, of course, "natural" to consideration of the drama, for, as Lessing argues, dramatic poetry seems to transform "the arbitrary signs completely into natural signs" (quoted by William Wimsatt and Cleanth Brooks in *Literary Criticism: A Short History* [New York: Random House, 1957], 270).

21. The line concerning "every like" occurs at an important moment: the unwitting Caesar has urged the conspirators, in a version of the Last Supper, to dine with him "like friends." The merely *figural* status of this ritual is underlined by Brutus's reply.

sure, then something of the gap between image and prototype might be overcome. As Thomas Heywood puts it,
"What English blood" would not respond to an enactment of English heroism by offering heart and will, "as if
the Personator were the man Personated."[22] Only the audience's surrender of critical faculties can serve this turn,
and given the inevitable contingencies of theatrical production, language would seem the most likely means for
the accomplishment of that conquest.[23] Indeed, like
Henry before Harfleur, the Prologue seems to wish that
language might overcome defenses; through words we
must see. Language will provide the pattern according to
which imagination can augment or abbreviate the otherwise intractable realities of stage performance. From the
first, the various speeches of the choric Prologue are designed to further this end. The initial speech, for example, establishes a binary opposition of "two mighty monarchies" and conveys a vision of cosmic hierarchy aligned
upon chivalric principles: from the martial masculinity of
"proud hoofs" down to the passive submission of the "re-
ceiving earth" (20–27), the world is patterned to order.
Later choric speeches will serve much the same function
in their attempts to marshal the "imaginary forces" of the
audience.

What this Prologue wants from its audience, Antony
desires from his own stage audience at Caesar's funeral:
not dispassionate judgment, not the sifting of rival interpretations, but wholehearted imaginative assent to a

22. Heywood, *An Apology for Actors* (1612; rpt. New York:
Scholars' Facsimiles, 1941), sigs. B_4^r.

23. Compare Dr. Johnson's point in the 1765 Preface, where he
argues that no "voice or gesture" could hope to add "dignity or
force" to the language itself of "imperial tragedy."

mythic reading of the past. Step by step, wound by wound, Antony shapes from the natural symbol, Caesar's cloak, an extended image to stand in place of the thing itself—the hidden historical ruin it covers.

> This was the most unkindest cut of all;
> For when the noble Caesar saw him stab,
> Ingratitude, more strong than traitors' arms,
> Quite vanquish'd him: then burst his mighty heart;
> And, in his mantle muffling up his face,
> Even at the base of Pompey's statue
> (Which all the while ran blood) great Caesar fell.
> O, what a fall was there, my countrymen!
> Then I, and you, and all of us fell down,
> Whilst bloody treason flourish'd over us.
>   (3.2.185–94)

Over us! The audacity of this call for undiscriminating identification complements the remarkable way in which these lines pattern Caesar's history for the crowd. There is no danger of mistaking the *meaning* of this "piteous spectacle" because it comes to us pre-patterned in the cloak of Antony's highly figurative discourse. The simple verbal and conceptual oppositions between "noble" and "great" Caesar and the "envious" (177) conspirators who are guilty of enacting the role of "Ingratitude" is realized iconically in that final significant image of "bloody treason," true to its name, flourishing in its crimson pride over the defenseless victim, "over us."

The theater audience, one might think, is not supposed to be taken in by all this. Watching the master image maker work his magic on others should serve to drive one quite out of his spell; however, it is difficult to conceive a similar explanation for Antony's powerful soliloquy in 3.1:

O pardon me, thou bleeding piece of earth,
That I am meek and gentle with these butchers.
Thou art the ruins of the noblest man
That ever lived in the tide of times.
Woe to the hand that shed this costly blood!
Over the wounds now do I prophesy
(Which like dumb mouths do ope their ruby lips,
To beg the voice and utterance of my tongue),
A curse shall light upon the limbs of men;
Domestic fury and fierce civil strife
Shall cumber all the parts of Italy;
Blood and destruction shall be so in use,
And dreadful objects so familiar,
That mothers shall but smile when they behold
Their infants quartered with the hands of war,
All pity chok'd with custom of fell deeds;
And Caesar's spirit, ranging for revenge,
With Ate by his side come hot from hell,
Shall in these confines with a monarch's voice
Cry havoc and let slip the dogs of war,
That this foul deed shall smell above the earth
With carrion men, groaning for burial.

(3.1.254–75)

Here are images to shape our own view of things. Here
are simple oppositions—conspiratorial "butchers" contrasted with the "noblest man" who ever lived; revenge
opposed to murder; domestic strife in future against the
tranquility of the past—and a clear hierarchy—from the
present "ruin" of Caesar's speechless body to the coming
autonomy of ghostly Caesar's "monarch's voice," itself
incorporate in the presence of Ate. Furthermore, Antony's use of the play's own imagery of blood, fury, and
bodily members, the general historical accuracy of his

prophecy, the similarity of his identification of power with the monologal self-sufficiency of autonomous language that the play makes so much of, and the congruence of his vision with conventional Elizabethan responses to the threat of civil disorder lend the speech enormous weight. It seems, in other words, the playwright's attempt to cast upon his own audience a spell of identification like that which Antony works upon his. We are being encouraged to accept and agree, to imagine, to identify.[24]

The play's various movements, of which this speech is one, toward the patterned world typical of myth repeatedly encounter strong counter thrusts that work to disenchant, to alienate rather than to envelop us in satisfying participation. The obvious differences between Antony's speech and the Prologue in *Henry V* are that Antony's speech neither comes from an unquestionably privileged perspective nor opens the play. It is, instead, a member of a series, an element in a context. Antony may be correct about what follows, but his own speech is only a follower in a long line of incidents that seem designed to make one unhappy with any one assessment of things. Even though it sometimes seems to want a response like that which the Prologue to *Henry V* desires, *Julius Caesar* fosters analysis and interpretation to a degree far beyond that encouraged in any other of the early plays.

Some measure of the extreme risks that *Julius Caesar* is prepared to run is indicated by the treatment accorded the great storm and its accompanying portents. Plutarch's mention of storm and portents is brief and enigmatic:

24. The echo of the Prologue's lines in Antony's figure of Caesar letting slip the hounds of Mars speaks for itself.

Certainly destenie may easier be foreseene, then avoyded: considering the straunge and wonderfull signes that were sayd to be seene before Caesar's death. For, touching the fires in the element, and spirites running up and downe in the night, and also these solitarie birdes to be seene at noone dayes sittinge in the great market place: are not all these signes perhappes worth the noting, in such a wonderfull chaunce as happened.[25]

This passage goes on to mention briefly the fiery figures and the sacrificial beast without a heart, but that is the extent of it. The play, by contrast, expands these few hints into a whole series of incidents extending over three scenes and touching most of the major characters. But beyond their temporal extent, the impact which they have on characters, or the intensity of their dramatic realization, the distinctiveness of Shakespeare's treatment of them lies in the way the play insistently couples the portents with disagreement about their meaning. It is as if Shakespeare had taken the passage from Plutarch and attempted to make it as theatrically impressive and convincing as possible, but had also decided to insist upon the ambiguities resonant in Plutarch's "perhappes," his "were sayd to be seene," and his interrogative syntax. The difficulty of interpreting the storm comes through despite the undeniable presence of thunder and lightning and despite the alacrity with which characters pronounce upon its meaning.

According to Cassius, storm and prodigies all exhibit features that clearly reveal their "true cause":

heaven hath infus'd them with these spirits
To make them instruments of fear and warning

25. *Lives*, 5: 341.

Unto some monstrous state.
Now could I, Casca, name to thee a man
Most like this dreadful night,
That thunders, lightens, opens graves, and roars
As doth the lion in the Capitol;
A man no mightier than thyself, or me,
In personal action, yet prodigious grown,
And fearful, as these strange eruptions are.

(1.3.69–78)

By this account thunder, lightning, and strange occurrences are not arbitrary events but iconic signs; as Caesar has grown "fearful" and "prodigious," so the storm and prodigies likewise exceed their own "pre-formed faculties" (67). What could be more appropriate or more aesthetically reassuring to the theater audience than the dramatic identification of such natural symbols of danger and disorder with the character from whom they originate and to whom they refer.[26] Yet within the same scene, Cassius himself suggests a completely different—in fact, a diametrically opposed—origin and referent for these same signs:

And the complexion of the element
In favour's like the work we have in hand,
Most bloody, fiery, and most terrible.

(128–30)

It is disconcerting to witness these cosmic portents so easily reinterpreted: referring either to the nature of

26. Compare E. M. W. Tillyard on the storm as iconic sign: "The portents that marked the death of Caesar were more than portents; they were the heavenly enactment of the commotions that shook the Roman Empire after that event" (*Shakespeare's History Plays* [1944; rpt. New York: Macmillan, 1962], 26).

the tyrant or to that of the conspirators. But it is even more disturbing to envision the playwright developing a scene in which major components of the play's verbal imagery—blood, fire, civil unrest—are given imposing physical embodiment and then going so gratuitously out of his way to deny the audience the twofold satisfaction of pattern and of significance grounded in that pattern. In fact, the scene seems to encourage some version of Cicero's scepticism:[27]

Indeed, it is a strange disposed time:
But men may construe things, after their fashion,
Clean from the purpose of the things themselves.

(33–35)

From Cicero's detached perspective, the sublime power of the storm and its symbols are reduced to mere "things"—things strange perhaps but no more wed to certain single significance or pattern of order than are the ciphers of everyday misconstruction—or of dramatic construction.[28]

27. It is interesting that both Maurice Charney, in *Shakespeare's Roman Plays* (Cambridge, Mass.: Harvard University Press, 1961), 42ff., and Wolfgang Clemen, in *The Development of Shakespeare's Imagery* (Cambridge, Mass.: Harvard University Press, 1951), 99–100, completely omit any reference to Cicero's remark in discussing the scene.

28. In "The Complexity of *Julius Caesar*," *PMLA* 81 (1966): 56–62, Mildred Hartsock argues persuasively for the centrality of Cicero's remark as setting the tone of "intellectual relativism" that pervades the play. Hartsock documents Shakespeare's modifications of the source material in order to render the dramatic situation ambiguous. For an interesting discussion of the play's ambivalences from a Freudian perspective see Lynn de Gerenday, "Play, Ritualization, and Ambivalence in *Julius Caesar*," *Literature and Psychology* 24 (1974): 24–33.

The case of the storm is most obvious, but the play is filled with similar instances in which totalizing devices and patterns are played off against one another and also against a sense of the arbitrary. Everywhere one encounters conflicts between the stable and natural and the arbitrary and shifting; even in so simple a "thing" as a name.

II

Pygmalion's frenzy is a good emblem or portraiture of this vanity: for words are but the images of matters and except they have life of reason and invention, to fall in love with them is all one as to fall in love with a picture.
(Bacon, *The Advancement of Learning*)

Who is so deluded and childish, Sidney asks his reader, as to believe he sees the real kingom of Thebes on the stage when the name "Thebes" is written over a portal.[29] Yet if he does not think that one could or should so confuse dramatic symbol with historical, geographical fact, Sidney does seem to believe that poetry—whether of the stage or of the page—somehow really "pictures what should be."[30] Even if there is a necessary disjunction between material limitations of representation and any *historical* fact represented, there should be a clear, convincing relationship between representation and a represented concept, idea, or pattern, a relationship that is, as Sidney's language suggests, more than merely conventional or arbitrary.

Sidney's values come through clearly in two aesthetic concerns: the use of names and the construction of

29. *Apology*, ed. Robinson, 57.
30. Ibid. On the "ground-plot" in Sidney see Robinson's *The Shape of Things Known*.

scenes. On naming, Sidney's theory is as explicit as his practice. "The poet nameth Cyrus or Aeneas," he writes, "no other way than to show what men of their fames, fortunes, and estates should do."[31] In application this dictum, which follows Aristotle, means that those who poetically represent such well-known characters are under obligation to keep their figures true to the outlines demanded by their names, ranks, and conditions—that is, under the control of the whole hierarchical pattern accompanying such a "signifying badge."[32] For poets who wish to create their own characters, the proper choice of names, remaining consistent with this prescription, may be illustrated by the practice of Sidney's *Arcadia*. The *Arcadia* is filled with characters bearing names such as Basilius ("ruler") or Philoclea ("lover of glory") and living up to the implications of such denomination. So, both in cases of invented and of inherited naming, the poet's choice of names ought to conform, to be fitted to the idea or pattern under which the character is to be subsumed.[33]

In a similar way, fictional scenes for Sidney tend to be carefully chosen manifestations of underlying and essential pattern. In Gervase Markham's continuation of the *Arcadia*, for example, Helen's arrival at Corinth with the half-dead Amphialus is depicted as an encounter with the masque of Hero and Leander:

> As soone as she had set her foote upon the shore . . . there might she see upon the sands, *Leander*

31. *Apology*, ed. Robinson, 58.

32. Ibid., 45; *Poetics*, ch. 9.

33. In keeping with such ideas, Sidney elsewhere recommends that the characters of comedy should "walk in stage names"— an apt combination of the visual/gestural and the verbally denominative.

drowned, and *Hero* lamenting over him, in her Nunne-like and virgin-stained apparell . . . in her amazement [Helen] looked first upon Hero, then upon her selfe; after upon *Leander*, lastly upon Amphyalus.[34]

Thus, for Sidney, name and scene are properly natural symbols, externalized (more than metaphoric) images for definable, internal truths rather than the arbitrary and essentially shapeless contingencies of history. Name and scene, insofar as they depart from the arbitrary in order to signify by resemblance—the name "Basilius" sounding like the Greek word for ruler, the character Basilius's actions looking like acts of dominion—aspire to the status of iconic images, as Puttenham, for one, clearly understood and appreciated.[35] In writing *Julius Caesar*, Shakespeare had ample opportunity to employ such means as Sidney recommends; the first scene is a case in point.

The various elements of Caesar's triumphal return to Rome and their significance were so well known that they could be used confidently in the form of similes. So, for example, in the chorus to Act 5 of *Henry V*, Caesar appears as the figure of the triumphant warrior, Roman no-

34. Markham, *The Second and Last Part of the First Booke of the English Arcadia* (London, 1613).

35. Puttenham praises the *Arcadia* for its use of "Icon," *The Arte of English Poesie*, ed. Gladys Doidge Willcock and Alice Walker (Cambridge: Cambridge University Press, 1970), 243–44. It is interesting that Sidney uses the terms "Eikastike" (perfect imitative likeness, the "Eikon") and "Phantastike" (fanciful semblance) from Plato's *Sophist* (235–36) to denote, respectively, moral art "figuring forth good things" and an immoral art that "doth contrariwise infect the fancy with unworthy objects," *Apology*, ed. Robinson, 59.

bility and citizenry as the embodiment of patriotic appreciation, and the return as a whole as a clear image of conquest celebrated:

> But now behold,
> In the quick forge and working-house of thought,
> How London doth pour out her citizens.
> The mayor and all his brethren in best sort,
> Like to the senators of th' antique Rome,
> With the plebeians swarming at their heels,
> Go forth and fetch their conqu'ring Caesar in:
> As, by a lower but by loving likelihood,
> Were now the general of our gracious empress,
> As in good time he may, from Ireland coming,
> Bringing rebellion broached on his sword,
> How many would the peaceful city quit
> To welcome him!
>
> (22–34)

As in the ancient past, so in the time of the play and in the future of English history, the audience is invited to take its place in a timeless continuity stretching from a mythic *illo tempore* ("antique Rome") into the living present and beyond.[36] However, when Shakespeare actually dramatizes Caesar's return, these metaphoric continuities and certainties give way to the interpretive disjunctions and difficulties of historical metonymy.[37]

Although its initial scene is occasioned by a triumph, *Julius Caesar* truly begins in confusion. Instead of the recognizable figures that any Elizabethan schoolboy would

36. In *An Apology for Actors*, Thomas Heywood, among many others, thinks of Caesar as the Conqueror.

37. The actual circumstances of Essex's return in September 1599 could teach a powerful lesson concerning the changing interpretation of character and action.

be looking for, the characters who take the stage are the tribunes and "certain Commoners." The scene becomes even more confusing when Flavius begins to talk:

Hence! home, you idle creatures, get you home:
Is this a holiday? What, know you not,
Being mechanical, you ought not walk
Upon a labouring day without the sign
Of your profession? Speak, what trade art thou?

(1.1.1–5)

If no certain rendering of Caesar's triumph, at least the scene provides elements for another "speaking picture." The men are mechanical, the day a laboring day, and yet they appear without the "signs"—rule, apron, awl, and so on—of their professions. The time and place would make their very lack of signs, insofar as the theater audience was ready to accept a mythic continuity between Roman days and its own time, significant of a present identity: they constitute a figure of the mob. Flavius and Marullus by their actions, costume, and speech represent authority. Authority confronting the mob—a clear opposition that would seem to demand certain audience response. The Homilies preached regularly and by law that subjection to authority was a duty validated by the very order and pattern of the universe, the same order that also dictated the hierarchy of trades and professions, demanding that each man keep himself "home" within prescribed limits of behavior and dress.[38] By such standards, the tribunes would be correct in demanding a return to proper decorum, a return to the well-known patterns

38. For the homilist's point of view see *Certain Sermons or Homilies* (London, 1623; rpt. Gainesville, Fla.: Scholars' Facsimiles, 1968).

that, officially at least, should obtain in Elizabethan life.[39] In this light, the fourfold reiteration of the question "What trade art thou?" makes sense. But the tribunes are not dealing with the *images* that the homilist can so easily assign to proper places; *characters* may talk back.

MARULLUS: You, sir, what trade are you?

COBBLER: Truly, sir, in respect of a fine workman, I am but, as you would say, a cobbler.

MARULLUS: But what trade art thou? Answer me directly.

COBBLER: A trade, sir, that I hope I may use with a safe conscience; which is, indeed, sir, a mender of bad soles.

FLAVIUS: What trade, thou knave? thou naughty knave, what trade?

COBBLER: Nay, I beseech you, sir, be not out with me: yet, if you be out, sir, I can mend you.

MARCELLUS: What meanest thou by that? Mend me, thou saucy fellow?

COBBLER: Why, sir, cobble you.

FLAVIUS: Thou art a cobbler, art thou?

COBBLER: Truly, sir, all that I live by is with the awl: I meddle with no tradesman's matters, nor women's matters; but withal I am, indeed, sir, a surgeon to old shoes: when they are in great danger I recover them. As proper men as ever trod upon neat's leather have gone upon my handiwork.

(1.1.9–26)

So long as the tribunes keep to the imperative, order seems almost realizable; when they venture to ask questions, things come loose. Dialogue threatens their order

39. Richard Levin attacks the critic's use of documents like the Homilies in his *New Readings vs. Old Plays* (Chicago: University of Chicago Press, 1979).

because it forces the once dominant consciousness of the speakers into an encounter with other languages, other possible orders perhaps in contradiction with the fore-conceit according to which they seek to pattern the world. The tribunes have a fore-conceit that the mechanical should fulfill. Perhaps he might have done so if denied the opportunity to speak.

Speaking leads to the admission that he is a "cobbler"—that is, in comparison to a skilled workman, no more than a bungler. Thus, he could be every and any man prone to error. Pressed to answer "directly," he specifies his trade as the mending of bad soles. The first answer escapes the fore-conceit of the tribunes by establishing the possibility of including the mechanical in another, quite different classificatory system. The second makes a parallel suggestion by hinting that one may call oneself a cobbler in respect of spiritual standards as well as material—one might recall a similarly humble designation, fishers of men. The tribunes do not want these sorts of extension. They want instead a clear one-word name that has only one privileged meaning, an equivalent of Sidney's "signifying badge"—an "awl" that will serve as the cobbler's "all," expressing his role and its "natural" limits. Rightly enough, only when that classification, that name, is unambiguously established does the cobbler begin to fit his image. Only then does he reveal his double motivation for leading the men through the streets: "to wear out their shoes, to get myself into more work. But indeed, sir, we make holiday to see Caesar, and to rejoice in his triumph" (29–31). Now these are more acceptable Elizabethan dimensions for a cobbler's existence—somewhere between the baser sorts of pecuniary desire and the scarcely more exalted level of popular and indiscriminate patriotism. It is striking how quickly the hints of a larger life for the individual get discarded once his role as a cobbler is clearly established, but other odd things are going on simultaneously with his reduction to the dimensions of his image.

As the personal role of the mechanical is reduced to arbitrary limits, his public role of the moment—member of a mob—takes on new complexity. One had, from the first speeches of the tribunes, identified the men as constituting a mob; now we begin to understand what their being a mob really means. As it turns out, from the tribunes' point of view, this particular mob is to be faulted not for disrespect toward authority but for paying too much respect to someone who happens to be in the place of authority. The men are to be blamed not for the abrogation but for the performance of ceremonial and civic duties—strange faults for a mob.

The tribunes want contradictory things. As individuals, the members of the crowd are supposed to conform to the role dictated by their social position—cobblers what cobblers should be. But as a group, this motley aggregation should act as "men of Rome" should. As men of Rome, they should retain both the image of Pompey's past triumphs and an awareness of what those scenes meant. Caesar's triumphal entry may look like Pompey's, but the resemblance is no more than arbitrary, for it *means* something entirely different, and under pressure from the tribunes' rhetorical onslaughts (32–60), the mob retreats "tongue-tied in their guiltiness." For the first of many times in the play, the verbal image is used to reduce one half of a dialogue to silence. And also for the first of many times, the course of future action is fore-conceived in imagery, as the tribunes' speaking picture of the past gives way to a vision of the ritual that *should be* the future.

"Every like is not the same"

Remarkably, after discouraging the ritual welcome for Caesar on the basis of its historical difference from a past prototype it superficially resembles, the tribunes do not go on to prescribe such mundane responses as political action or a return to work. Instead, they propose a counter-ritual. By reconstituting itself as a congregation for a ceremonial lamentation, the mob is supposed to create a scene of grief to expiate the guilty scene of holiday. And this expiatory rite is envisioned as anything but perfunctory observance:

> weep your tears
> Into the channel, till the lowest stream
> Do kiss the most exalted shores of all.
>
> (58–60)

Men whose semblance of patriotic duty has been established as a compound of idle escape, hope for monetary gain, and conformity are supposed to enact such an exalted, such a poetic scene? Here are paradoxes.

At first the cobbler's playful remarks hint at greater human potential than the tribunes and their order will grant. As a result of probing, however, another, more reduced view of the mechanicals as merely "base mettle" emerges. Yet, subsequently, the tribunes attempt to mold this base "rabble" into the shape dictated by an exalted image of cosmic expiation. Reduction alternates with amplification.[40] Whatever a character is or might be in fact,

40. Nicholas Brooke's *Shakespeare's Early Tragedies* (London: Methuen, 1968) is particularly good on the double perspective of *Julius Caesar*. The alternating perspectives, with their tendency to ennoble and trivialize, are reminiscent of the amplification and diminution mentioned by Aristotle (*Rhetoric*, bk. 2) and subsequently developed by rhetoricians into set figures. One might also think of the flexible method of Margaret's curses in *Richard III*, with their bettering and worsening.

his reality and its potential is first condensed to the limits of the speaker's fore-conceit; then the speaker refashions this image to fit a new schema. This violent process is immediately repeated when the tribunes turn their full attention toward Caesar.

The plan to strip Rome's images of Caesar's decorations would be an unambiguous act of animosity, dictated by easily understood principles, if, that is, the playwright had not altered his historical source. By changing dates in order to make the triumphal entry coincide with the feast of the Lupercal, Shakespeare might seem to be exercising that "poetic" right of alteration that Sidney acclaims. However, this particular rearrangement of history complicates and entangles instead of clarifying.

MARULLUS: May we do so?
   You know it is the feast of the Lupercal.
                    (66–67)

And because it is the feast of the Lupercal such decoration is fitting, proper, and in keeping with civil and ceremonial decorum. The tribunes would deprive the statues of the signs of recognition that Rome rightfully grants its supreme ruler, any ruler, as Marullus's remark suggests, during the feast. By their action they intend, despite the fact that the decorations belong to Caesar as recognition given to any member of his class, to reduce Caesar to the image of cruel political faction. Once this course is established, the two then proceed to mold Caesar anew into a figure of vaunting ambition:

These growing feathers pluck'd from Caesar's wing,
Will make him fly an ordinary pitch,
Who else would soar above the view of men
And keep us all in servile fearfulness.
                    (72–75)

This is the way the Sidneyan poetic would work—with a vengeance. The "bare was" of history, with all its untidy qualifiers—Caesar's legitimacy, the commoners' many possibilities, the crowd's right of assembly—is sacrificed. The poet-tribune suppresses these qualifications and complications in order to figure and re-figure character and scene into patterned images that reveal clearly and unequivocally an essence—or, more honestly, the tribunes' own representation of what that essence *should be*: Caesar's ambition, the crowd's guilt. Henceforth, one might expect the characters to act as icons of that essence; in neither case is this precisely true—or precisely false.

Certain recent critics speak of an Elizabethan "image consciousness" or of an "emblematic" mode of perception that accorded with the Neoplatonic notion that percepts (especially visual percepts) could reveal the Idea lurking within men and things.[41] For the most part, these critics presume that significant numbers of Elizabethans were trained to see emblematically, not only in their imaginative response to poetry, or merely when visually confronted with the painted cloths and public pageants that surrounded them, but even in the course of everyday nonaesthetic experience.[42] Evidence in support of such an idea may be detected, for example, in Fynes Moryson's

41. For criticism of this sort, see Introduction, above. On the notion of perceiving the Platonic Idea, Lieselotte Dieckmann's "Renaissance Hieroglyphics," *Comparative Literature* 9 (1957): 308–21, is particularly useful.

42. Dekker, for instance, describes a Fleet Street pageant of 1603: "Having tolde you that her name was Justice, I hope you will not put me to describe what properties she held in her hands, sithence every painted cloath can informe you" (cited in Glynne Wickham, *Early English Stages, 1300–1660* [London: Routledge and Kegan Paul, 1959–63], 1: 107).

pronouncement on French women, "And they use a strange badge of pride, to wear little looking glasses at their girdles."[43] Even outside an aesthetic context, Moryson views the women iconically, as symbols or emblems—speaking pictures much like those Sidney sees as the proper product of the poet. The same sort of approach to reality gives Elizabethan portraits their peculiar, iconlike quality—transforming historical individuals into natural symbols for Ideas.[44]

But there were also counterforces at work in the Elizabethan cultural and intellectual world. There was Montaigne, for one, who considers the self so shifting and unstable that the very idea of such portraiture would appear factitious.[45] And the actions and pronouncements of some reformers challenged the assumption that men like the cobbler could be fully characterized by what they "should be," by their "awl"—the sign of their place in a rigidly ordered universe. The doctrine of the world order, with its basis in Neoplatonic notions of identity according to the idea of one's function, might be proclaimed by the official homilists; but, as Raymond Southall argues and as events make clear, such a view of man and the limits of the individual is inconsistent with the spirit of the Refor-

43. Fynes Moryson, *An Itinerary* (London, 1617), quoted in John C. Meagher, "Vanity, Lear's Feather, and the Pathology of Editorial Annotation," in *Shakespeare 1971*, ed. Clifford Leech and J. M. R. Margeson (Vancouver: Proceedings of the World Shakespeare Congress, 1971), 252–53.

44. Roy C. Strong, *The English Icon* (New Haven: Yale University Press, 1969), 14.

45. See chapter 1 above.

mation.[46] The vision of order promulgated by the Homilies was under pressure, and men like the orthodox divine John Walker could see lamentable evidence of its collapse:

> One . . . who was the Hogsherd's son of Little Houghton, had been bred a knitter, became afterwards a horsebuyer, but then Mayor of Northampton, Colonel of the Town Regiment. . . . If a cobbler or a tinker get into a pulpit and preach four or five hours for the Parliament, these are the men nowadays. . . . They did put out good ministers and put in peddlers, tinkers, and cobblers.[47]

If both the Sidneyan aesthetic and an official Elizabethan ethic tended to value iconic fixity, they existed in conflict with counter-views that were, in thought and deed, in art and life, profoundly iconoclastic.

Victor Turner draws an enlightening parallel between this English iconoclasm and certain rituals in traditional societies. Among the Bemba of northeastern Zambia, for example, a girl's initiation into adulthood requires the modeling of clay emblems that figuratively reproduce the various roles of her society, and it also requires her subsequent destruction of them. Turner suggests that such iconoclasm may originate in the same

46. Raymond Southall, *The Courtly Maker* (New York: Barnes and Noble, 1964), 55.

47. Walker's *Suffering of the Clergy* is cited in Patrick Cruttwell, *The Shakespearean Moment* (London: Chatto and Windus, 1954), 148–49. Compare Socrates' ideal republic in which "we shall find a shoemaker to be a shoemaker and not a pilot also" (Plato, *Republic*, bk. 3). Christopher Marlowe was, of course, son of a shoemaker.

human needs that prompted Henry VIII's commissioners, Cromwell's Roundheads, and the Scottish Covenan-
ters to their iconoclastic acts—that is, the impulse "to assert the contrary value to structure that distances and
distinguishes man from man and man from absolute reality, describing the continuous in discontinuous terms."[48]

It is true that the first scene of *Julius Caesar* exhibits
various, more or less ineffectual and violent, attempts to
capture the flux of human reality within the borders of
image or class. Throughout the play, characters are
shown attempting, with only questionable success, to
turn others and their actions into figures, even trying to
fashion themselves according to such images. The play is
remarkable for the extent to which the dramatist examines such processes from every angle, while exposing
them to searching and sceptical enquiry. Yet Turner's
sense of ritual iconoclasm cannot lead one very far in pursuit of the complexities of *Julius Caesar* or of Reformation
iconoclasm. For this we need to refine the definition of
iconoclasm, to recast Turner's ritual dichotomies into historical dimensions. After all, simple destruction is only
one form of European iconoclasm, and hardly the most
prevalent or interesting.

For all of its occasional apocalyptic fervor, the iconoclasm of the Reformation period is often strikingly selec-
tive in word and action, and this selectivity has an important historical dimension. At the cost of considerable time
and effort, the verbal form of historical exposure and the
physical act of partial mutilation are often chosen over

48. Turner, *Dramas, Fields, and Metaphors* (Ithaca, N.Y.: Cornell
University Press, 1974), 297.

complete destruction. Indeed, the evidence suggests, as Martin Warnke has argued, that the Protestant iconoclasts often had a substantial interest in preserving the very icons whose sanctity they insisted upon violating.[49] The point of such paradoxical activity is not so much the affirmation of human continuities as a desire to reveal certain cultural and social patterns as both historically real and yet ultimately arbitrary in nature. Following the tactics of the Book of Wisdom, the European iconoclast often chooses to use pen rather than hammer, reinscribing the icon in the history of its origins, giving it a context. Or, in wielding his hammer, the iconoclast of Münster, as discussed by Warnke, chooses to scrupulously preserve those features of his figure that signify social rank. The complexity of such acts, ultimately aesthetic as well as historical, that simultaneously preserve and destroy is obviously something more than the either/or ritual of the Bemba. More properly considered, they seem to be attempts to drive home the merely arbitrary status of specific symbolism, to mark the symbol as an empty cipher—a fiction born of desire instead of cosmic reality. As Turner elsewhere observes, such attacks indicate a rethinking of the symbolic order in general: "Iconoclasm does not recognize any necessary linkage between signifier and signified. It denies that there are 'natural symbols.' "[50] The iconic statue, after all, is the most obvious example of

49. Warnke, "Durchgebrochene Geschichte? Die Bilderstürme der Wiedertäufer in Münster 1534/35," in *Bildersturm: Die Zerstörung des Kunstwerks* (Munich: Carl Hanser Verlag, 1973), esp. 83ff.

50. Victor and Edith Turner, *Image and Pilgrimage in Christian Culture* (New York: Columbia University Press, 1978), 144.

what a nonarbitrary "natural" symbol would be.[51] Verbal accounts of origin and physical acts of desecration seem intended to force the viewer of such a statue into recognizing the all-important role of the human maker, into seeing the dependence of the apparently self-sufficient image on the shaping consciousness of the interpreter. Such an act insists that the image be recognized as "historical"—*made* rather than given in the nature of things.

Far from being an absolute innovation or aberration, this active attack on the "natural" status of the symbolic has a history running back through the prophetic strain of the Judaeo-Christian tradition.[52] Despite periods in the Middle Ages in which the idea of natural symbolism assumed prominence, the prophetic tradition has perennially reasserted itself in calls to alienation from the various signs, symbols, and formulaic fixities of human representing. One time-honored means of verbal attack on the visual image is just such a reinscription of it in the history of its production—making clear that the same material could equally, to cite Tertullian's polemic, serve either as a god or as a cooking pot.[53] But the focus of traditional

51. In this regard, the play's use of statuary is very interesting. Statues of the ancestors—Pompey, Brutus—represent a compromise: the dramatic use of symbol instead of the medieval practice of actually violating historical limits by bringing the "dead" into scenes as contemporaries of the "living" characters. Erwin Panofsky discusses the use of statuary as "concealed symbolism" and finds its emergence as artistic practice to coincide with the introduction of a perspectival treatment of space in the Trecento (*Early Netherlandish Painting* [Cambridge, Mass.: Harvard University Press, 1953], 1: 140–43).

52. On this whole subject, see Schneidau, *Sacred Discontent*.

53. See *The Apology of Tertullian*, trans. Wiliam Reeve (London: Griffith Farran, n.d.), 41.

attacks is not limited to such obvious targets as the physical image of pagan worship. Never for long at ease with
any of the norms and forms of human creation, the
prophetic inheritance repeatedly recalls the merely
made, arbitrary quality of such things as personal reputation, cultural systems and observances, even linguistic
forms. As Tertullian reminds his readers, the word for
formula is derived from the Greek term for idol; all formulae are potentially idols.[54] Thus, it is not surprising
that Jahweh should have neither face nor abode nor
name. Unknowable by symbols, which like the ark of the
covenant are merely empty ciphers, the divine can only
be approached through the "bare was" of His actions,
themselves often contradictory and extremely difficult to
bring to pattern. Moreover, the fact of this difficulty
makes it imperative that one continually sift through history and reinterpret it in a search after the truth. Even the
incarnation of the Son in the world of nature does not
blunt this imperative. The parables of the Gospels themselves constitute a series of challenges to wrestle with the
inarticulable and uncapturable—calls to interpretation
and yet again to reinterpretation.[55]

54. "On Idolatry," trans. and ed. S. L. Greenslade, in *Early
Latin Theology*, The Library of Christian Classics, vol. 5 (Philadelphia: Westminster Press, 1956), 85.
55. On Hebrew historicism and the call to interpretation, see
Erich Auerbach, *Mimesis*, trans. Willard R. Trask, (1953; rpt.
Princeton: Princeton University Press, 1968), esp. 14ff. Auerbach notes that the text of biblical narrative is "greatly in need of
interpretation on the basis of its own content" (15). See also Tom
F. Driver, *The Sense of History in Greek and Shakespearean Drama*,
esp. ch. 2. On the troubling parables of the New Testament see
John Dominic Crossan, *Raid on the Articulate* (New York: Harper
and Row, 1976). Cf. Donne's sense of the "evermore something

The alienating strategies of *Julius Caesar* drive its audience into the sort of interpretive state of mind that is demanded by a truly historical consciousness, a consciousness fundamentally antithetical to the assumptions of myth and ritual.[56] In part, one sees evidence of this fact in the frequently expressed criticism that the play lacks a true tragic hero; yet such criticisms are responding to the more fundamental attack upon the idea of natural symbolism that runs throughout the play.[57]

In the second scene, for example, Caesar's majestic entrance with his train of noble Romans at first seems designed to image the absolute power and presence predicted in the tribune's extravagant verbal fore-conceits. In the context of these expectations, the scene quickly disappoints: the ruler who works his will on the Roman nobility is revealed caught in circumstances beyond his hope of control, dependent on superstitions, ceremonies, old saws, and obsequious treatment. And when it comes to his dealings with the soothsayer, Caesar is reminiscent of the tribunes in his oddly urgent attempt at

reserved to be inquired after" of Scripture (The *Sermons of John Donne*, ed. George R. Potter and Evelyn M. Simpson [Berkeley: University of California Press, 1953–62], 7: 316).

56. Schneidau is particularly good on this hostility. For a strong statement of the opposing point of view see Peter S. Anderson's "Shakespeare's *Caesar*: The Language of Sacrifice," *Comparative Drama* 3 (1969): 3–26. Anderson argues for a mythic reading of the play and assumes that "there is not so much suspension of disbelief during the play as there is participation in the larger life through the play."

57. On the play's attempts to keep our sympathies divided see G. Wilson Knight, *Wheel of Fire* (1930; rpt. London, Methuen, 1949), 151; and Adrien Bonjour, *The Structure of "Julius Caesar"* (Liverpool: Liverpool University Press, 1958), 3.

classification. Three times Caesar reiterates his demand
to know the identity of the speaker; and three times the
response instead warns him to "Beware the Ides of
March." As in the first scene, the image of authority confronts a figure whose identity is questionable, but whose
message is both clear and repugnant: the cobbler means
to honor Caesar, the soothsayer to warn him of doom. In
both cases, the scene's commanding presence devotes inordinate attention to determining the identity of the
speaker—as if proper naming might somehow establish
control over both the speaker and what he has to say. The
differences between the two encounters is nevertheless
worth considering.

Despite the fact that Caesar knows the speaker to be
a professional "soothsayer," he demands to see the man
behind the name:

CAESAR: What say'st thou to me now? Speak once again.
SOOTHSAYER: Beware the ides of March.
CAESAR: He is a dreamer. Let us leave him. Pass.

(1.2.22–24)

In this encounter, the terms of identity have changed.
Caesar's designation of the speaker as "a dreamer" is
more obviously subjective as an assessment than is the
name "cobbler"—and the results of this judgment, as any
acquaintance with history would lead the audience to realize, more patently ironic. Yet in calling a character
"dreamer," Caesar is exercising precisely the sort of
power that Sidney claims to to be the essence of the poetic. Caesar may even be correct; the soothsayer may
dream more than others, but Caesar is wrong, obviously
and tragically, to assume that every action of a man who
dreams is nothing more than a dreamer's act, nothing

more than it "should be." As a cobbler may be *more* than the name "cobbler" can suggest, a ruler of Rome may be *less* than imperious in his inability to soar above prescription and circumstance, and a dreamer may actually possess the clearest vision of all.

Once Caesar and his train have departed, the stage is left to Brutus and Cassius, and these two quickly reveal themselves as alienated, unhappy characters, who define themselves most characteristically as unlike others: Brutus unlike "gamesome" Antony (28–29), but ultimately unlike "other men" in general; Cassius no "common laughter" or performer for the rabble (72–78). Cassius's stories about Caesar take up most of the exchange, and in those stories, it is Caesar's physical weaknesses—tired limbs, plaintive cries, fits, shakes, and so on—that are made definitive. If Cassius is defined by being unlike others, Caesar is made out to be rather too much like them, to share too many of their frailties. As if Caesar's pretensions to "honor," which Cassius claims as his subject, were somehow negated by physical limitation. Paradoxically, the "sick girl" of Cassius's images grows to the stature of an inflated colossus by the end of his speech, while the once proud Romans, inhabitants of the "majestic world," are reduced to "petty men" who "peep about":[58]

Why, man, he doth bestride the narrow world
Like a Colossus, and we petty men
Walk under his huge legs, and peep about
To find ourselves dishonourable graves.

(133–36)

58. In *The Governour*, Sir Thomas Elyot cites the incident of the swimming match as an example of Caesar's physical prowess, see citation in Bullough, 5: 23. Plutarch is favorable to Caesar

The course is familiar by now. Caesar is recast as a mere "thing" (95) and then reduced to the image of a "sick girl" only to reappear in the deliberate amplification of Cassius's later figure. Neither the reduced nor the inflated figure quite squares with our own perceptions of the slightly inept, yet politically commanding, character we have seen on the stage. Before he reappears, his opponents are themselves first put through a series of image changes: from their identity as petty, futile figures, they are recalled to their larger role as "men of Rome." Brutus is reminded of his rightful place in the historical family of noble Romans who, like their father—that mythic figure also known by the name of Brutus—are defined by their opposition to tyranny. Reduction changes to amplification.

Whatever reality might be, the characters and the play repeatedly draw attention to the multiple possibilities of interpretation. Even background elements, such as the Lupercal, get this treatment. While for Caesar it is a ceremonious "holy chase," demanding strict observance of elder prescription (1.2.6–11), for Brutus it appears a trivial pastime for those who, unlike himself, are "gamesome" (28). Casca's account of these particular "games," however, represents them as neither frivolous nor closely adherent to prescribed form but as an empty cipher, a mere pretext for Caesar's political theatrics. Or so Casca sees them—to his thinking.[59] Thus one must use the historical sieve, going after truth through discordant accounts and evidence. And these accounts are given am-

---

both in the report of this incident and in the matter of Caesar's illnesses.

59. Casca's repeated reference to the limits of his own perception is reminiscent of the tentative tone in Plutarch.

ple opportunity to conflict: even Caesar, the enigmatic
center of observation, observes his observers—and himself—in his exchange with Antony concerning Cassius.

To be distrusted for his lean and hungry look, Cassius exhibits to Caesar signs of danger (189–92). Yet to Antony, Cassius is "not dangerous" because he is "a noble
Roman" (193–94). Initiated in this disagreement over the
relative reliability of perceptual symbols (fatness, bald-
ness, smiles) versus names ("noble Roman") in determining identity, their dispute raises complicated questions about symbols and reality. The terms (sign/name)
are reminiscent of Caesar's encounter with the soothsayer and that of the tribunes with the cobbler, but the
outcome raises still more questions.

Questions, above all, about identity. If Caesar's
"name were liable to fear," he would, he admits, fear Cassius. An odd phrasing in a passage that rejects another
name, "noble Roman," as a sufficient determinant of
someone's character, but there have been other instances
of such concern with names and the act of naming. Most
of these are easily understandable: Brutus loves the
"name of honor" more than he fears death (89); Cassius
encourages Brutus to wonder why the "name" of Caesar
should be sounded more often than his own (143); and
Cassius plans to send Brutus forged messages that reveal
"the great opinion / That Rome holds of his name" (315–
16). In these examples, the name is little more than the
sort of everyday public designation or reputation with
which each of us lives. In Caesar's remarks, however, it
becomes something quite different, the degree of this difference confirmed with that majestic declaration of fear-
lessness "always I am Caesar."

Caesar has come to define himself by his own name,

but that name is for him obviously more than merely arbitrary. To Caesar, the name "Caesar" has taken on a kind of independent existence as an image or figure. Like a metaphor, this name has come to highlight certain qualities of its referent while disregarding others; in this case, "Caesar" designates the fearless constancy that the character called by that name desires—the Caesar that Caesar *should be*. If Cassius's accounts are to be credited, or indeed if our own perceptions in this very scene are to have their proper weight, then the image Caesar desires to claim for himself represents precisely what he has been unable to realize in the "bare was" of his actions. More than capable of detecting the gap between his Roman contemporaries and *their* "noble Roman" name and image, Caesar ignores the obvious incongruities between himself and this ideal pattern. It was not great "Caesar" who cried out like a sick girl, or that now finishes a rather too lengthy elaboration of what he ought *not* to fear with signs of physical vulnerability and insecurity of judgment.

Come on right hand, for this ear is deaf,
And tell me truly what thou think'st of him.
(210–11)

Caesar clearly sides with Sidney and against the historians when it comes to representing himself.

A well-chosen name, like a good metaphor or portrait, cannot be wholly arbitrary but must speak in some way to the sense of similitude.[60] This iconic component is

60. According to C. S. Peirce, signs are iconic insofar as they signify by virtue of similarity rather than due to mere arbitrary convention (*Collected Papers*, ed. Charles Hartshorne and Paul Weiss [Cambridge, Mass.: Harvard University Press, 1931–58], vol. 2, pt. 2, ch. 3). This sense of "icon" corresponds to Renais-

most notably present in the name Caesar claims for himself. In fact, the name is something more than a metaphor; it appears to be a natural symbol, for, as the play will twice make evident, the personal name "Caesar" is a homonym for the name given to the class of Roman rulers. Brutus himself is almost made "Caesar" by the crowd (3.2.52), while Octavius wins the same title from Antony (5.1.24). Now, it is important that Caesar possess *some* similarity to "Caesar," or the figure of speech would not even be figural but merely ridiculous. The importance of such a nonarbitrary, iconic component of just resemblance between the image and its referent wil be underlined in the very next scene.

Because Cassius is alienated by political events, he is, as Caesar has anxiously observed, able to see quite through the affairs of men. He is particularly acute, it seems, at recognizing and naming the discrepancy between Caesar and the images, the names, he claims for his own. This alienation enables Cassius to operate with ruthless verbal power, his sense of the merely arbitrary enabling him to use names and images with dangerous freedom. The measure of his freedom from the constraints of necessary categories in thought and language is revealed by the ease with which he can alternately employ the image of the sick girl or that of the colossus for Caesar. This easy irony stands in marked contrast to the clumsy difficulties experienced by Brutus in his own attempts to employ imagery for similar ends.

---

sance usage in which the classical rhetorical term (which itself originated as meaning statue or image) came to find use for any sensuous, vivid image. On metaphor as icon see Paul Henle, "Metaphor as Icon," in his *Language, Thought, and Culture* (Ann Arbor: University of Michigan Press, 1958). On naming see Lévi-Strauss's *The Savage Mind*.

Through the contortions of his first soliloquy, Brutus attempts to support a fore-conceived conclusion on the basis of a patently *un*natural image:

> It must be by his death: and for my part,
> I know no personal cause to spurn at him,
> But for the general. He would be crown'd:
> How that might change his nature, there's the question.
> It is the bright day that brings forth the adder,
> And that craves wary walking. Crown him?—that;—
> And then, I grant, we put a sting in him,
> That at his will he may do danger with.
> Th' abuse of greatness is when it disjoins
> Remorse from power; and, to speak truth of Caesar,
> I have not known when his affections sway'd
> More than his reason. But 'tis a common proof,
> That lowliness is young ambition's ladder,
> Whereto the climber-upward turns his face;
> But when he once attains the upmost round,
> He then unto the ladder turns his back,
> Looks in the clouds, scorning the base degrees
> By which he did ascend. So Caesar may;
> Then lest he may, prevent.
>
> (2.1.10–28)

Bright day brings out the snake. If Caesar be crowned, he will have the power to harm, as does the awakened snake with its sting. Such power without remorse is, moreover, the common "abuse of greatness." These commonplace images might seem unexceptionable in themselves, but Caesar as a particular individual rather than the member of a general class has, Brutus admits, always kept his will under the control of reason; therefore, the analogy does not hold. In a crucial point, there is simply not enough similarity between the image and the imaged. Yet again, according to "common proof," it must be admitted that "lowliness is young ambition's ladder." Following the logic of this image, Caesar, enacting the pattern of "ambition," seems destined to kick aside the lowliness of reasonable restraint. Since he—or it—*may*, steps must be taken to prevent the fulfillment of the pattern. The doggedness, the sense of strain behind these artificial images and conjectural patterns becomes most obvious in the lines that prepare the way for a recurrence of that admittedly inadequate snake image:

> And since the quarrel
> Will bear no colour for the thing he is,
> Fashion it thus: that what he is, augmented,
> Would run to these and these extremities;
> And therefore think him as a serpent's egg,
> Which, hatch'd, would, as his kind, grow mischievous,
> And kill him in the shell.
>
> (28–34)

Caesar as he is, the "thing" that he is, the "bare was" of his historical actions, offers no support for the quarrel that Brutus would pick with him. Looking at Caesar has refuted the contention that he is by nature a passionate tyrant; his actions do not furnish satisfactory similitude for the image that Brutus needs and desires in order to reach his fore-conceit. They provide no "colour."[61] One must first be a thing before speech can incorporate one into a figure, but since the actions of the historical Caesar, in effect, talk back, the reduction into silent thingness is

61. On "colour," see Jewel's remarks cited in Introduction. Brutus's use of the snake for Caesar's dangerous qualities accords precisely with the sort of usage described by Puttenham as "iconic."

difficult. Thus, what should be an instantaneous fusion in the unity of the metaphor becomes a prolonged, highly self-conscious fashioning. Brutus is able to close off his dialogical encounter with the otherness of Caesar only by invoking a hypothetical, fictional image of the future.[62] By placing Caesar, or more properly neither Caesar nor "Caesar," but the image of Caesar-as-he-should-be-*for-Brutus* in the patterned world of this mental text, a text in which whatever Brutus most fears may be "augmented" to extremity, Brutus wins for himself poetically the grounds upon which to act. The choice of serpent *en ovo* for the final figure is thus highly appropriate, since by its inactivity the egg is conveniently unable to refute claims made about its essence or nature. In discussing the unborn snake, one may avoid the risks of refutation that would be run in making claims or names for a hatchling— that is, perhaps as an individual more interested in sleep than attack. Stories of lions, bears, and unicorns behaving according to the patterns of bestiaries might be good enough to flatter Caesar (2.1.203–6); but even the rudimentary seventeenth-century equivalent of observation would soon mean the end of the acceptance such stories once enjoyed. King James would learn how little the im-

62. As Paul de Man observes, "The metaphor that connotes Achilles' courage by calling him a lion is correct within the textual situation of the *Iliad* because it refers to a character in a fiction whose function is to live up to the referential meaning of the metaphor. As soon as one leaves the text it becomes aberrant—if, for example, one calls one's son Achilles in the hope that this will make him a hero " ("Theory of Metaphor in Rousseau's *Second Discourse*," *Studies in Romanticism* 12 [1973]: 475–98; pp. 490–91). Or, we might add, if one calls another character an adder in a fiction that does not have the future built into it upon which such a denomination is based.

ages of beasts could have to do with the actions of actual animals.[63] But at least with animals one may speak of likelihood according to kind. Of what kind may man properly be said to be? Cobbler? Tyrant? Noble Roman?

The self-conscious quality of Brutus's attempt to enclose Caesar in the shell of his image lends the whole process a strange status, somewhere between argument and ritual. It is as if the right image could silence the conflicting elements of a divided mind, bringing them, in spite of themselves, into a semblance of agreement, an agreement of semblance. What could be a clearer example of working one's thoughts? Yet the image that is both the product and the process of that work is here shown to

---

63. In the sixteenth century, one finds fables recommended as good sources of fictitious examples. Thomas Wilson, for example, writes that the "brute beasts" provide excellent "paterns and Images of diverse vertues," in his *Arte of Rhetorique* (1560), ed. G. H. Mair (Oxford: Clarendon Press, 1909), 191. Thomas Browne attacks the animal stories for their falsity in his *Pseudodoxica Epidemica* (*The Works of Sir Thomas Browne*, ed. Charles Sayle [Edinburgh: John Grant, 1912], 1: 322). For King James's difficulty in getting animals to behave in properly emblematic fashion, see Angus Fletcher, *Allegory* (Ithaca, N.Y.: Cornell University Press, 1964), 39–40. Tyndale offers an interesting parallel to Brutus in his use of the unborn serpent to discuss the fallen nature of all men rather than the failings of any one individual: "And as an adder, a toad, or a snake, is hated of man, not for the evil that it hath done, but for the poison that is in it, and hurt which it cannot but do: so are we hated of God, for that natural poison, which is conceived and born with us, before we do any outward evil" (cited in Stephen Greenblatt, *Renaissance Self-Fashioning* [Chicago: University of Chicago Press, 1980], 94). As Greenblatt's other citations suggest, Tyndale's proclamation needs to be seen in the context of his belief in the power of Christ to free the penitent from such bondage by nature.

refer more directly to the nature of the maker/interpreter than to that of its ostensible subject. Here most clearly, but elsewhere in this scene and in this play, characters will be shown in the act of disregarding matters of historical, political cause and effect in the interests of questionable figures—of speech and of posture.[64]

The conspirators intrude into Brutus's orchard, and they arrive much like an earlier group of our acquaintance, lacking "any mark of favour" (2.1.76). This very absence of visual signs betrays, as in the case of the mechanicals, a collective identity: "conspiracy" incarnate (77). Brutus's remarks about the "monstrous visage" that is conspiracy's true, though hidden, face are troubling. Are there no saving images, no better colors available to him? Does not a cause favored by Cassius, Casca, and the others lend itself to more elevated imagery than this, to a better name than "conspiracy"? Brutus soon finds a better construction when he comes to argue against the swearing of oaths: the conspirators reappear as "secret Romans" opposing "high sighted tyranny," Romans whose "honesty" and virtuous cause are now more definitive than their conspiring, to the extent that they need not swear allegiance to one another before undertaking

64. Cicero, alone among the noble Romans, effectively resists the call of the figure; witness his dismissal of the opportunity offered by Casca and his concern with political realities: "Comes Caesar to the Capitol tomorrow?" Fitting, I suppose, for the historical character who observed: "There is nothing in the world, the name or designation of which cannot be used in connection with other things" (*De oratore* 3.40.161). In this context it is striking that Brutus associates the absence of "figures" with the untroubled sleep of servants—i.e., with those incapable of aspiration to the "formal constancy" of the noble Roman "actors" (2.1.227–31).

the task of "redress" (114–38). His timing is not quite right, but somehow between the first reaction and these later remarks, Brutus has switched from the reductive mode to the amplifying one. Here, too, one has the uncomfortable feeling that neither the pejorative nor the laudatory figure quite fits. And this sense of discomfort increases as we watch Shakespeare's Brutus make the first of what Plutarch considered the fatal errors of the historical Brutus.

The increased speed with which Brutus is able to arrive at the right image for his purpose might suggest that, under the pressure of public life, Brutus is quickly learning the ways of Cassius. But his treatment of Antony reveals to what degree Brutus is not Cassius.[65] Brutus objects to killing Antony because he is only a "limb of Caesar." The conspirators, after all, oppose Caesar's spirit rather than his body, and Antony can do "no more than Caesar's arm / When Caesar's head is off" (2.1.165–83). Cassius immediately suggests an important inadequacy of this image: "Yet I fear him; / For in the ingrafted love he bears to Caesar—." Brutus breaks off this reply in mid-sentence, countering Cassius's counter-image with another assertion. Cassius's point will be proven proper: venerable tropes of the body of state and of servants as the limbs of their masters do not provide reliable guidelines for the behavior of particular men. Men are not objects so easily separable from one another, nor are their ties so easily defined as the physical model—any physical

65. Does the playwright's interest in preserving this difference between Cassius and Brutus cause him to omit from the play Brutus's reported remarks against virtue as a mere "unsubstantial name"? See the New Variorum *Julius Caesar*, 250; cf. Sidney's *Apology*, ed. Robinson, 40.

model—may suggest. Brutus briefly admits this ob
tion but only in order to reduce its terms to trave
through an unlikely amplification: if Antony truly lo⌐es
Caesar, he will pine helplessly away at his loss.

Alas, good Cassius, do not think of him:
If he love Caesar, all that he can do
Is to himself: take thought and die for Caesar.
(185–87)

If the first image reduces Antony to a senseless physical
extremity, the second amplifies the spirituality of his affection, casting him as an exaggerated figure of bereaved
love. Is either of these alternative identities any more convincing than are the two characterizations of the faction?
Even Brutus feels the falsity of his sentimental Antony
and quickly produces yet a third version: "he is given / To
sports, to wildness, and much company." Thus Brutus
ultimately recurs to the terms of his very first dismissal of
Antony as "gamesome"; as if the one objective attribute
of gamesomeness would be as sufficient as the cobbler's
awl or the soothsayer's dreams, a "signifying badge" for
all that might be said.

In any case, the outer world of experience has once
again undergone a distorting schematization under the
direction of inner needs and designs. Brutus may be making his own figures, but his seeming faith in their very
meager reality seems scarcely more critically judicious
than is Casca's response to Cassius's world of figures during the storm scene. There Casca is won to the cause of
rebellion by nothing more substantial than Cassius's imagery for Caesar. Agreeing to redress "all these griefs,"
Casca joins the conspiracy even though no griefs have
been enumerated beyond a series of images opposing the

"thing" that is Caesar—wolf, lion, incendiarist—to the Roman populace—presently sheep, hinds, trash (1.3.103–15).[66] Given their basis in desire—and Casca's desire to kill the ruler he believes contemptible has already been established in his report of the abortive coronation (1.2.265–90)—images need only contain enough semblance of truth to make them entertainable; once entertained they seem to become compelling enough to halt the exchange of dialogue. All the characters seem to need a patterned image of the world against which to define themselves and their situations. This need finds expression in the attraction of various characters to signs and portents. Caesar most emphatically recurs to the idea that events may be natural symbols, and even Cassius does so. This is certainly Cassius's belief in 5.1 when he reads the flight of birds as pointedly inauspicious, in spite of his former avowal of Epicurean skepticism (and in spite of his quick denial in subsequent lines). In addition, there is the problematic incident in 1.3 that suggests much the same attitude: Cassius's walking about "unbraced" in defiance of the elements may be designed as a rhetorical gesture for Casca's benefit, but the possibility suggests itself that he might be taken rather more seriously. Confronting the elements wherein Caesar's spirit is "infused" would, after all, be only an extension of the logic that underlies the idea of natural symbolism. Brutus himself reads no entrails, and bares his chest to no cosmic por-

66. Bullough points out that the only "concrete reference" to a specific evil action of Caesar's occurs in 4.3 when Brutus mentions Caesar's having supported robbers. The omission of reference to this crime in 2.1 makes Brutus's decision, in Bullough's opinion, lack a "sufficient cause" (5: 48).

tents, but he does seem to take his patterned reading of events to have some sort of objective reality; and, whether in the case of his suicide or in that of his military decisions, his metaphors announce the end of dialogue. Cutting off Cassius's arguments concerning the course of battle, Brutus claims a summary power to envision the way things go:

The enemy increaseth every day;
We, at the height, are ready to decline.
There is a tide in the affairs of men,
Which, taken at the flood, leads on to fortune.
(4.3.215–18)

That the pretense to objective certainty contained in lines such as these is merely pretense is a fact underlined in a whole series of ironic incidents, a series culminating in the suicide of Cassius, in which Pindarus, acting in place of Cassius's eyes, sees *all* and still misconstrues everything (5.3).[67]

In the face of difficulty and division, the peculiar Roman art and occupation is the attempt to fashion events, themselves, and their fellow Romans to pattern. In this pursuit, figurative language is their chief instrument. Even seemingly literal designations, such as those which class Antony among the harmlessly social and the worker in leather as but a cobbler, are shown to be merely figurative. Aristotle defines metaphor as "the transfer to a thing of a name that designates another thing, a transfer from the genus to the species or from the species to the

67. The suicide of Brutus has a place in this list. Over the objections of Volumnius, Brutus asserts his ability to see the way the world goes (5.5.22).

genus or according to the principle of analogy."[68] The task of the tribunes, like that of Brutus pronouncing upon the tide of times or upon the gamesomeness of Antony, is to fit the individual under the name of a class on the basis of resemblance. But, unlike Sidney's ideal characters, the characters inhabiting *Julius Caesar* resist such easy fashioning into figures. Even though they may in part resemble their images, they are not the same. The absurd expression of this conflict between the purposes of the characters and the strategies of the play occurs in the *sparagmos* of Cinna the poet.

Closely imaging the play's initial confrontation, while inverting its social allocation of power, this incident represents another putting to silence with a name. But this time—again, even though the name is in some senses "correct"—the wielding of verbal power appears simply absurd, the expressed belief in a necessary congruence of name and the named—"It is no matter, his name's Cinna" (3.3.32)—scarcely even a pretext for a naked exercise of an arbitrary will to power. In the spirit of men there may be no blood, as Brutus claims, but this play (at least until the appearance of the ghost) does not represent the confrontations of spirits. Here, despite desire, there is neither the marriage nor the divorce of "true minds," but only the confused impedimenta of human encounter. Characters face men, men whose reality is never quite congruent with the limits artfully prescribed by the images that surround them. Furthermore, what is

68. *Poetics* 1,457b. On this whole issue cf. de Man, "Theory of Metaphor." Similarly, the use of "all" as a substitute for "many"—the problem of the cobbler and tribunes—is also a "metaphor" according to Aristotle (*Poetics* 1,461a).

true in the general class of figurative language and in the particular class of names proves equally true of their scenic equivalents.

The significance of great and portentous happenings in Rome is as subject as the identities of the noble Romans to the designs of interpreters. And, as they see fit, these interpreters may reduce the happening to the mere working of chance or of base human motives, or they may inflate it into an iconic embodiment of some transcendent principle. Brutus assumes the amplified version of Caesar's assassination, calling the act an expression of noble sacrifice. Antony sees in it only the action of ambitious "butchers." Paradigmatic of the play's refusal to treat its scenic elements as stable, "natural" symbols might be the scene unseen in which Caesar is offered the crown by Antony. This, the most important piece of evidence for Caesar's "tyranny" or his "nobility" comes to us only through Brutus's conjectures and Casca's far from unambiguous account. Reading the cheers from off-stage according to his own fears, Brutus introduces us to the idea that the people may be crowning Caesar. As Casca's account subsequently reveals, however, all has been misconstrued: the common people actually cheer for Caesar's refusal of the badge of kingship, the shouts of the "common herd" representing in fact the voice of noble Roman principle. Ironically, if we are to believe Casca's account, the visual posturings of Caesar have conveyed their meaning all too well; the natural symbols of humility have caught up both performer and audience in a ritual reaffirmation of antique Roman values—this despite the fore-conceived pattern of Caesar's directing intelligence. Caesar's performance may appear to Casca no more than the sort of duplicitous image work typical of the Roman stage (1.2.260), but to the audience his words and gestures seem to embody truth indeed. Thus, the interpretations conflict: What Casca "for [his] own part" as an ill-disposed political analyst takes things to mean is not what the crowd believes—"He would not take the crown; / Therefore 'tis certain he was not ambitious" (3.2.114–15). Furthermore, the progressive movement of Caesar from designing, fore-conceiving intelligence searching for a way to realize his designs upon the crown, to the public being who is caught perforce and unexpectedly in dialogue with the audience he had originally conceived as silent and passive, to his collapse as the helpless, physical figure wracked with fits, might suggest to us the ironic history of the play's other attempts at fashioning the world to the figures of desire. Like the tribunes before him, Caesar's seemingly successful attempt to assume dominance through the use of imagery ends in his own being "put to silence."

Standing above the play's other important scenes, the murder of Caesar and its aftermath clearly express this sense of historical irony. Trapped into going to the Capitol by his own images of fearless constancy and his desire for the crown, led into disregarding Artemidorus's warning by his assumed posture of noble disinterest ("What touches us ourself shall be last served"), drawn into the dangerous circle of kneeling conspirators by the need to demonstrate his aloofness ("Let me a little show it"), Olympian Caesar fashions only his own death. And once dead, he becomes little more than the stuff for the figures of others, his very blood of use to his enemies.

BRUTUS: Stoop, Romans, stoop,
    And let us bathe our hands in Caesar's blood
    Up to the elbows, and besmear our swords:
    Then walk we forth, even to the market-place,
    And waving our red weapons o'er our heads,
    Let's all cry "Peace, freedom, and liberty!"
CASSIUS: Stoop then, and wash. How many ages hence
    Shall this our lofty scene be acted over,
    In states unborn, and accents yet unknown!
BRUTUS: How many times shall Caesar bleed in sport,
    That now on Pompey's basis lies along,
    No worthier than the dust!
CASSIUS: So oft as that shall be,
    So often shall the knot of us be call'd
    The men that gave their country liberty.
               (3.1.105–18)

"So often" as it shall be repeated, this scene will include a necessary denomination: the "knot" of them will be called "The men that gave their country liberty." The irony of course is that Cassius's dreams of ritual reenactment—in which symbols are "natural," certainly fixed to the truths they embody, where every like is the same and every unlike clearly different—are set in the middle of a dramatic representation that takes the existence of history and the problems of interpretation seriously. As inhabitants of a later age, the Elizabethans would know that the designation here applied has only dubious, figural status; as members of the audience for *this* play, they would have this sense of the arbitrary reinforced.

Dialogue, dissonance, and discordant response invariably counter the monovocal delusions of its characters. In this play, one cannot, one suspects, except in very limited and eventually ironic ways, autonomously fashion the world or name oneself.[69] The "knot of us" must necessarily include the *not* of us. The "knot" seems to need its "not" in a way that inextricably knots them all together; only by naming Caesar "tyrant" can the conspirators lay claim to the honorific title of "secret Romans" in the sense they intend. And calling themselves the givers of liberty depends upon the clear sense that they have opposed tyranny—and it must be "by his death." The conspirators are, in Antony's phrase, quite rightly "Sign'd in [Caesar's] spoil" (3.1.206). The tyrant—the symbol of tyranny—is essential in the birth of liberty. In their passionate conviction that this scene, this arbitrary image of their own creation, will persist through the ages as a natural symbol, the conspirators have, like Caesar, fallen into a deluded, idolatrous relationship with an image of their desires, of themselves. And what are they?

III

Only for a detached, alien onlooker is the bond between the signans and signatum a mere contingence.
    (Roman Jakobson, "Quest for the Essence of Language")

The character of Brutus most clearly evidences the extent to which the play is prepared to go in demonstrating that every like is not the same nor every different an absolute other. Whatever his problems in the first three acts—illusions and short-sightedness of one sort or another—

69. Consider Marcus Cato, who marches around declaiming his identity—

I am the son of Marcus Cato, ho!
A foe to tyrants, and my country's friend.
I am the son of Marcus Cato, ho!

(5.4.4–6)

—only to fall immediately thereafter.

the play goes to some lengths to establish his nobility.[70]
This unwavering nobility occurs to other characters as *the*
defining quality that makes Brutus "like himself":

> Brutus is safe enough.
> I dare assure thee that no enemy
> Shall ever take alive the noble Brutus.
> The gods defend him from so great a shame!
> When you do find him, or alive or dead,
> He will be found like Brutus, like himself.
>   (5.4.20–25)

Lucilius's conception of Brutus's identity, unlike the Prologue's vision of Henry V, is not grounded on a mythic
figure, yet the word "noble" is employed here as though
it could just as clearly define the borders within which
Brutus can truly be himself. Whether alive fighting or
dead—either by enemy hand or his own—Brutus will be
unsubjected to the ignoble shame of captivity. When in
fact he is found a suicide, Lucilius expresses relief that
this figure has been fulfilled: "So Brutus should be
found" (5.5.58).

So a fore-conceit is satisfactorily realized—or, rather,
"should be" realized. The "bare was" appears rather dif-
ferently to our own eyes because the play has taken from
its source more than one interpretation of this defining
act of suicide. True to Plutarch, Shakespeare includes
Brutus's remarks denouncing Cato's suicide—a death
that would be exemplary by the standards of Lucilius. Re-

70. Roman Jakobson, "Quest for the Essence of Language,"
Diogenes 51 (Fall 1965): 21–35; p. 25. Charney has traced the
honor words that surround Brutus (*Shakespeare's Roman Plays*,
227).

plying to Cassius's enquiries concerning the proper response to failure, Brutus maintains that he will act

Even by the rule of that philosophy
By which I did blame Cato for the death
Which he did give himself, I know not how,
But I do find it cowardly and vile,
For fear of what might fall, so to prevent
The time of life, arming myself with patience
To stay the providence of some high powers
That govern us below.

(5.1.101–8)

Since the identity of Brutus seems to hinge upon the act
itself, it is troubling that this very unflattering interpretation of suicide should intrude thus upon our attention.
And Shakespeare goes well beyond his sources in creating problems, for, unlike Plutarch's *Lives*, which had presented this negative pronouncement on Cato as a re-
counting of Brutus's *former* opinion, contrasting it with
his present judgment in favor of suicide, the play represents Brutus's change of opinion as an abrupt response to
taunts from Cassius:

CASSIUS: Then, if we lose this battle,
    You are contented to be led in triumph
    Thorough the streets of Rome?
BRUTUS: No, Cassius, no: think not, thou noble Roman,
    That ever Brutus will go bound to Rome;
    He bears too great a mind.

(108–13)

Under the pressure of potential circumstance—in this
case nothing more substantial than Cassius's *image* of a
possible future—the same act that was a moment ago
"cowardly and vile" undergoes revaluation, becoming

the sign of a mind "too great" for the shame of bound captivity.[71]

This abrupt contradiction is made all the more noticeable in the striking switch, so frequent in the play, from Brutus's self-designation under the first person pronoun to his use of the third person. This switch emphasizes the self-division, that changeableness and being unlike oneself that the change of opinion itself expresses. If the weight of a single taunt, of a single negative image can swing the balance and realign Brutus's entire system of values, are we not justified in questioning the assumption of certainties that support Lucilius's faith in a stable identity that can be designated by the name "Brutus"? Furthermore, if the same terms "noble" and "nobility" can be used for the mere dominance of Caesar (3.1.256), the hysterical self-mutilation of Portia (2.1.303), the character of Cassius as well as that of Brutus (1.2.194), then what stability of meaning can it possess? Like the elements of the storm, both the play's chief character and one of its most important verbal elements are treated as empty signifiers, names no more firmly fixed to a particular Idea or concept, no more infused with a particular spirit than are the great signs and portents. This drifting usage might seem intended to drive one away from an unthinking identification with these noble Romans and their readings of the world, but the fact that the play has not often been so taken demands that we investigate further.

Far from being an icon of Roman nobility or even the

71. Plutarch specifically rejects hints of cowardice in Cato's suicide as the unjust conjectures of unreliable historians ("The Malice of Herodotus," 856). Compare George Chapman's treatment of Cato in *Caesar and Pompey*.

embodiment of the name "Brutus," the Brutus that emerges into view after the assassination turns out to have a great deal in common with the so-called opposition. Like the idol that is exposed as first cousin to the cooking pot, the "noblest Roman of them all" appears as a figure carved upon the human material that constitutes the others. Nowhere is this clearer than in the fourth act.

Following a practice Shakespeare had employed for similarly pointed purposes in *Richard II*, the fourth act of *Julius Caesar* allows for an intersection, an exchange between the dominant pattern of the first acts, with its well-established oppositions, and a new pattern that undermines those oppositions.[72] The act opens in Antony's camp, where we see Antony, Octavius, and Lepidus cynically trafficking in lives. We hear Antony contemptuously image Lepidus as ass, horse, and "property," and we also learn that Antony intends to alter Caesar's will in order to defraud the commoners. We would expect things to be absolutely different in the camp of Brutus.

Yet when we join Brutus in the second scene, he is passing judgment on Cassius and making use of familiar images:

> Thou has describ'd
> A hot friend cooling. Ever note, Lucilius,
> When love begins to sicken and decay
> It useth an enforced ceremony.
> There are no tricks in plain and simple faith;
> But hollow men, like horses hot at hand,
> Make gallant show and promise of their mettle;
> [*Low march within*]
> But when they should endure the bloody spur,

72. I think here of the treatment of Bolingbroke.

They fall their crests, and like deceitful jades
Sink in the trial.

(4.2.18–27)

Is this, not forty lines from Antony's own cavalier use of
the horse image, supposed to be the sober Brutus speaking? Hard upon this speech, Cassius arrives and attempts
to defend himself.

CASSIUS: Most noble brother, you have done me wrong.
BRUTUS: Judge me, you gods; wrong I mine enemies?
    And if not so, how should I wrong a brother?
CASSIUS: Brutus, this sober form of yours hides wrongs;
    And when you do them—
BRUTUS: Cassius, be content.
    Speak your griefs softly; I do know you well.
    Before the eyes of both our armies here,
    Which should perceive nothing but love from us,
    Let us not wrangle. Bid them move away.

(4.2.37–45)

From "Judge me, you gods!" to that parenthetical aside,
so conscious of their appearance to the watching armies—Brutus has problems of consistency that remind
one of Caesar. But the movement from exalted principle
to realpolitik concerns about appearance repeats a shift
that Brutus has made before—for example, when he concludes his oration on Caesar's spirit with a reminder that
indiscriminate bloodletting might not appear right to
"common eyes" (2.1.162–80). And Cassius puts a linger-
ing suspicion into words: Brutus's characteristically
"sober form" hides wrongs. Brutus no more recognizes
the contrast between his admonition to Lucilius concerning the incompatibility of "enforced" ceremony and true
love and his aside cautioning Cassius that the armies

must see nothing but shows of love between them than Caesar can admit the incongruities between his own actions and his grand posturings.[73] In Caesar's case, the "form" is a public persona—the brave, noble, generous, and constant ruler—after which he attempts to model himself for easily understandable motives. Like Casca playing the fool, Caesar projects an image from which he hopes to profit. Brutus might chance to profit from the role he assumes—the plebeians do momentarily at least consider making him their Caesar—but the play never hints that any simple motives of gain impel Brutus to fashion his own life according to his sober, Roman standards. Nevertheless, the third scene of the fourth act goes to remarkable lengths in suggesting a "hollow" beneath his "sober form."

The scene opens with Brutus and Cassius at odds because Brutus has ignored Cassius's pleas on behalf of a man accused of taking bribes. The situation might remind us of two earlier scenes of judgment: the conspirators begging pardon for Publius Cimber, and the members of Antony's faction pricking off friends and relatives. But against the backdrop of these other judgment scenes, the distinctive quality of the encounter between Brutus and Cassius becomes quite apparent. Caesar had refused to reconsider his judgment of Publius because, unlike other men, he cannot, he says, be "moved." Others are mere men, "flesh and blood, and apprehensive," but Caesar himself is "constant as the Northern Star." Antony and his crew, on the other hand, make no pretense to such

73. Moody E. Prior finds evidence in the quarrel scene and elsewhere that Brutus is incapable of confronting reality or himself ("The Search for a Hero in *Julius Caesar,*" *Renaissance Drama*, n.s. 2 [1969]: 81–101).

"noble" qualities as personal constancy. They are as ready to trade a stranger as a brother in the unprincipled reciprocity of their machinations. By contrast to Caesar and to Antony, Brutus seems to be constant *on the grounds of principle* in rejecting Cassius's pleas. However, we quickly learn that there is more going on here than at first appears.

Cassius argues that the times being such as they are, it is not right that every offense be chastised; and Brutus responds, touching off an explosion by accusing Cassius himself of the avarice first charged against his underling. Their anger quickly reduces the two to exchanges such as the following over Cassius's claim to greater experience as a soldier:

BRUTUS: Go to! You are not Cassius.[74]
CASSIUS: I am.
BRUTUS: I say you are not.
(4.3.33–35)

It is hard to respond to exchanges like this without wondering how silly these two are supposed to appear. Here is the Roman preoccupation with name and identity being travestied. And, as if in likeness of Caesar, Brutus goes on to grow more rigid with every line, insisting upon his immovability:

BRUTUS: Away, slight man!
CASSIUS: Is't possible?
BRUTUS: Hear me, for I will speak.
  Must I give way and room to your rash choler?
  Shall I be frighted when a madman stares?
CASSIUS: O ye gods, ye gods! Must I endure all this?

74. I here follow the Folio punctuation, which omits any comma before the name of Cassius.

BRUTUS: All this? Ay, more: fret till your proud heart
    break;
    Go show your slaves how choleric you are,
    And make your bondmen tremble. Must I budge?
    Must I observe you? Must I stand and crouch
    Under your testy humour?

                 (37–46)

Beneath the petty, querulous tone, there is evidence of
something like Caesar's typical posing in Brutus's refusal
to budge or observe. In both cases, a posture signifying
aloofness precludes proper response. Furthermore,
there is a similarity to Caesar's rejection of the soothsayer
as a "fool" in Brutus's emotional denunciation of Cassius
as "madman." In fact, even the power of hearing seems
to begin to abandon Brutus in this exchange; witness his
misquotation of Cassius and the rebuff with which he dismisses correction (51–57). The Brutus who can answer
such legitimate correction with "I care not" has gone
more than a little way toward being, as Caesar is, deaf to
the empirical evidence contradicting his postures and figures. Furthermore, the Brutus who can take the money
wrung from the commoners so long as he himself does
not have to do the wringing has a certain duplicity in common with the plainly hypocritical Antony (65–77).

    These observations give Brutus's subsequent re-
sponse to the death of his wife a disturbing resonance,
for in that response we may detect an extreme instance of
posing. If one accepts the majority editorial judgment on
4.3, then the scene first shows us Brutus and Cassius
aware of Portia's death before Messala arrives bearing
news of it:

MESSALA: For certain she is dead, and by strange
    manner.

"Every like is not the same"

BRUTUS: Why, farewell, Portia. We must die, Messala.
    With meditating that she must die once,
    I have the patience to endure it now.
MESSALA: Even so great men great losses should endure.
CASSIUS: I have as much of this in art as you,
    But yet my nature could not bear it so.
                    (188–94)

Even without the expressed suspicion that Brutus is staging this both for himself and for an admiring audience,
the "Why, farewell, Portia" would be too much to take.
One would still want to use Cassius's terms and ask how
such a response could be anything but "art," and I assume one would be likely to wonder how much else that
had seemed "nature" in Brutus might better be thought
artificial.

    The charge, of course, need not of itself be damning.
But the charge when made in this play and in this scene
is something else. Stoic tradition should respect the
lonely indifference of the principled mind to any sort of
public recognition.[75] But here, as in the case of his about-
face in the matter of suicide, Brutus, like Caesar, seems to
depend upon public recognition rather too much, despite
his expressed preference for "plain and simple faith" and
his detestation of the "gallant show and promise" that is
characteristic of the men he deems "hollow." Brutus's reversal of inner and outer might be reconcilable with cer-

75. On the stoic ethic see John Anson's "*Julius Caesar*: The Politics of the Hardened Heart," *Shakespeare Studies* 2 (1966): 11–33.
Anson accuses Caesar of a similar distortion of stoic values—
confusing public validation with internal qualities. T. J. B. Spenser's discussion in "Shakespeare and the Elizabethan Romans,"
Shakespeare Survey 10 (1957): 24–38, is useful.

tain minor trends of Stoicism, but it cannot escape judgment when set in the context of this scene, of this play.[76]

The man who is not hollow—the symbol infused with spirit, the icon—has significance regardless of public recognition, by virtue of its participation in some timeless essence. The golden image of the saint or divinity is important independently of any audience; stories about the miraculous ability of holy images to retaliate against profanation attest to this belief.[77] And in its treatment of Caesar's ghost and Pompey's bleeding statue, *Julius Caesar* suggests some sympathy with such assumptions: the ghostly image of Caesar and the marble image of Pompey do incite revenge upon their profaners. But the play also undercuts the basis of such ideas by directing attention to the arbitrary figurative process by which such icons are generated out of confusion, contradiction, and resistance. The process by which, in his ghostly form, Caesar becomes a visible icon of authority is, in truth, only a grander version of the way he is made into serpentine and colossal verbal images of tyranny by Brutus and Cassius, and a more exalted instance of the process by which the loquacious mechanical is reduced by the tribunes to a "cobbler." In each of these cases, a contradictory and recalcitrant character is arbitrarily schematized into an image that *should* have nothing to do or say beyond the ghostly repetition of one meaning.

Figuration operates on the assumption of likeness;

76. I think of the stoic Epictetus, who resolved to commit suicide rather than suffer the loss of the badge that publicly identified him as a philosopher—his beard (J. M. Rist, *Stoic Philosophy* [Cambridge: Cambridge University Press, 1969], 252).

77. See Richard Bernheimer, *The Nature of Representation* (New York: New York University Press, 1961), 11.

its successes depend on the falling away of the contingent facts that complicate such likeness into an indistinct ground, like the shadow surrounding an iconic figure.[78] Those contingent facts that should be relegated to background by the metaphors and images of *Julius Caesar* represent the untidy stuff of life in time. So, for example, the figure of Ceasar as adder depends on Brutus's ability to suppress his memory of the historical Caesar, the man whose actions have never been dictated by passion. Ritual, as analyzed by Mircea Eliade, is also an attempt to get outside historical time and its discontinuities and to reembody in its observances a nontemporal, essential reality.[79] In its elaborate structures of gesture and word, ritual attempts to repeat, to be like and to be more than like, to be the same as a primal act, an act whose context has been reduced to the schematic demands of significant figure. In other words, the central act that ritual reenacts is both remembered and forgotten. In deference to its assumed significance, the complicated political, social, and personal circumstances that once made up its full historical context are, of necessity, relegated to obscurity. To the ritual consciousness, such factual ground would only serve to hide the pattern with irrelevant associations and, in effect, rob the act and its actors of their single significance. Thus, the blindness of ritual is a *desired* blindness that intends to preserve the fictitious autonomy of the defining act in *illo tempore* from the encroachments of historical interpretation. The believer does not want to hear that there are other meanings for that first act or that there

78. On metaphor and boundary see Max Black, *Models and Metaphors* (Ithaca, N.Y.: Cornell University Press, 1968), 41.

79. Mircea Eliade refers frequently to the notion, for example, in *Cosmos and History* (New York: Harper Torchbooks, 1959).

are historical reasons why the cult repeats this act, reveres this figure and no other. Rather, his attention is focused on the original figure and the attempt at scrupulous repetition of it; he demands, with Caesar, that no ceremony be left out. The end result of this process is to transfer an inner need—the desire for participation in holiness or power—to an external observance.

The Protestant attack on the "idolatry" of Catholic ritual and writ takes the form of a new insistence on the importance, indeed, the constitutive value of internal factors (belief, conscience) that give external observance its meaning. Thus, one might say that the reformers were, in effect, calling attention to the "metaphorical" character of the Eucharist when they cautioned their followers that true communion was not a repetition, a re-sacrifice of Christ, but rather an interpretive remembrance of a single, historical act to which proper response would be a reconciliation with one's neighbors.[80]

The conspirators attempt to establish a timeless, ritual significance for the killing of Caesar, but Caesar does have blood, does have a temporal existence admitting of more than one interpretation. His will represents one tie that binds Caesar to the world in a network of different patterns; his regard for Brutus and the loyalty of Antony to him are others. The image that proclaims Caesar as "sacrifice" overlooks the fact that the sacrificial victim must be one for whom society has renounced such ties and complications—must, in fact, be a natural symbol rather than a historical being. The effect of Shakespeare's dramatization is, however, to make such spiritualization

80. On Protestantism and metaphor see Barbara Kiefer Lewalski, *Protestant Poetics and the Seventeenth Century Religious Lyric* (Princeton: Princeton University Press, 1979), esp. ch. 3.

unbelievable: Caesar is no icon of Tyranny nor Brutus of noble Roman Liberty. No amount of imagery or posture can simplify the mixture of base and admirable qualities in either, nor can one "lofty scene" harden their actions into the simplifying scheme that gives rise to ritual. The play's iconoclasm is not the simple, overt destruction of the Bemba girl smashing her images, but rather an insistence that one notice the merely arbitrary metaphors upon which such images are founded.

This sense of the way the play works has not been popular, but it has some precedent. There is a hint that Ben Jonson sensed what the play was doing when he cited one of Caesar's speeches as an example of lines that "could not escape laughter." He means that the sense of the line—"Caesar did never wrong, but with just cause"—is ridiculous, but the line as he quotes it (before, as we assume, Shakespeare revised it) makes sense if its purpose was to call attention to Caesar's exaggerated poses. If Jonson's is the first recorded divergence from the enraptured assent of Leonard Digges and his followers, it is not the last.[81] Pope found reason to be uneasy with the play's assignment of speeches to certain characters and claimed that "nothing is more inconsistent with [Brutus's] mild and philosophical character" than the speech in which he encourages the conspirators to bathe themselves in Caesar's blood.[82] In this vein, the criticisms of John Dennis and Thomas Rymer are particularly interesting.

81. Jonson's remark appears in his "Timber or Discoveries," *Ben Jonson*, ed. C. H. Herford and Percy Simpson (Oxford: Clarendon Press, 1925–52), 8: 584. Digges's poetic response is included in the 1640 edition of Shakespeare's *Poems*.

82. For Pope's remarks, see the Variorum edition of *Julius Caesar*, ed. Howard Furness (Philadelphia: Lippincott, 1913), 145.

Dennis finds a number of things wrong with *Julius Caesar*. The scenes with the rabble offend the "Dignity of Tragedy," for instance, but the most damning complaint concerns the handling of Caesar. Shakespeare should have rendered that Caesar, "who did greater Things and had greater Designs than the rest of the *Romans*," so that he would have "outshin'd by many Degrees all the other Characters of his Tragedy."[83] In particular, Dennis recommends changes that would render Caesar so undeniably noble that his fall would seem lamentable even to the conspirators themselves. In other words, he wants *Julius Caesar* to be *Henry V*. All these recommendations are in contrast to the manner in which Dennis judges Shakespeare to have treated Caesar—that is, as "but a Fourthrate Actor in his own Tragedy." Dennis elaborates:

> How could it have been that seeing *Caesar*, we should ask for *Caesar*? That we should ask, where is his unequall'd Greatness of Mind, his unbounded Thirst of Glory, and that victorious Eloquence, with which he triumph'd over the Souls of both Friends and Enemies, and with which he rivall'd *Cicero* in Genius as he did *Pompey* in power.[84]

To Dennis, Shakespeare's Caesar lacks the characteristics of grandeur, eloquence, and power. Furthermore, he makes quite a bit of the fact that Shakespeare has failed to take advantage of the many chances provided him by his subject; instead Caesar appears hardly different from the lowest of his stage contemporaries.

83. Quotations from D. Nichol Smith, ed., *Eighteenth Century Essays on Shakespeare* (Oxford: Clarendon Press, 1963), 31 and 19.
84. Ibid., 32.

Rymer had already taken this last criticism to its more extreme position in his *A Short View of Tragedy*.[85] There he accuses Shakespeare of putting Caesar and Brutus in "Fools Coats." Their characters are said to be filled with unfortunate "self-contradiction," and Rymer goes on specifically to denounce the third scene of the fourth act:

> But pass we to the famous Scene, where Brutus and Cassius are by the poet represented acting the parts of *Mimicks*: from the Nobility and Buskins they are made the *Planipedes*; are brought to daunce *barefoot*, for Spectacle to the people. Two Philosophers, two generals (*imperatores* was their title) the *ultimi Romanorum* are to play the Bullies and Buffoon, to shew their Legerdemain, their *activity* of face, and divarication of Muscles. They are to play a prize, a tryall of skill in huffing and swaggering, like two drunken Hectors, for a two-penny reckoning.[86]

Both Rymer and Dennis assume that Shakespeare has failed to provide a drama of characters who oppose one another on the basis of their absolute difference of principle. They want no discrepancy between the noble character and the lines he utters—no "self-contradiction"—and, above all, no breach of decorum such as that which occurs when Brutus and Cassius square off. Such breaches after all suggest that those noble Romans, far from being the iconic embodiments of grand truths, are mere men striking poses in their attempts to pass for stat-

85. *The Critical Works of Thomas Rymer*, ed. Curt A. Zimansky (New Haven: Yale University Press, 1956).
86. Ibid., 168–69.

ues. Adopting a phrase from Schelling, we might say they aspire to the condition of frozen rhetoric.[87]

The voices of Dennis and Rymer are lonely. More typical are the readings of such critics as Lawrence Danson. Danson believes that the play expresses a kind of nostalgic longing for a lost ritual order. When Brutus manages his own self-slaughter, it seems to Danson that the play has finally achieved the "proper sacrifice" for which it has been searching in a world where words and ritual gestures have "lost their conventional meanings."[88] Thus have critics joined—as if in fulfillment of Antony's final figure coercing "all Nature" to "stand" however unnaturally erect—in witness that "This was a man!" But let us not forget the alternative reaction of Pindarus, who feels the need to put some *distance* between himself and these noble Romans and their ways:

Far from this country Pindarus shall run,
Where never Roman shall take note of him.

Nor take the *not* of him.

87. Erasmus found the stoic ideal no more than a "stony semblance of a man" (*The Praise of Folly* [Ann Arbor: University of Michigan Press, 1958], 46). Cf. Montaigne's remarks on the flight from change in stoicism as transforming men, not into angels, but into beasts (*Montaigne's Essays*, trans. John Florio [New York: E. P. Dutton, n.d.], 3: 13).

88. *Tragic Alphabet* (New Haven: Yale University Press, 1974), 65.

4

"How the wheel becomes it!":

MONUMENT, MUTILATION, AND
THE IMAGES OF CAUSE
IN *Hamlet*

An absence which would not be death's reflection, but death in life it-self, in the replication of a lack, as it traces it and shifts it. The theatre takes up the wager of invoking this absence in the most scandalous manner, since nowhere does language hold forth with more ostentation the discourse of presence. . . . In the theatre absence must be sought lurking in the redoubling of speech spoken again.
   (André Green, *The Tragic Effect*)

Hamlet propels us beyond the historicism of *Julius Caesar* and into an encounter with the more violent, more prob-lematic end of that spectrum of iconoclasms first indi-cated in *Lucrece*, displaying both the violence and the im-position of sign upon sign that characterize acts of mutilation. Furthermore, as we shall see, the play seems haunted by the same fundamental questions—about the relationship of image to prototype and of mutilation to

Epigraph is from André Green's *Un oeil en trop*; I use the trans-lation appearing in J. F. Lyotard's essay "Jewish Oedipus" (see below, n. 33) for its clarity.

monument—that complicate any attempt at a single account of iconoclasm, or, for that matter, of the act of
judgment.

I

Unlike such tightly constructed plays as *Caesar*, *Othello*,
and *Macbeth*, in which each incident leads necessarily to
the next, the movement of *Hamlet* is often staccato, a para-
tactic leap from one incident to another incident that follows only in a seemingly random, imprecise way.[1] It is
perhaps because of this episodic plot construction that
apparent repetitions of elements and sequences become
so important as unifying devices in the play and in its criticism. Everywhere, as critic after critic has told us, there
are doublings, foils, and mirrors: characters for other

1. The placement of speeches, such as the "To be or not to be"
soliloquy, or incidents, such as the nunnery scene, is notoriously debatable. As paradigmatic of this problem in the play,
one might consider Claudius's first confession, which actually
comes before the play within the play as a response to one of
Polonius's off-handed platitudes (3.1.45–54), or Hamlet's seemingly double decision in 2.2 to use the play within the play—first
commissioning the players for the play (511–16) and *then*, after-
wards, deliberating about doing so while uttering an audible
"hum" of consideration. Among those who have commented
with insight on the seemingly accidental character of action in
Hamlet is Nicholas Brooke in *Shakespeare's Early Tragedies* (London: Methuen, 1968), 189. The criticism, however, has a long
history. The digressiveness of *Hamlet*'s plot, for example, is one
of Wilhelm Meister's complaints against the play. Harold Fisch
compares the Goethean criticism of *Hamlet* with Aristotle's demand that a tragedy's parts be nontransferable, nonarbitrary,
and goes on to contrast the classical unity of *Julius Caesar* with
the apparent arbitrariness of *Hamlet* (*"Hamlet" and the Word*
[New York: Frederick Ungar, 1971], 138–39).

characters, events for other events, lines for lines, and situations for situations.[2] Where else, for example, does one find anything to match the chain of varied, but related, images that includes Hamlet, Fortinbras, Laertes, Pyrrhus, and Lucianus as revengers? Thus, it might seem fitting that two small dramatic segments—a pass of foils between Hamlet and Laertes and a verbal duel between Hamlet and Polonius—should appear, as do so many of the play's recognizable subunits, surprisingly suggestive, commenting on each other, on the text in which they are embedded, and on our relationship as audience to that text.

The foiling sequence between Hamlet and Laertes begins with the emergence from the amorphous flux of "play" of an assertion of existence, of distinctive, singular identity, which immediately finds its opposing negation, its inverse:

[*They play.*]

HAMLET: One.

LAERTES: No.

(5.2.267)

Two words of two characters by virtue of their proximate opposition constitute a dramatic figure—the conflict that constitutes drama's minimal unit.[3] Mere play is not *a* play until there is, at least, some such opposition. The words

2. This mirroring effect needs to be set against the play's unique length. Sometimes this time factor works to put things out of joint by defeating our memory; at other times it allows us to forget about differences.

3. Madeleine Doran represents combat as the minimal form of dramatic conflict in *Endeavors of Art* (Madison: University of Wisconsin Press, 1954), 302.

that express this particular conflict—one/no—form, moreover, the poetic figures of palindrome. How fitting that a play which repeatedly displays its characters in duels of one sort or another, that articulates a comparison between the whole of a man's life and the momentary pass of foils that precedes the fencer's cry of "one," should choose to cast conflict in palindrome. The same forward and back, from beginning or end, palindrome asserts stability and a unity that transcends the flux of time and syntax. Even amid the volatile back and forth movement of combat, the work of art here suggests the stillness of form, its words taking on the nonarbitrary appearance of singular things rather than of common words. And as it delineates a fragment of the text as a distinct unit, this palindromic conflict suggests further features of the whole, for as criticism has demonstrated, even if the plot of *Hamlet* seems dramatically nonsequential, the play is nevertheless possessed of a surprising unity of form, in which scene answers to scene and element to element in an overall ABC/CBA palindromic configuration.[4]

Yet there remains something oddly contingent about this very figure that apparently offers to still time and to reveal, within the contingencies of conflict and flux, the

4. The palindromic structure of *Hamlet* is described in Keith Brown's " 'Form and Cause Conjoin'd': *Hamlet* and Shakespeare's Workshop," *Shakespeare Survey* 26 (1973): 11–20. Brown's point is that the play is comparable to "a statue constructed upon a symmetrical armature" (20). Mark Rose describes the play as employing a "full circle technique" that at the end "brings back the two or three hours of traffic of the stage for contemplation as a whole" (*Shakespearean Design* [Cambridge, Mass.: Harvard University Press, 1972], 124).

necessity of detemporalized form. Under scrutiny, palindrome reveals that it is itself rather an action than the
thing it might appear to be; for the very existence of the
one/no conjunction as a palindrome, as a thing, depends
upon our activity as well as upon its form. Not only must
the words be isolated in their visual dimension so that
one may see what one does not hear (the sound of "one"
backwards in "no"), but, in addition, it is only the interpreter's act of disposing the letter "e" from its original
home in order to connect it with "no" that lets the palindrome exist at all. Without this silent, hidden movement,
there could not be the apparent monumental stability of
the figure. In fact, without the interpreter's double disposition—dividing the letters one way in the linear time
of the text's progress and quite another in the conceptual
space after time of judgment—significance fails, the image disappears. But even this choice so to dispose elements within the figure is already dependent on a previous act of detaching it from its syntactic context.

How easy it would be for the distinctive identity of
this figure to be lost if it were not isolated from the tide of
common dialogue:

> [*They play.*]
> HAMLET: One.
> LAERTES: No.
> HAMLET: Judgement.

What need for the interpreting eye to stop before "Judgement"? In fact, bracketing this word in order to concentrate attention on the isolated, detached figure of the palindrome necessarily blinds one to a realization that is
only to be had if the figure is left embedded in its text. The
one/no conjunction may be most properly linked, not es-

sentially as an image for the prototypal idea that it may embody, but temporally to the next word that follows in the text, since standard Elizabethan practice employs the *none*, *mine*, *thine* forms of negation or possession before words with initial vowels—so the King James version's "none other Gods," or the play's own "thine own self" and "mine own treachery." In other words, whether the special formal appeal of the palindromic figure dictated its shaping order through the flux of play or whether the attractiveness of "judgement" as the dramatically exact final word in this sequence worked its way backward, ruling out, by an altogether different, totally temporal set of preferences, the possible use of the 1603 Quarto's "none," remains a question.[5]

Furthermore, the slightly enlarged sequence—one/ no/judgment—itself constitutes a competing configuration, which might, given the larger play in which it occurs, seem far from arbitrary, representing as it does the compact schema of much that one encounters: Hamlet's private ruminations opposing one to no (true king and father to the uncle who is neither, being to not being, the player's grief to his own silence, Fortinbras's action to his own inaction), as well as his public representations, which bring together positive images of the past king and negative images of his present opposite for Gertrude, Horatio, and the audience of the *Mousetrap*. In each case, out of flux and confusion, Hamlet isolates positives and

5. The 1603 Quarto reads:

HAMLET: I'le be your foyle *Laertes*, these foyles
    Have all a laught, come on sir: *a hit.*
LAERTES: No none.
HAMLET: Iudgement.

opposes them to negatives, ostensibly for the ultimate purpose of judgment. Then, too, there is the further similarity between this sequence and the play's visions of life at the Globe and on the globe. In the prince's ideal theatre, the "necessary question" is to be limned out for the eye of the "judicious" (3.2.25–40). In Claudius's fears, we are reminded of a larger command performance—that "action" (3.3.61) played before the judicious eye of heaven, that "trial" none may refuse by answering "no." Life in *Hamlet* is more than "to say one," not because any positive value asserted always encounters its "no" in others—already is a "no" for others—but because there is so often a sense that the verdict, no matter how strongly felt, is still undecided. Since judgments, whether in the universal weal, the lesser world of the court, the representational domain of the stage, or the interior globe of the brain, are both provoked and invoked so frequently in *Hamlet*, it would be useful to consider the act of judgment both in itself and in the telling similarities it shares with palindrome.

As its etymology (from the Latin *jus*, "law") might suggest, judgment has often been thought to depend upon the firm establishment of a fixed relationship between an individual instance and a stable, prototypal category. According to one widely held Renaissance view, the faculty that exercises this disposing capability is the very foundation of the human self, the Ratio of the reasoning being, without which one would be, as mad Ophelia is said to be, a picture or mere beast (4.5.86)—either silent or speechless because dispossessed of that stable interior order and hierarchy that both constitutes a self within and achieves outer articulation in meaningful speech. This valuation of a judicial "sovereignty of reason" as the defining human quality carries certain dangers with it.

The troubling aspect of judgment, as Montaigne realized, is that although, like a palindrome, a judgment may seem certain and permanent in its product, the whole actually represents process exercised upon process: "Thus can nothing be certainely established, nor of the one, nor of the other; both the judgeing and the judged being in continuall alteration and motion."[6] From constitutive acts of isolation and detachment, judgment may result in something that seems to be stable, monumentally out of time, but memory first demands forgetting, relationship, a putting out of relation.[7] The terms of

6. *Montaigne's Essays*, trans. John Florio (New York: E. P. Dutton, n.d.), 2.12.323. See also Raymond C. La Charité, *The Concept of Judgment in Montaigne* (The Hague: Martinus Nijhoff, 1968), esp. 20 on the opposition of memory and judgment. On the numerous Montaignean echoes in *Hamlet*, see G. C. Taylor, *Shakespeare's Debt to Montaigne* (Cambridge, Mass.: Harvard University Press, 1925). Harry Levin points out formal similarities between the *Essays* and Hamlet's soliloquies in his *The Question of Hamlet* (1959; rpt. New York: Oxford University Press, 1970), 72. But compare Fisch, *"Hamlet" and the Word*, 60–68, on the difference between the essayist's and the playwright's concerns and tone.

7. As Justus Buchler has put it, the exercise of judgment "presupposes a set of limiting conditions, a perspective within which it functions to define properties," and, as he adds, "All judgment to some extent detemporalizes nature, holds it in suspense" (*Nature and Judgment* [New York: Columbia University Press, 1955], 17, 25). Palindrome, supremely among figures of language, seems to promise a detemporalized vision; so, in what is perhaps its most widely known European form—the Rotas-Sator square—palindrome promises that, when seen

this description might remind one that within *Hamlet* the act of choosing limitations within which to exercise judgment, within which to remember and to forget, forms a crucial locus of contention. Hamlet's "particular" judgment opposes the "common" one of Gertrude and Claudius in a struggle over the proper category under which to consider Old Hamlet's death. Is that fact properly to be seen within the universal context of natural undifferentiated dissolution, wherein it can only appear "as common / As any the most vulgar thing to sense" (1.2.98–99)? Or is it rightly isolated in the infinitely narrower confines of Hamlet's personal experience, where it assumes the huge dimensions of a tragic loss that is not nor cannot come to good? Either perspective demands the bracketing of the other; and, as the intensity of parry and thrust between the two sides indicates, a great deal rides upon establishing the proper frame for such isolation. According to choice, the death becomes, for judgment, a different thing—an unindividuated member of a group of images embodying a common theme ("all that lives must die"), or a singular, unrepeatable fact.

The play reveals an acute awareness of potential ironies in the exercise of this most human power of ordering and disposing. Mad Ophelia's discourse, for instance, sufffers under the disposing activities of others, its "nothing" forced into "collection" by their attempts to

---

from opposite ends of time, sowing and reaping, beginning and end are actually one, not two, as time might have it seem. The Rotas-Sator square may be seen in the word square of Cirencester, Gloucestershire; see R. G. Collingwood and Ian Richmond, *The Archaeology of Roman Britain* (1930; rev. ed. London: Methuen, 1969), 207–8. Renaissance terminology identifies judgment with disposition (from *disponere*, put or place).

make something stable of its flux (4.5.7–10). Hamlet himself wars with the disposing that goes on around him, his
own aggressively shapeless usage provoking one attempt
after another: from Rosencrantz and Guildenstern, who
would have him put his discourse "into some frame"
(3.2.294–95) and to this end suggest for him the commonplace framing category of "ambition" (2.2.246); to Claudius with his displeasure at the "nothing" (3.2.90) that
he gets from Hamlet's words, even as he attempts to
cast him in the image of "son"; and to Polonius, who in-
clines to fixing Hamlet and his words, no matter how resistant they may prove, as the embodiment of "love"
(3.1.177–78).

The small duel has taken us some way into the workings of the larger play, but not far enough, for the progression of the foiling sequence from one to no to judgment offers only one model, and a deceptively simple one
at that, by which to understand the play's attitudes toward the faculty of judgment and toward the images that
are judgment's tools and product. In a text that makes
much of speaking daggers (3.2.379), of tongues as weap-
ons steeped in venom (2.2.488), of ears poisoned, forti-
fied, and assailed, it is hardly surprising that additional
light on the difficulties haunting the exchange of dueling
sword strokes is furnished by an incident involving an
exchange of dueling words.

Responding to an especially long-winded attempt at
judicious disposition by Polonius, Hamlet offers a puzzling exclamation concerning the Old Testament judge,
Jephthah:

POLONIUS: The best actors in the world, either for tragedy, comedy, history, pastoral, pastoral-comical, his-

torical-pastoral, tragical-historical, tragical-comical-historical-pastoral, scene individable, or poem un-limited; Seneca cannot be too heavy, nor Plautus too light. For the law of writ and the liberty, these are the only men.

HAMLET: O Jephthah, judge of Israel, what a treasure hadst thou!

(2.2.378–85)

And since Polonius seems ignorant of Jephthah's story, Hamlet repeats a portion of the narrative specifying the particular nature of the judge's treasure, which offers Polonius a reason for its mention at this particular moment:

POLONIUS: What treasure had he, my lord?
HAMLET: Why,
> "One fair daughter, and no more,
> The which he loved passing well."
POLONIUS: [*Aside*] Still on my daughter.

(386–90)

Ever ready to interpret by the image of his cause, Polonius immediately identifies Ophelia with her antitype, Jephthah's daughter. Hamlet's next line confirms this conjunction across time and space of two in one by directly identifying Polonius with Jephthah: "Am I not i' the right, old Jephthah?" In sum, Hamlet's lines present an openly figural text that first prompts, and then even demands, acceptance of its figuration of extra-textual reality. Yet no sooner has Polonius, the audience for this text, responded to its figures with an exercise of the most minimal speculative activity—the near tautology of his next line "If thou call me Jephthah, my lord, I have a daughter I love passing well"—than Hamlet objects. What truly "follows" is not this backward inference that acts to annul

193

difference, not this act of judgment, but the ineluctable forward progress of the text:

POLONIUS: If you call me Jephthah, my lord, I have a
    daughter that I love passing well.
HAMLET: Nay, that follows not.
POLONIUS: What follows, then, my lord?
HAMLET: Why,
    "As by lot, Got wot,"
    and then, you know,
    "It came to pass as most like it was,"—the first row
    of the pious chanson will show you more; for
    look, where my abridgements come.—
    [*Enter four or five Players.*]
                  (392–401)

That which "follows" does not help much either. First of all, because, despite Hamlet's assertion of relevance to the present company and situation, the text itself resists treatment as an image of general applicability. Things come to pass in it "most like" only what they "were." Not *like* the outer image of an inner conceptual content—the pattern of doting fatherhood confounded or the mirror of careless swearing punished, as the allegorically adept reader might take them to be—the events recorded by the text are inescapably particular, their "bare was" even aleatory ("as by lot") rather than timelessly patterned and symbolic. By no means will Hamlet allow Polonius to see in the text the image of his own cause—i.e., an expressive embodiment of the love for Ophelia that he persists in believing to be Hamlet's obsession—despite the fact that Hamlet has warranted his seeing precisely this. The other reason that the text will not give Polonius much satisfaction is that it relates things that are themselves already doubtful, things that have come to pass only as *most like* they were, not *as* they were. Neither a repository of likenesses for general application nor quite of one substance with a stable prototype, the text, although beginning in such promising fashion, turns into a perverse denial of itself.

Its end, furthermore, is not that predicated in its beginning, not only because of internal contradictions, but also because it has no end. The "pious chanson" of the Quarto reading is actually a deceiver, a "pons chanson" as the Folio calls it, because its narrator/interpreter refuses to isolate its text from the flow of events that is the temporal context of its presentation. An event that can only find its fulfillment in other unforeseeable "abridgments" yet to come, the text appears in Hamlet's rendering as openness itself, any conceptual ends or conceivable endings abandoned for the uncharted future action to come in the play of the players.

From an initial assertion of identity, this curious sequence has proceeded through a contradictory insistence on difference to an ultimate deferral of significance. The paradoxes attendant on such a progress are much like those that characterize Christian typological interpretation, a mode sometimes invoked by interpreters to explain the workings of *Hamlet*, but this particular challenge to identification and unity, which foreswears conceptual reduction and formal closure within textual limits, is not quite, or rather is not only, what it seems.[8] Its progress

8. Mark Rose has suggested that the structure of *Hamlet* is at times "not entirely unlike" a progress past typological paintings toward an encounter with the New Testament scenes they foreshadow (Rose, *Shakespearean Design*, 105). For Shakespeare's knowledge of typology see Alice-Lyle Scoufos, *Shakespeare's Typological Satire* (Athens, Ohio: Ohio University Press, 1979). On

significantly reverses that of the actual pass of foils between Hamlet and Laertes. Beginning with an act of judgment by Polonius in his catalogue of playing, the sequence follows with the suggestion of an identity
between Polonius and Jephthah on the basis of their possession of "one" fair daughter, a claim in turn contradicted in Hamlet's own "nay," only to be surrendered to
the playing of the "players." By putting this inverse progression—judgment, one, no, play—up against that of
the other sequence, one may begin to catch sight of the
double businesses to which *Hamlet* is bound.

Among the multiple ironies of the physical foiling sequence is that the ultimate judging is turned over to Os-
ric. But this is only one of the problems with this tiny
drama, for no matter who occupies the judgment seat,
any act of judgment passed upon the duel itself may be
utterly correct without being in any way adequate. The
isolation of the incident as we have seen it is far too complete. It is not itself a whole but a part. An all-important
act of judgment has actually preceded this moment of
trial—the constitutive act of already judging the two foils
to be equal, the same sort of *thing*:

---

the incomplete nature of the typological figure see Erich Auerbach, "Figura," in *Scenes from the Drama of European Literature*
(New York: Meridian, 1959), esp. 58. Compare Michael T. Beehler's discussion of this issue in his *"Murder in the Cathedral*: The
Countersacramental Play of Signs," *Genre* 10 (1977): 329–38.
Beehler relates Eliot's criticism of *Hamlet* in "Hamlet and His
Problems" to the problem of signs in *Murder in the Cathedral*
(334). Sacvan Bercovitch provides a bibliography of literature on
typology in the Renaissance and seventeenth century in his *Typology and Early American Literature* (Amherst: University of Mas-
sachusetts Press, 1972), 245–337.

"How the wheel becomes it!"

LAERTES: This is too heavy; let me see another.
HAMLET: This likes me well.—These foils have all a
length?

(5.2.251–52)

The relationship between this judgment and the sequence that follows is underlined by the use of verbal parallels—from Hamlet's suggestion of brotherly "play"
(240), Laertes' claiming of "one" for himself (242), Hamlet's "no" (245), and the ultimate judgment that accepts
the equality of the swords. Process built upon process,
but even to intersect the action here is to come upon the
scene too late and to leave it too soon. The foils do "have
all a length," but beyond this one positive quality they
share, which makes them conceptually *one* for Hamlet,
there lie negative temporal particulars: the point un-
bated, the edge envenomed. Baited with a likeness and
betrayed by a difference, Hamlet loses his life through his
readiness to isolate a part as the definitive sign of a conceptual whole. Judgment comes before play, and in fact,
prejudgment before that judgment, for even Hamlet's
mistake about the foils is predicated on the prior mistake
that judges Laertes by the image of his own cause—i.e.,
the two as brothers (5.2.231,240), two in *one* act of revenge, rather than as Laertes sees them, one a murderer
and the other a revenger. In judging, Hamlet misjudges
how he has already been disposed by another, and he,
like Laertes, ends up slain by an illusory confidence in his
powers of isolation and disposition. Again, there are important relations to be recognized between the plight of
the dueling prince and that of the character who taunts
Polonius.

If Hamlet's double intention is to try old Jephthah by

providing him with a text in which to demonstrate the blind and guilty error of his own judging ways—to show the world what Polonius is, and by inversion to confirm his own clear-sighted innocence, demonstrating how different he is from the old man—then the play's intentions redouble those of its namesake. For if Polonius is mistaken in isolating the one element of fatherly love as the positive conceptual factor that underlies the figural relation between himself and Jephthah, and thus shows himself to miss the hidden poisonous negative point that follows within the story—that both he and Jephthah are capable of sacrificing their daughters in their foolishness—then it is also true that it is the very mode of Hamlet's own representation that necessarily elicits, and even guarantees, Polonius's error. The prince has already prejudged Polonius, and the form of his "play" cannot but confirm this prejudgment. Thus, despite the semblance of safeguards in this incident—Hamlet's careful deference to the tentativeness of text and time—it is neither tentative nor without preestablished, although tacit, conceptual reduction of Polonius, its target. Appearances of openness to the contrary, Hamlet's text is already open and shut, a trap for its audience.

Here is a warning concerning the apparent openness of typology and the seemingly open field of judgment provided for us by the typological conjunctions the play offers. For all its apparent regard for the protection of individuals and events from the violence of conceptual reduction in the name of some hidden, provisional quality they may contain, typological practice may already secretly presuppose the very violence it shuns. The discovery of figural likenesses between type and antitype, foreshadowing and realization, already depends on con-

ceptual thinking. Yet this presupposition, this prejudgment by which two things are judged to be one sort—for
example, Jewish Exodus and Christian Resurrection seen
as two instances of one rebirth; foil one and foil two perceived as the same—is doubly hidden from the figural
intelligence interpreting the text. Although it may appear
to those who stand outside the circle of belief every bit as
much an instance of the self-closed self-representations
that are the allegorist's stock in trade, to the maker the
figure appears the natural testimony of *things*, to which
he is merely *open*. Appearances to the contrary, Hamlet's
play on Polonius ought to be seen not as a trial but as an
act of mutilation.

II

It was Tolstoy's attack, so far as I know, that first employed the idea of mutilation in discussing the abuse of
characters and events that appears in Shakespeare's "disfigured" version of the Hamlet story.[9] Tolstoy is particularly incensed by the way Shakespeare's characters are
made to say and do "unnatural" things, but one need
share neither his novelistic conception of the stage nor
the ethical assumptions upon which it rests in order to
find something valuable in the terms of his attack. In the
act of mutilation one encounters what appears to be the
opposite of palindrome. Insofar as palindrome represents the illusion that arbitrary signs may have the time-

9. "Shakespeare and the Drama," in *The Complete Works of Lyof
N. Tolstoi* (New York: Crowell, 1899): *Shakespeare, Christian Teaching, Letters*, esp. 405–9. Shakespeare plays on the mutilating nature of representation in Quince's line from *Midsummer Night's
Dream* (3.1.56) concerning the mechanical who will "disfigure,
or present" the person of Moonshine.

less stability of a monument, the act of mutilation furnishes an inverse: revealing the arbitrariness of what had seemed certain. The disfigured figure denies in a second set of signs what is asserted in the first—the otherwise regal bishop suffering humiliating de-coronation, the sometime judicious old Jephthah associated with the infantilism of Hamlet's epithet "great baby." An assertion that one is actually more than one, the act of mutilation would seem a graphic representation of the opening of the world of things to debate about claims of truth and falsity—to judgment. But mutilation may actually be more complicated, as is demonstrated in the treatment accorded Ophelia by Hamlet and by *Hamlet*. Through her case, one gets a better sense of the reasoning behind Tolstoy's attack on Shakespeare himself as the father of mutilation and a clearer conception of the gulf that separates mutilation from trial or debate.

Hamlet's mutilating treatment of Ophelia is concentrated in the nunnery scene. There, the original elevated image of her, like that of Hamlet's love letter with its characterization of her as his "soul's idol, the most beautified Ophelia" (2.2.109), recurs in the form of the prince's initial greeting. But his "fair Ophelia?—Nymph, in thy orisons / Be all my sins remember'd" (3.1.89–90) is abruptly contradicted by its opposite. Hamlet's "Ha, Ha! are you honest?" follows hard upon the return of his letters, and the force of this verbal blow to Ophelia is subsequently redoubled with gathered violence until its fury is fully realized in the elaborate image of the nymph turned whore:

> I have heard of your paintings too, well enough; God has given you one face, and you make yourselves another; you jig, you amble, and you lisp, and nick-

name God's creatures, and make your wantonness
your ignorance. Go to, I'll no more on't; it hath made
me mad.

(3.1.142–46)

Or rather of the nymph/whore, for these lines claim that
Hamlet's abusive image of her is not belated supplementation but a necessary part of the original monument itself. Swept away in his own intensity, the mutilator
seems to lose sight of his own instrumental role in this act
of mutilation; not his own choice to appear mad but
Ophelia's sinful nature has made him mad indeed. Thus
denying the reality of time and his own acts of cognition,
he seems unwittingly to inscribe his present awareness
backward over past reality: "I loved you not" over "I did
love you once." Her erstwhile innocence now appears in
the two-faced form of an outer affected "ignorance" and
the inner "wantonness" that is revealed as having always
been its true cause. So Hamlet's blows claim to free a significance that had been hidden yet is *already* present in
the lines of Ophelia's original icon: the "idol" now appears to have been, as the term might well suggest, a corrupted seeming indeed, and the otherwise hidden con-
notation of artificiality that occasioned Polonius's
judicious rejection of "beautified" as a "vile phrase" has
also risen into view. The once dominant hierarchy by
which such suspicion was relegated to ground has been
inverted. Judgment confronts judgment; in mutilation
both sets of opposing signs must be preserved, not as a
means of rationally testing their claims of validity, as in a
debate or trial, but in service of a new transvaluation.
Ophelia could not appear the maddening monster of
Hamlet's mutilated image if the signs of her identity as

chaste nymph and beautified idol were not both preserved in the lines that enact his mutilation of her.

The play seems to treat her in precisely the same
way. The innocent figure of the first acts, who is as note-
worthy as the image of daughterly "duty and obedience"
(3.2.107) as she is as that of loving concern for Hamlet,
praying for his health and restoration to himself even as
he curses her (3.1.150–61), is violated by the second face
that emerges into view in the later acts. The beauty of innocent deference and maidenly concern reappears as the
necessary public aspect of indiscriminate subservience
and erotic abandon.

From what one is able to see, she first appears innocent of such a corrupt nature. Yet when Polonius's death
sets loose her madness, her lines openly express the
fallen sexuality of Hamlet's accusations. Retrospectively,
his mutilating attack upon her in the nunnery scene begins, on the basis of the play's later evidence, to take on
the stability of a true iconic rendering. Strikingly, it is particularly in the case of her pious terms that corruption
shows itself the rankest:

By Gis, and by Saint Charity,
    Alack, and fie for shame!
Young men will do't, if they come to't;
    By Cock, they are to blame.
Quoth she, before you tumbled me,
    You promised me to wed.

(4.5.56–61)

In recognizing "God" deformed to the wanton's deity,
"Cock," are we not supposed to remember Hamlet's attack on her pious seemings, on the wantonness that uses
ignorance for its public aspect? To take things so and sim-

ply so, however, would be to overlook significant complications that haunt Hamlet's attacks, and *Hamlet*'s attacks,
with the further complexities potential to the act of
mutilation.[10]

In its simplest form, mutilation aims its blow
through the image at the prototype of that image; the attack so intended enacts a negative version of the honor
rendered the prototype through traditional homage to
the image. Seen from this perspective, Hamlet's violent
verbal attack on Ophelia's innocent image would obviously be an attack upon her and less obviously an attack
upon the physical father whose living image she is, as
well as upon the conceptual principle—frail woman-
hood—she embodies. Yet the warfare of signs is as capable of alternative interpretations as the nunnery scene itself has proven to be, for, paradoxically, the symbolic acts
through which the iconoclast insults his enemies may be
read in precisely the opposite way.

When the figure of the infant cradled in the arms of
a statuary Virgin is desecrated so as to make it appear a
deformed, premature fetus, as in a case mentioned by
John Stow, the act is something more than a blow struck
against the artist of the scene, the conceptual principle of
representability it embodies, and the Roman Catholicism
it connotes.[11] In such cases, the act of mutilation is itself
split by opposed senses: on the one hand, a blow at the
enemy; on the other, a belated attempt to rescue the prototype from an original desecration embodied in the very

10. For a typical reading of Ophelia's songs as the expression
of erotomania see Carroll Camden, "On Ophelia's Madness,"
Shakespeare Quarterly 15 (1964): 247–55.

11. John Stow's account may be found in *Stow's Survey of London* (1598; rev. ed. 1956; rpt. New York: Dent, 1970), 238–39.

fact of representation. The blow that appears to violate an absent enemy as present in the representation may also seek to preserve the iconoclast's own beloved Lord as absent from the original violence of representation itself. And it is by no means unfitting that this particular defacing should take the form it does, for the iconoclast is not engaged in a version of Luther's undertaking, which gently attempts to rescue the babe of the nativity by unmetaphorical reminders of the child's human functions.[12] This is not an entryway for naturalism, not a patient attempt to resurrect human life from the shroud of conceptualization. Rather it is an attempt to cancel the first murder with the violence of a second, while preserving the figure that represents the infamy of the first crime. Thus the place of the timeless One, that concept made flesh in the aged baby of traditional Christian iconography, is usurped by the iconoclast's rendering of the mutilated one, who appears, in Stow's turn of phrase, born "out of time"—i.e., premature, helpless, ignorant, untimely rather than timeless.[13] Concept counters concept, image image, not in the rendering of an envisioned or reenvisioned nature, not in the creation of a more perfectly inclusive monument, not in an attempt to show how it was and is, but intending through disfiguring misrepresentation to unseat the thoughtless arrogance of representation itself, exposing its fictionality.

Could not this formula—violent misrepresentation intended to both defeat and accuse a representation that is blind to its own violence—serve equally to describe

12. On Luther's "unmetaphoring" of the nativity see William Mallard, *The Reflection of Theology in Literature* (San Antonio, Tex.: Trinity University Press, 1977), 66.

13. *Stow's Survey of London*, 239.

Hamlet's attack upon Ophelia? Certainly, from the lines of his first speeches on, Hamlet repeatedly casts himself as a partisan of the unrepresentable "that within" both self and events, which may not be caught in the conventional figures of language and gesture. Neither his father's death nor his own "me" is truly denotable by word or show. Is not his self-mutilation in putting on the signs of madness presumed, however unconvincingly, to be a form of self-defense?[14] Similarly, the abuse of Ophelia's image might well appear truly defensive, though pursued in the form of offense—an affront intended to counter the representational activities of Polonius, whose shaping presence is audible in her insipid couplets, a misrepresentation intended to sunder Ophelia from passive enthrallment in Polonius's shows.[15] Once again the activities of Hamlet parallel those of the play.

If the very improbable extremity of Hamlet's violent attack might lead one to read its *offendendo* backward as an odd instance of *defendendo*, the play's own violent treatment of mad Ophelia raises enough uneasiness to

---

14. Hamlet's self-defense by self-mutilation—i.e., putting on the signs of madness—recalls Sir Walter Raleigh's similar actions during the Salisbury charade, a tampering with the truth that Raleigh felt compelled to defend from the charge of sinfulness, in John Chamberlain's words, excusing "the disfiguring of himself by the example of David who fained himself mad to avoide daunger: and never heard yt imputed to him for a sinne" (from a letter to Sir Dudley Carleton of 1618, reprinted in Albert C. Baugh and Thomas Cable, *A History of the English Language* [1957; rpt. Englewood Cliffs, N.J.: Prentice-Hall, 1978], 416. On the Salisbury performance and Raleigh's subsequent defense of his actions see also Robert Lacey, *Sir Walter Raleigh* (New York: Atheneum, 1974), esp. 372–73.

15. See 3.1.100–101.

suggest the playwright's similar possession of a Hal-like capacity to make offense a skill.

By its very sexual and blasphemous violence, the mad language of Ophelia almost seems designed to assure that one will reject its accusatory implications. Her lines, as Claudius suggests, might rather denote the absence of herself, of her judgment, from her words and actions than the shape of a self behind them. Perhaps part of the point is that one does inevitably botch her lines in the collection and should rather hear in them only "nothing sure, yet much unhappily" (4.5.13), the discoursing of mad grief, occasioned "all" by the death of her father:

Oh, this' the poison of deep grief; it springs
All from her father's death.

$$(4.5.72–73)$$

Devoid of her isolating, disposing faculty of judgment, Ophelia is left an undiscriminating compendium of any and all expressions of loss and mourning, whether appropriate or not to the chief instance of her loss. Instead of the "discourse of reason," which looking before and after confidently selects and arranges its *parole*, choosing the *mot juste* from the set of available alternatives, Ophelia's mad language is discourse in its etymological sense—a running back and forth, confusing lovers and parents, negatives and positives, desire and fact. This distracted and distracting ebb and blow of signifiers performs, but performs "too much," the necessary work of mourning:

> there is nothing of significance that can fill that hole in the real, except the totality of the signifier. . . . The work of mourning is first of all performed to satisfy the disorder that is produced by the inadequacy

of signifying elements to cope with the hole that has been created in existence, for it is the system of signifiers in their totality which is impeached by the least instance of mourning.[16]

The great demand of grief cuts signifiers loose from their conventional moorings to one signified or another, letting them drift about in the vortex of Polonius's absence—without ending or intended ends. A sense of this overpowering effect of mourning might permit one to resist, in credibly dramatic terms, both the suspicions aroused by Hamlet's denunciations and even the seeming confirmation of these suspicions in Ophelia's own lines. In effect, she is lost in grief, her one's and no's, signs of innocence and sin, left to do ghostly battle in a field from which she herself has departed. The accusations that the play arouses against her die in the "plurisy" (4.7.118), from *plus*, *plethora*, of their own excess.

Yet for all that, her case must remain, in the clerk's term, "doubtful" because it is not just her language that might cause in us a judicious running back again to the terms of Hamlet's original accusations. Gertrude's eulogy, against all dramatic likelihood of her own character and of the play's action (how could she know?) manages to resurrect the suspicious reading of Ophelia outside the dramatic contexts of either Hamlet's obscure strategies or Ophelia's own mad utterances. A character whose lines are dominated, even in madness, by her appropriate and explicit use of the language of emblematic vegetation dies into an iconic scene dominated by the willow of forsaken love and, more disconcertingly, by the "long purples"

16. Jacques Lacan, "Desire and the Interpretation of Desire in *Hamlet*," *Yale French Studies* 55/56 (1977): 11–52, p. 38.

pendant from her fantastic garlands. The gratuitous reference to the "grosser name" of these "dead men's fingers," protruding as it does from the conventional *florilegia* of maidenly mourning, quickens the ghostly figure that first showed itself in Hamlet's attack.[17] If, as Laertes suggests, "praises may go back again" (4.7.27), then surely blame can follow the same crablike route. On the basis of this judgment, from outside, from after the conclusion of her line of life, are the accusations of Hamlet finally to be credited? Or is the ghostly image that walks here meant to be securely laid in the burial scene, with its echoes of the wedding ceremony and its bestowal of "virgin crants"? Does ultimate position dictate judicious supremacy, or are the conflicting images of Ophelia left grappling, like brother and lover, in the obscure place of her absence?

Sign against sign—with the final violent twists of this conflict one might seem to be left with something resembling the open uncertainty with which the typologist's incomplete chains of figuration conclude; left waiting, that is, for a fulfillment which is not yet. The difference is that this chain begins and ends with overt judgments and conscious conceptualizations: Ophelia signifies to Hamlet alternately nymphic chastity and feminine corruption; however an "idol" and in whichever sense "beautified," she is fit for disposing to a nunnery in one of its two diametrically opposed senses. Judgment, instead of remaining hidden beneath the pretense of de-

17. The willow appears as the emblem of forsaken love in *Much Ado About Nothing* (2.1.209). On the shape and sexual significance of dead men's fingers, the *Orchis mascula*, see Geoffrey Grigson, *The Englishman's Flora* (London: Phoenix House, 1955), 194.

conceptualized "historical" treatment, challenges us from the first to the last by violently pitting conception against conception: judgment to play, a play of judgments, as in Hamlet's verbal foiling with Polonius. Oddly enough, this reversal of the physical duel sequence (from play to judgment) ends in the very ambiguity that its structure seems initially to deny, for the precise point at which the play of judgments is played out, over and done, is left unclear, surrendered, in fact, to the judgment of the audience.

Once again a part seems to offer to tell us something about the structure of the whole, for in similar fashion things within the play itself are handed over finally to Horatio, who appears to embody so well the audience's important role. Called by a name that suggests the double sense—both rational and orational—of *logos*, Horatio everywhere evidences the function of ratio, of measure and discrimination.[18] To Hamlet he appears "e'en as just a man" as his conversation ever "coped" (3.2.49–50), one in whom "blood and judgment" are so well "commingled" (3.2.64) that neither passion nor fortune seems capable of prevailing against his proper equilibrium. To us he presents a similar image from the first time we meet him. In the first scene, as the "scholar," Horatio speaks from a perspective of detachment: by his own report only a "piece of him" attends upon the seemingly foolish errand of ghost watching, while his acquiescence to the superstitions of vulgar legend is, even despite the "sensible and true avouch" of his own eyes, but "in part." By virtue

18. Sidney uses the oratio/ratio pun, demanding rhetorically, "if *oratio* next to *ratio*, speech next to reason, be the greatest gift bestowed upon mortality" (*An Apology for Poetry*, ed. Forrest G. Robinson [New York: Bobbs-Merrill, 1970], 53).

of this detachment, certain features of his language seem appropriate as well: his oddly tentative assessment of history since Old Hamlet's triumphs, for example, with its interesting stylistic similarities to the characteristic self-qualifying mode of Plutarch—"our valiant Hamlet— / For so this side of our known world esteem'd him" (1.1.84–85), or Fortinbras's enterprise "As it doth well appear unto our state" (1.1.101).[19] Horatio repeatedly speaks in quotation marks, distancing himself from his relation of something that he has "heard"—whether concerning the political causes of Denmark's nightly labors, the legendary behavior of spirits at cockcrow, or Christian tales of Christmas.

Unlike any other character in the play, Horatio is privileged to combine an insider's knowledge with an outsider's detachment. This remarkable combination of inside and outside is early demonstrated in his command of the precise details of Danish history (how would he recognize the very armor in which the old king had confronted ambitious Norway thirty years before?), but is most strikingly evidenced in the play's final moments. There, even in the throes of enacting an irrational, passionate identification with the plight of Hamlet, even as he reaches for the cup that contains the fatal "union," Horatio manages to speak the rational, hierarchical and conceptual language that is his own: "I am more an antique Roman than a Dane" (5.2.328). From outside and by election rather than from inside the necessity of birth and blood, he chooses the attempt to throw off consciousness

19. On Plutarch and style, see the chapter on *Caesar* above. Ernest Schanzer points out an echo of North's Plutarch in *Hamlet* in his *The Problem Plays of Shakespeare* (New York: Schocken Books, 1963), 47.

and individual identity in language that carefully pre-
serves the distinction of three terms, the limits and the
hierarchy of their relationship: his "I" is "more," though
not entirely, of the type denominated "antique Roman"
(notice the nice historical distinction of kind in "antique")
than that defined by "Dane." The mode reminds one of
the style of Brutus' funeral oration with its proportional
qualifications, "Not that I loved Caesar less, but that I
loved Rome more," or of the general feeling in the case of
Julius Caesar that one is only being called to a partial identification with characters and their actions while being
warned to keep one's categories and distances in working
order.

Thus, it seems fitting that Horatio should be the one
to isolate the corpses, to dispose them "High on a stage"
(5.2.365), and to order "things" under a conceptual "upshot" that has already twice been suggested by the play:

And, in this upshot, purposes mistook
Fall'n on the inventors' heads. All this can I
Truly deliver.[20]

(5.2.371–73)

But in the light of the play's final gesture of surrender to
an audience as embodied in Horatio, Hamlet's own longing for a "judicious" audience, his taste for plays that are
a cut above the vulgar capacities of the "general," his
dream of a theatre of ideas in which no unruly contingencies of particular production will hinder the procession of

20. For other enunciations of this principle see 3.4.207–11 and
5.2.306–7. For a reading that is more optimistic about Horatio's
adequacy as a storyteller see Eileen Jorge Allman, *Player-King
and Adversary* (Baton Rouge: Louisiana State University Press,
1980), 253.

"necessary questions" from printed script to performance to audience, his insistence upon decorous congruence of word and action among the players, and his concern that his own act of revenge will be properly "scann'd," all take on a certain futile poignance. Having seen all that we have seen in Denmark, how many of us have ever been satisfied with Horatio's common upshot? Never Hamlet.

But if Horatio's judicious principle is not true enough to satisfy, it is also not untrue. When placed in properly enlarged contexts, even the encounter between Hamlet and "Old Jephthah" in Act 2 reveals levels of significance that seem to render it an iconic embodiment of Horatio's motto. Examined closely, the incident shows, in fact, that it is the very ability of Hamlet's discursive reason to look cognitively both forward to Polonius's future treatment of Ophelia and back to Jephthah's parallel treatment of his own daughter that occasions a kind of blindness in him. He himself is not proof against the enticements of the very figure with which he tempts Polonius. Polonius, despite his eager responses, is not even the primary offender revealed by the scene, for even if Hamlet's judgment of him turns out to be correct, even if Polonius actually appears elsewhere in this scene as quite ready to sacrifice his daughter by loosing her to Hamlet, the old man is not, as the scene also reveals, the only one prepared so to use her. The prince has been perfectly willing to sacrifice her himself in his own act of sorting her, without discernible provocation, among harlots (2.2.173–85)—an act of conceptual violence scarcely to be preferred over Polonius's own mistreatment of her, nor, for that matter, much better than the scandalous strategies for which Polonius commissions Reynaldo in spying on Laertes. The prince may intend the exposure of another through his Jephthah/Polonius conjunction, but he has, in his very act of likening, of rendering an image, transposed his own readiness to violate Ophelia onto that other and attempted to isolate it there.

For this attempt Polonius is indeed a "capital calf" because his thick-witted and graceless manipulations of others make him by nature a fit bearer of the loathing such misuse of poor Ophelia might arouse. At this level, then, the incident might remind one of the scapegoat's role played by Caesar, who, in his own play, is naturally unattractive enough to bear the burden of sins that he actually shares with the other, more attractive Romans. And the extent to which Hamlet's lines, and indeed the play itself, succeed in dramatically isolating the quality of self-blind guilt in the figure of Old Jephthah might obscure the place of this whole incident in what is surely one of the more obvious patterns of the play: despite the fact that they may be sound in themselves, acts of judgment appear to be readable as inverted self-representations of the judge.

The idea that the judge's own acts of isolation and disposition may be read in two different directions is a recurrent Shakespearean theme. In *As You Like It*, for example, Duke Senior argues that Jaques's satirical scourgings of the world are really acts of self-representation, voidings of his own sins upon others (2.7.45–87). The mad Lear vehemently denounces the justice who whips whores for enacting the secret lust in his own heart (4.6.163–65). As in the case of Angelo's punishment of Claudio in *Measure for Measure*, the point is clearly not the exact proportion of guilt or innocence in the accused but the bi-directional significance of the act of judgment it-self—openly representing the world to the judge and se-cretly unfolding the judge to the world: his very *one* re-vealed through the *no* he proclaims to another.

An awareness of this double potential in judging is not incompatible with the manner and matter of *Julius Caesar*, but part of the difference between that play and *Hamlet* lies in the differing approach to this problem. In *Caesar* event is matched to event, character to character, to reveal that the factions are ultimately similar where they believe themselves to be different and different where they believe themselves the same. The formula is that of the couplet—two signifying halves that need one another for balance, unity, and ultimately for a kind of resolution: the party of Caesar and that of Brutus to-gether, as the play's shifting use of the term suggests, embodying the concept of "noble Roman." This interde-pendency complicates the simple idea of univocal signif-icance, of one signifier to one signified (wherein Brutus might image either factious usurpation or Roman no-bility, but not both) since signifier so obviously needs signifier. But from *outside*, from after the fact, from the playwright's and audience's safe position of historical irony and alienation, judgment of the entire body of an-tique Rome remains possible. From this distanced per-spective, across the discontinuities of ages and faiths, the particular Romans might all appear as a group to embody the common pathology and cause of Romanness. In the case of *Hamlet*, by contrast, the play does not so much drive one out as pull one in, performing instead of an ex-posé of Polonius and Hamlet a mutilation of what is, as generations of commentators have understood, an image of author and of audience.[21]

By virtue of its double potential—offense or defense—the act of mutilation makes extraordinary demands upon its audience. It is we who must interpret, must judge, whether, for example the alteration of Becket's features into feminine form represents a hostile statement about his whoring after Roman domination or a defense of some sort.[22] By the very violence of its terms, mutilation does not leave one the luxury of distant neutrality, but forces one to judge where the finger of accu-

21. As Stephen Booth puts it, from the prince's first speech, he "gives himself to the audience as its agent onstage. Hamlet and the audience are from this point in the play more firmly united than any other such pair in Shakespeare, or perhaps in dramatic literature" ("On the Value of *Hamlet*," in *Reinterpretations of Elizabethan Drama*, ed. Norman Rabkin [New York: Columbia University Press, 1969], 150). The idea of Hamlet as a stand-in for Shakespeare is ubiquitous; see, for example, Tolstoy, "Shakespeare and the Drama," 413. Coleridge observes, with regard to Hamlet, that "one of Shakespeare's modes of creating characters is, to conceive any one intellectual or moral faculty in morbid excess, and then to place himself, Shakespeare, thus mutilated or diseased under given circumstances" (*Lectures and Notes on Shakespeare and Other English Poets*, ed. T. Ashe [1884; rpt. Freeport: Books for Libraries, 1972], 344). Even a reader so alert to the ironic as A. W. Schlegel saw in Hamlet a merging of playwright and prince, *August Wilhelm von Schlegel's Sämmtliche Werke*, ed. Edvard Böcking (Leipzig: Weidmann, 1846), 6: 202.

22. On the mutilation of Becket's image see David Freedberg's "The Structure of Byzantine and European Iconoclasm," in Anthony Bryer and Judith Herrin, eds., *Iconoclasm* (Birmingham: Center for Byzantine Studies, 1977), 169. See also Tancred Borenius, "Some Further Aspects of the Iconography of St. Thomas of Canterbury," *Archaeologia* 83 (1933): 171–86, esp. 182.

sation points. But not only must one decide upon the intended meaning of the mutilator's act, one must also determine whether or not the finger is actually a phallus—a pointed disposition of the judge's own lack, his desire. So it is that in the nunnery scene, the possibility presents itself that Hamlet's icon of feminine duplicity, instead of representing Ophelia either offensively as he believes her to be, or defensively as he believes her not to be, represents instead Ophelia as he unwittingly *needs* her to be. If she were, always had been, and would be the figure that he envisions, then her unquestioning obedience to the commands of her father would not be yet another standard against which to judge his own shortcomings as a child. She would not be another "mirror"— another ideal he is unable to measure up to—but a mere "semblable"—a likeness for the lapsed character who oddly turns upon himself the very names of "whore" and "drab" (2.2.560–62) that his icon would make appropriate to Ophelia.

Surely some sort of unintended self-exposure of the judge's needs is operating in the closet scene. Even the syntax of the prince's attack suggests that we are not being shown an objective rendering of Gertrude but something within Hamlet, as he wantonly desecrates her through his images of her seduction:

HAMLET: One word more, good lady.
GERTRUDE: What shall I do?
HAMLET: Not this, by no means, that I bid you do:
    Let the bloat king tempt you again to bed;
    Pinch wanton on your cheek; call you his mouse;
    And let him, for a pair of reechy kisses,
    Or paddling in your neck with his damn'd fingers,
    Make you to ravel all this matter out.
                (3.4.180–86)

In this "one word" are heard not the singular ghostly Word but the many words contributed by the speaker—*one plus* rather than the simple "Not" that he owns for his own. This may be an attack on her, may be an attack against what others have made her to seem, but it is also obviously an exposure of needs so obscure to the attacker that it is only through such occasions that they can find expression. Only through such violence wrought upon another does his own nameless "that within," that "something dangerous" find an outer shape.[23] The secret fact is that the mutilator may need the image the way the judge needs the criminal to represent, to image upon another—his "dearest foe" (1.2.182)—what he would not own in himself, to himself.

Through such acts, the fingers of righteous accusation appear as the dishonest "pickers and stealers" of Hamlet's joke, for in their selecting and disposing they corrupt the pious office of judgment even in the act of executing its formal demands—as Hamlet's lying witticism to Rosencrantz and Guildenstern violates both trust and the Catechism while employing the forms of both:

ROSENCRANTZ: My lord, you once did love me.
HAMLET: So I do still, by these pickers and stealers.
(3.2.320–21)

As Coleridge saw, the word "So" in Hamlet's lines enables him to lie even while speaking truth: Rosencrantz is bound to take Hamlet's word to mean that his love is a permanent unity, today still one as yesterday, not the

23. For a reading of the closet scene in terms of Neoplatonic emblematics see Paul Hamill's "Death's Lively Image: The Emblematic Significance of the Closet Scene in *Hamlet*," *Texas Studies in Literature and Language* 16 (1974–75): 249–62. Hamill sees Hamlet as embodying a profoundly Christian and iconic vision.

mixed one and no that we see elsewhere enacted in his treatment of the "adders fanged."[24] But what if the accusing member is a dead man's finger?

III

The ghost enwraps Hamlet in what sounds like a couplet:

HAMLET: Speak; I am bound to hear.
GHOST: So art thou to revenge, when thou shalt hear.
(1.5.6–7)

Such a wedding of two into one that the couplet represents, such a fitting of time and tension into a culminating resolution, is in form like revenge, which belatedly comes on the scene to complete the movement begun by murder. Thus revenge is, or would seem to be, as Alexander Welsh has argued, an appropriate antidote to mourning.[25] The hole in the "real" that Lacan discusses as the occasion for mourning would seem to be plugged decisively in the act of revenge, the endless melancholy drift of signifiers stopped by revenge's insistence on the one proper signified, the one victim that will do precisely for its need. The Polonian son's focus on the precise signified exactly opposes the daughter's loss in the floating substitution of signifiers; mourning would go on forever, revenge resolve everything now.

The intention of revenge is fitness and resolution, but in its longing it reaches beyond human limitations toward a state of immediate natural fitness without the de-

24. See the Variorum notes to this passage for Coleridge's remarks.

25. For Welsh's argument see "The Task of Hamlet," *Yale Review* 69 (1980): 481–502.

lays, substitutions, and mediations characteristic of the symbolic social order. So Laertes' appearance as revenger must appear to the keepers of that order as absolute threat:

> as the world were now but to begin,
> Antiquity forgot, custom not known,
> The ratifiers and props of every word.
>
> (4.5.99–101)

Slitting throats in church would indeed "thoroughly" demonstrate, as Claudius and Laertes agree, Laertes' natural sonship because such an act would graphically enact his denial of the mediate social realm within which he has other roles—allegiance, vows, conscience—besides that of immediate heir to his father (4.5.117–19;131–36).[26]

It is fitting, then, that the ghost's lines demanding revenge from his son actually do more than form a couplet with the son's words, for as they take those very words and repeat them (hear/hear), they point to a union that longs, ultimately, for timeless identity rather than the mere successive resonance of words joined in a couplet. Ideally, the son should not be "bound" by hearing *words*, by his belated decision as a cognizant, separate individual, but pre-bound, already caught up in his task by

26. Eleanor Prosser notices that Laertes' rejection of patience echoes the ghost's appeal to Hamlet's "nature," the only difference being the compression of Laertes' sentiments into one moment of fury and their direction against "our hero" (*Hamlet and Revenge* [Stanford, Calif.: Stanford University Press, 1967], 214). The ironies that attend upon the fact that Laertes' "natural" impulsiveness falls under the anything but impulsive cold-bloodedness of Claudius are explored by Nigel Alexander, *Poison, Play and Duel* (Lincoln: University of Nebraska Press, 1971), 191ff.

the very nature of *things*.[27] Such is the dream—to be already bound utterly by "nature" (1.5.81) to undo the "unnatural" (1.5.25,27)—as "swift as meditation or the thoughts of love" but without either. Hamlet dreams this dream, wishing to have been impregnated by his cause, to be, like the actor, a living image of that cause, but not like the actor through an effort of personal force based on "conceit." Instead, without thinking about ratio and relation—himself to Hecuba, Hecuba to him—he longs to have that cause in him, or, more accurately, to be already himself within it.

Lamenting the fact of "conscience," of the thought whose sickly "pale" compromises the "native hue" of resolution (3.1.84–85), Hamlet speaks as if resolution were not properly the end of human thought, not a re-solving of thought's distinguishing, paling questions, but rather nature itself, native and given in the world of things themselves long before thought comes limping along behind to cloud nature's clarity with words, with individual judgments.[28] From such a perspective, "occasions" might truly seem to inform on their own (4.4.32), "foul deeds" themselves to rise up (1.2.257), tongueless murder, Gertrude's trespasses, and Laertes' fitness all to speak (2.2.579; 3.4.147; 5.2.190). Even such contingencies as the vicissitudes of theatrical fashion might be "not very strange" but necessary, "more than natural" signs of universal falling off (2.2.355–59). Fittingly, Hamlet threatens

27. The Variorum note contrasts Hamlet's use of "bound" as "ready, addressed" with the ghost's use of it as a past participle of the verb "to bind."

28. This sense is reinforced by the fact that "hue," according to the *Oxford English Dictionary*, is another Elizabethan term for "apparition." Thus, the "native hue" would be a resident spirit.

Polonius by warning that even Ophelia might perforce be brought to intelligent conception, understanding bred in that unlikely location by the natural operation of things, as maggots are engendered by the sun in the passivity of a dead dog's remains (2.2.180–84).

Considered in this regard, the precise moment of the ghost's initial appearance to Hamlet is especially significant. The way for that apparition is prepared by the noise of Claudius's cannon, a thing with a meaning, as Horatio's question—"What does this mean, my lord?"—assumes. Hamlet's answer returns us to the terms of his first soliloquy:

The king doth wake to-night and takes his rouse,
Keeps wassail, and the swaggering upspring reels;
And as he drains his draughts of Rhenish down,
The kettle-drum and trumpet thus bray out
The triumph of his pledge.

(1.4.8–12)

Claudius enacts his bestial nature, swaggering, reeling and wassailing—publicly embodying, in other words, the satyrlike (both Lapithian groom and wine-crazed demi-beast) rank grossness "in nature" of Hamlet's earlier private assessment, while the musical instruments abandon their proper human office to "bray" the triumph of the "lord of Beasts" (5.2.87). Dramatically, this would be fine if this were all. One would be fitly prepared for the silent martial stalk of the ghost and the echo of Horatio's questioning in Hamlet's own subsequent query, "What may this mean?" The parallelism of the two sequences and the opposed natures of the two kingly figures would say it all: drunken noise opposed to sober silence, each character a thing with a timeless meaning, a signifying icon imaging its cause.

And so it is in the Folio and first Quarto versions, but in other texts the incident is altered profoundly, for between this *one* and its *no* there intrudes a surprising wound, an extended temporal gap during which Hamlet verbally exercises his own power of judgment—without the ghost.

This heavy-headed revel east and west
Makes us traduced and tax'd of other nations;
They clepe us drunkards, and with swinish phrase
Soil our addition; and indeed it takes
From our achievements, though perform'd at height,
The pith and marrow of our attribute.
So, oft it chances in particular men,
That for some vicious mole of nature in them,
As, in their birth,—wherein they are not guilty,
Since nature cannot choose his origin,—
By the o'ergrowth of some complexion,
Oft breaking down the pales and forts of reason,
Or by some habit that too much o'er-leavens
The form of plausive manners; that these men,—
Carrying, I say, the stamp of one defect,
Being nature's livery, or fortune's star,—
Their virtues else—be they as pure as grace,
As infinite as man may undergo—
Shall in the general censure take corruption
From that particular fault; the dram of eale
Doth all the noble substance of a doubt
To his own scandal.

(1.4.17–38)

Verbose, as Pope says, circular, even obsessive in its repetitions, this speech is utterly wrong dramatically but crucial morally. The son is carving for himself a moral vision that is in matter completely at odds wih the preeminent natural demands of the revenge code and in manner opposed to the uncompromising pronouncements of his own first soliloquy.

Then and there he has no problem with the assumed unchanging negative and positive values of Claudius and Old Hamlet, no hesitation in likening one to the singular sun god Hyperion and the other to an unindividuated member of a group—like a satyr, any satyr—constituted by the eternal common theme of satyrs: the double signs of bestiality and humanity under the domination of the brute. Gertrude's own doubleness, it is true, at first presents something more of a problem, for in her case time and change are less easily ignored in favor of the claims of essence: from Niobe once "all tears" to the worse than bestial being who actually chooses, rather than simply and passively embodying, the bestiality of Claudius. Hamlet's solution to the dilemma posed by Gertrude occurs through his generation of an image, an eternal dead (because unchanging) monument to Frailty, a timeless quality upon which his mother's two otherwise disparate temporal moments may both be held as one—external aspects of an internal concept. "Frailty, thy name is woman"—so he judges her lack of judgment, and, as in the case of Ophelia's own caricature, nothing is lost in this Janus-like icon. Gertrude may even keep her tears; only by virtue of her iconization, they now appear not sincere but "most unrighteous," their double temporal significances subordinated to the single hierarchy implied in her retrospective designation as woman, as Frailty. Nothing is lost, nothing, that is, except her life, except her inner human life, for in this belated reduction to the embodiment of general feminine Frailty she is robbed of the full complement of individual human complexity. No longer a person to him but a thing, Gertrude and her actions become predictable to him; even her very particular act of incest more or less expected, common to kind, at worst offensive for its "dexterity" and "speed" rather than its evil. It is the complexity of Hamlet's own life within that seems to speak, suddenly and unexpectedly, through the lines that immediately precede the ghost's arrival, as they fly in the face of the testimony of things without and put the question to the mode of his first soliloquy.

By driving Hamlet's lines into the gap between Claudius's noise and Old Hamlet's dumb show, the play mutilates its own stage tableau physically, while the sense of the prince's lines attacks the presumptions that would allow, and already in the first soliloquy have allowed, such schematic oppositions their validity. In "particular" men, as in whole races and groups, the "particular" fault, whether derived from birth, nature, or consistent habit, often wrongly outweighs a host of virtues in the scale of judgment. In judging, men privilege the *isolated* part, the flaw, or the piece of behavior congruent to the outlines of type ("common theme"), even when such signs ought to be seen against the competing evidence, the "all" or ground of the individual's entire "substance." It is a fault of human judgment that it cannot attend both to flaw and to substance without *disposing* the one in domination over the whole of the other. Here, in Hamlet's ever-shifting near-repetitions is a powerful antidote for the poison that made his first soliloquy a mockery of justice, with its violent confusion of parts and wholes, nature and guilt, timebound acts and timeless essences. Here for others, as elsewhere for himself, Hamlet asserts and defends a something more, an uncircumscribable "that within," which cannot without violence be subordinated to the image of a cause.[29]

Judgment turned against judgment. If, as Hegel claims, conceptual thinking amounts to a kind of murder of its object, then in Hamlet's lines there dawns the promise of a second life born of a second murder.[30] Perhaps if Hamlet had been allowed to continue, his verbal blows directed against the encroaching tableau of this scene would have reclaimed Gertrude and Claudius as human beings rather than leaving them petrified images of concepts. Even the imagery Hamlet uses when he rejects the testimony afforded by a "dram of eale" (1.4.36) refers pointedly to the case of Claudius. "Enter Ghost"—perhaps this unspoken line is the most tragic of the play, for with the entry of the ghost *Hamlet* and Hamlet seem inevitably driven back to the terms of the first soliloquy. The tragedy of Hamlet is not so much that he is restricted, that

---

29. He angrily rejects not only Gertrude and Claudius's attempts to read him by his outside but also the attempts of Rosencrantz and Guildenstern to make a "thing" out of him by plucking from him the heart of his human "mystery" (3.2.346–50). Of course, this uncatchable "that" is also shown to be a mystery even to Hamlet himself, leading him to admit:

> I do not know
> Why yet I live to say "This thing's to do."
> Sith I have cause and will and strength and more,
> To do't.
>
> (4.4.143–46)

30. Hegel's argument is in Book 7 of the *Phenomenology of Mind*; see Alexandre Kojève, *Introduction to the Reading of Hegel* (New York: Basic Books, 1969), 140ff. Shakespeare plays on a similar notion of mental incorporation of the object into the subject in Sonnet 112: "You are so strongly in my purpose bred, / That all the world besides me thinks y'are dead."

he may not do as the "unvalued" and "Carve for himself" (1.3.19–20). Rather, the tragedy is that, with such supplementation as occurs here, *some* of Hamlet's own carvings are accorded retrospective stability and external authority. At such extremely important moments, the process of mutilation is forgotten in the apparent permanence of the monument.

"Permanence" is the word for the dead father, who exists in the past, present, and future tenses of Hamlet's language as a pure, timeless concept, the same from any direction:

He was a man, take him for all in all,
I shall not look upon his like again.

(1.2.187–88)

As a silent monument in Hamlet's mournful internal vision, the father not only represents but constitutes a class of one, singular without likeness among dead, living, or yet unborn, who are only definable by dissimilitude, by the absolute extent to which they are all fallen off. The absent one comprises the essence of manhood, dead empirically and frozen spiritually, standing forever erect as the lonely, unconjoined "all in all," the self-identical idol of Hamlet's mind, an eternal *one* before which all others are merely *no*'s. This is the ghost who walks; the ghost who talks, however, is something more. As might be expected from a play that is so hard on the "idol" of Hamlet's soul, *Hamlet*'s treatment of the idol of the prince's mind is surprisingly vexing.[31]

True, some of the ghost's words when conjoined to those of Hamlet seem also to constitute a palindromic fig-

31. Prosser offers a representative account of the ambiguities of the ghost in *Hamlet and Revenge*.

ure, confirming after the fact and from another direction the pre-judgments of Hamlet's own "prophetic soul" (1.5.40). Not only in matter but in very manner, the ghostly imagery of beastliness and radiant spirituality carry one back again to the son's first soliloquy, giving that speech an added appearance of stability and objectivity. The personal and arbitrary now appear objective and natural. It is this very look of solidity, however, this apparent sameness from forward and back, that marks the palindromic conjunction's diabolic potential.[32]

When satanic legions recite the Mass backward, they plainly assert, however futile and deluded the assertion, a choice of meaningless chaos over significant form, an enactment of the simple will to independence of orders human and divine. Palindrome, on the other hand, far

32. For the diabolism of palindrome see Benno Tschischwitz's note to *Hamlet* 1.5.42 in his edition of *Hamlet* for *Shakespeares Sämmtliche Werke* (Halle: Barthel, 1869). Of course, it also had its sacred uses, particularly in the popular inscription of Gregory Nazianzus's "nipson anomemata me monan opsin" (wash my transgressions, not only my face) on baptismal fonts. The interesting aspect of the Rotas-Sator palindromic square, which was known all over medieval Europe, is that it may be read, according to Walter O. Moeller, as either Christian *or* Mithraic, its anagrammatic references to a father-centered religion ("oro te pater" and "pater noster"), its central cruciform design, and its use of alpha and omega all being interpretable from either religious context. Here would be temptation incarnate, but hardly an isolated instance, in which Christianity and a non-Christian religion use the same outward forms. See *The Mithraic Origin and Meanings of the Rotas-Sator Square* (Leiden: E. J. Brill, 1973). The threat of Hamlet's situation is suggested by his odd comparison of himself to the Nemean lion—the victim of Hercules—in the simile that immediately precedes his encounter with the ghost (1.4.83).

from being the form of such simple rebelliousness, is the form of allowance, of temptation. Its formal properties may give it the appearance of objective singleness and monumentality by making it look the same from any direction, but this seeming stability marks the hidden danger of the form. It seems necessary, not contingent, and this look of necessity and objectivity seems to constitute it, not as an arbitrary syntactic unit, but as an "eternal blazon," a significant thing. Yet, as our previous analysis has argued, the figure actually depends to a remarkable degree upon the individual interpreter's own readiness to isolate and dispose, to judge, to cognize.

In this, the couplet with its marriage of two independent, signifying entities into a harmony of relationship and hierarchy provides a fitting foil. Since the couplet's qualities consist of balanced tension and temporal evolution progressing to a culminating rest and resolution, it is obviously appropriate as a seal of closure for the action of a play or a scene. Palindrome, by contrast, presents itself, not as wedding and culmination, but as atemporal fixity, as a pre-existent identity—like Ophelia's alleged wantonness, already there from the beginning even if not at first apparent—rather than a resolution. But despite this appearance, it is in fact the occasion for a kind of specular life after life that silently and after the fact directs the interpreting consciousness to run back again, playing within the empty husks that the living voice has left behind. Posing as an eternal certainty, it is actually a figure of restlessness, of eye and intellect at play. No more one found to be two than two made one, it is rather *one plus*, for it is only the reader's contributed act of judgment, not the necessity of the form, that decides, first, that it exists, and then decides when to leave behind its formal enclosure and follow instead the course of the discourse in which the figure is contained.

This is the temptation: that apparent stability created by its form allows one to exercise one's own power of judgment, to cut oneself free, violating rather than following (as in couplet) the course—from left to right, from beginning to end, from Alpha to Omega—of the Word, but without knowing oneself rebellious. The reader thinks for himself, exercising his own powers of isolation and disposition, treating the Word as mere words but without realizing what he is doing. If cognition, as J. F. Lyotard suggests, appears in the Judaeo-Christian tradition as "the usurpation by the self of the place of the Word," then it is easy to see why the palindrome could be thought the perfect form for diabolical temptation.[33] In its secret alliance with that usurping cognition, palindrome offers it a place to exercise itself without recognizing its own blasphemy. It need not be a lie, need not be double speech, because by virtue of the illusions of its form, palindrome may, to twist Hamlet's express fear, actually *disabuse* one in truth, only to damn one indeed by providing one with a place in which to exercise judgment, in which to have a self without knowing it.[34]

33. Lyotard's quote is from his excellent meditation on Freud and *Hamlet,* "Jewish Oedipus," *Genre* 10 (1977): 410. In this same line of thought, it should be noted that for Luther the contrary of *ratio* is not *irratio* but obedience; see Robert S. Kinsman, *The Darker Vision of the Renaissance* (Berkeley and Los Angeles: University of California Press, 1974), 5. Luther's "Tu ratio stulta est" (cited in Kinsman, 1) might remind one of Hamlet's pointed remarks on the limits of "your philosophy."

34. Cf. Luther: "For faith speaks as follows: 'I believe Thee, God, when Thou dost speak.' What does God say? Things that are impossible, untrue, foolish, weak, absurd, abominable, he-

The return of Hamlet's own words in the ghost's lines provides the prince with a perverted version of the Christian promise of gaining one's life in the losing of it, for it enables him to meet himself coming and going without recognizing his own image. No sooner has the ghost departed than Hamlet enacts precisely this movement:

> Remember thee?
> Ay, thou poor ghost, while memory holds a seat
> In this distracted globe. Remember thee?
> Yea, from the table of my memory
> I'll wipe away all trivial fond records,
> All saws of books, all forms, all pressures past,
> That youth and observation copied there;
> And thy commandment all alone shall live
> Within the book and volume of my brain,
> Unmix'd with baser matter; yes, by heaven!
> O most pernicious woman!
>
> (1.5.95–105)

Apparently totally unaware that these lines disregard that portion of the ghost's Word marred by the overt contradiction between a manner that condemns Gertrude as

---

retical, and diabolical—if you consult reason" *Luther's Works*, ed. Jaroslav Pelikan and Walter A. Hansen [St. Louis, Mo.: Concordia, 1963], 36: 227. Compare *Macbeth* (1.3.123–26):

> And oftentimes, to win us to our harm,
> The instruments of Darkness tell us truths,
> Win us with honest trifles, to betray's
> In deepest consequence.

One thinks of the difficulties of Calvinist predestination in which hints of one's own pre-judged status might lead one precisely into sin; on this problem see Robert G. Hunter, *Shakespeare and the Mystery of God's Judgments* (Athens, Ga.: University of Georgia Press, 1976).

"lust" preying on garbage (55–57) and a Christian matter that forbids contrived act or tainted thought against her (85–86), Hamlet's isolating consciousness apprehends only monuments. The "most pernicious woman" is his first thought.

And if it is obviously something within Hamlet himself that is active in the selection that is going on here, that something within is itself clearly more than one thing. Accompanying the attack on Gertrude, there is mixed the baser matter of his disposition of Claudius:

O villain, villain, smiling, damned villain!
My tables, meet it is I set it down,
That one may smile, and smile, and be a villain;
At least I'm sure it may be so in Denmark.—
So, uncle, there you are.

(106*–10)

The commonplace about smiling villainy would be merely fatuous, akin to Ophelia's vapid "There's tricks i' the world" (4.5.5), or tautological, of a kind with his own later "never a villain ... But he's an arrant knave" (1.5.123–24), if it did not complete itself in the bizarre triple qualification—"At least I'm sure it may be so in Denmark." Here, exactly reversing his treatment of his mother, is ratio and proportion where one would expect absolute commitment. His locution echoes, in fact, the careful tentativeness of Horatio's assessment of Old Hamlet. Alternately violently absolute where he is explicitly commanded to restraint and tentative where he has been commanded to certain violence, Hamlet's lines show him possessed of an "I" that is everywhere evident even if not precisely definable. Indeed, even at the moment in which he seems to be enacting the role of abso-

lute son by his passive quotation of the father's very
words, one may hear a parricidal potential at work in his
language:

Now to my Word:
It is "Adieu, adieu, remember me."[35]

(110–11)

The difference between natural re-membering such
as occurs in the case of characters who feel, as does Or-
lando, the silent spirit of their fathers rising within them
to take them over and the unsettled potential of actual
human memory, dependent as it is upon words, is epito-
mized in the dangerous workings of the shifters—my,
me—within these lines.[36] Even as Hamlet repeats it, *the*
Word is already becoming *his* Word, the ghost's words
providing an opportunity for substitution and a potential
locus for Hamlet's thinking "on him / Together with," in
Claudius's diabolically perverted usage, a "remembrance" of his own "me." The son will die, of course, urg-
ing Horatio with a command that fully articulates this
substitution: "report me and my cause" (5.2.328), not remember the long since forgotten ghost and his cause.

35. Even to take "Remember me" as the ghost's sole command
is to take his word as only a command to keep on doing what
Hamlet has already been doing. Martin Scofield is good on this
passage as an expression of the "relativity of human judgment,
which runs through the play" (*The Ghosts of "Hamlet"* [Cam-
bridge: Cambridge University Press, 1980], 143–44). I quote
from the Second Quarto, which capitalizes "Word."

36. The opposition of deceptive verbal memory, particularly
writing, to an ideal personal memory founds Sonnet 122. For a
useful discussion of shifters see Anthony Wilden's note to
Jacques Lacan's *Language of the Self* (New York: Dell, 1968), 179–
85; on verbal memory, see Wilden's note on 195–96.

"How the wheel becomes it!"

If these lines suggest that there is no self-effacement sufficient, no passivity passive enough to lose the self, to leave it open completely, if even quotation presents temptations to a foreclosing selfhood, then it is part of Hamlet's greatness that he elsewhere refuses to blink such matters away. Quite the opposite of Polonius, he may doubt that which he has most inclination to believe—i.e., what seems most natural to him.

> The spirit that I have seen
> May be the devil; and the devil hath power
> To assume a pleasing shape; yea, and perhaps
> Out of my weakness and my melancholy,
> As he is very potent with such spirits,
> Abuses me to damn me. I'll have grounds
> More relative than this. The play's the thing
> Wherein I'll catch the conscience of the king.
>
> (2.2.574–81)

Precisely because the "spirit" presents itself in a shape—its "form and cause conjoined"—fit to please Hamlet, it is, he reasons, to be mistrusted as a possible external representation of his own inner "spirits" of weakness and melancholy. Insofar as the ghost seems right, conforming on the outside to what Hamlet feels on the inside, the conjunction is to be mistrusted. The effort to test, not to take the "natural," or even the supernatural, as givens, but to make them, no matter how attractive, stand before the bar of truth, is the supreme task of Western thought. However, the complex way in which this noble demand is treated by the play is nicely captured in Hamlet's word "relative."

The term is rich in implication. On the one hand, Hamlet's projected play would be more "relative" in the sense of being less immediate than the ghost to Hamlet. According to this meaning, the word betokens an ascetic act, the play becoming a self-denying exercise undertaken in the cause of the sovereignty of reason, an effort to stand back and be like Horatio, unbound by otherwise preemptive claims. Such an act would be to Laertes the calm bastardy that he himself rejects in favor of the more natural bloody haste (4.5.113). But on the other hand, the term "relative" was also current with quite an opposite sense among the defenders of visual imagery within the Church. Against those who championed purely verbal means of worship, the defenders of visual representation argued that images, because of their status as natural signs, offered, to a degree quite beyond the power of mere words, a means of access to the actual presence of that which was being worshipped. Acts of respect and attention paid to physical images actually passed through the image to its prototype, the near relation of the two being something like the shared substance of Father and Son in which prototype and image are one thing rather than the arbitrary linkage of word and its conceptual prototype.[37] Assuming this sense of "relative," one is prepared by Hamlet's lines for the fact that his moment of doubt in the ghostly father as an unchosen and unconscious representation of his own is only prologue to a new

37. The analogy between prototype/image and parent/child relationship is employed in A Midsummer Night's Dream when Titania and Oberon are called the "parents and original" of the natural disorders which surround them (2.1.115). Thought about representation in terms of the shared substance of image and prototype dates back to a misappropriation of a text from Basil of Caesarea and remains a standard of defense through the sixteenth century (see Bryer and Herrin, Iconoclasm, 167).

faith in the natural adequacy of his own *chosen* representations. His new faith would be that his representation of Claudius's deed will so effectively make present that prototypal crime, will be so "relative," that Claudius cannot but be bound naturally, by the force of *things*, to respond; his very "occulted guilt" forced "itself" to "unkennel" (3.2.77–78).[38]

But whatever he means by "relative," the prince's decision to put on the play enacts the choice of representation over naive, natural succession; in effect, electing the arduous route of re-fathering himself by means of his cognition. In the play, his images, his mental children (Sonnets 17, 26, 32, 38, 76), become, by virtue of his deliberative choice, "more relative" to him than the Father and his Word. However, instead of opening the unpaled world of thoughtless spontaneity to the demands of truth by clearing an open space for a valid test of judgment,

38. Hamlet's precedent is in such stories as that of the townswoman of Lynn who confessed to the murder of her husband as a result of a performance of *Friar Francis*; see O. B. Hardison, "Three Types of Renaissance Catharsis," *Renaissance Drama* n.s. 2 (1969): 3–22, pp. 4–5. Compare Iago's lying use of this notion as he projects his own guilt for the attack on Cassio onto Bianca:

Behold her well; I pray you, look upon her.
Do you see, gentlemen? Nay, guiltiness will speak,
Though tongues were out of use.

(5.1.108–10)

Hamlet's belief corresponds in principle to Claudius's own professed faith that "variable objects" will forcibly "expel" the ills that have settled in Hamlet's heart (3.1.172). God, of course, is the only "author" who can communicate through "things" with any certainty; see St. Thomas Aquinas, *Summa Theologica*, part 1, question 1, article 10, in *Aquinas on Nature and Grace*, ed. A. M. Fairweather (Philadelphia: Westminster Press, 1954), 48.

Hamlet's images both open *and* foreclose that possibility because they actually provide him a further means to self-deception, an opportunity to isolate and dispose, to have prejudged without realizing it. Hamlet's play, after all, is pulled by double chains of relevance: its dumb show is exactly, *wordlessly* relative to Claudius's prototypal crime, an unambiguous testimony of things, yet it fails to elicit guilty self-incrimination from him. The actual play within the play may look the same, but it speaks in words that are actually more relative to Hamlet's own avowed (the murder of Claudius) and unavowed (the resentment of the father, the wooing of the mother) desires than to Claudius's guilt.[39]

Thus, although it had seemed at first to promise a means to become cognitively independent, father to himself, by offering an arena in which to wrestle further with the claims of the paternal Word in order to make it his own conscious word, the image allows Hamlet to become unwittingly all the more the unthinking heir to a part of himself, to his own affection.[40] His representation turns out to be an idolatrous self-deception—both a thing and a part of himself.[41] It is precisely here that I find *Hamlet*

39. For a lengthy consideration of the relationship between the dumb show and the play see Lee Sheridan Cox, *Figurative Design in "Hamlet"* (Columbus, Ohio: Ohio State University Press, 1973).

40. The line is Florizel's from *The Winter's Tale* (4.4.481).

41. These facts about the play seem to me utterly to compromise statements like that of Robert Egan, who takes Hamlet's mirror for Shakespeare's: "Mimesis, then, the ability to reflect reality in an effective image that codifies and communicates the artist's vision: this is what Shakespeare defines as the utmost power of drama in *Hamlet*" (*Drama within Drama* [New York: Columbia University Press, 1975], 11). Similarly, critics have often

most perverse, for although, by virtue of its confusions, the play within the play is no true "thing" and its place of performance no true "thing" in the Anglo-Saxon sense of court of justice, Hamlet is far from the only one to overlook this fact. Neither Horatio, Claudius, nor most audiences give sign of realizing that the play within the play reads one way forward *and* another way back in the time after time of judgment, its meaning ultimately reversed by the *no* in Hamlet's unexpected identification of the poisoner with, not Claudius, but himself: "This is one Lucianus, nephew to the king" (3.2.233). In the tide of the play, everything goes along as if this *one* were in Hamlet's words a "whole one" (268), proof positive, one only, not itself both one and no.

One plus, monument and mutilation, thing and judgment, like diabolical hendiadyses, play within as well as play without repeatedly tempt not only the characters on stage, but also the audience to exercise the power of judgment, while at the same time they thwart satisfactory translation of process into permanence.[42]

---

disregarded the gap between Hamlet's abstract pronouncements with their optimism about the theater as, in H. D. F. Kitto's phrasing, "the true image of life," and what we see of theatrics in the play. For Kitto, see *Form and Meaning in Drama* (London: Methuen, 1956), 297. Cf. Oscar Wilde, who thought the mirror up to nature speech had been given to Hamlet "in order to convince the bystanders of his absolute insanity." Michael Baxandall mentions the Reformation criticism of religious art as inevitably referring to its commissioners in his *Limewood Sculptors of Renaissance Germany* (New Haven: Yale University Press, 1980), 82.

42. Among the many who have felt the unsatisfactory nature of much of the play, Matthew Arnold puts the matter most succinctly when he writes that the play "will never . . . be a piece to

There is always more to be said. Is there any more telling monument to the futility of judiciousness than the tableau in which Hamlet pauses with drawn sword over the kneeling Claudius? Reading the Variorum commentary impresses one with the extent to which this tiny scene makes it literally impossible for one not to judge and equally impossible to judge comfortably. The contradictory verdicts of the "judicious" who attempt to deal with it, like latter-day Horatios, by weight and measure—assigning culpability "in part" to the semi-repentant Claudius for his wishing forgiveness without really willing it, awarding "half a share" of virtue to Hamlet for not killing Claudius, or, paradoxical converse, approving of Hamlet for exceeding the ghost in the bloodthirstiness of the thoughts that prevent him from taking action—make for chilling reading.[43] And is the incident not set up to guarantee precisely such confounding consternation? Bound, double bound, perhaps the point turns on us, the judges judged. But why are we—even as we try, with our attention to "necessary questions," to be the very kind of judicious audience that Hamlet asks for—why are we put through such tortures when we try to set things right?

---

be seen with pure satisfaction by those who will not deceive themselves" (cited from "Hamlet Once More," in Arthur M. Eastman, *A Short History of Shakespeare Criticism* [1968; rpt. New York: Norton, 1974], 399). George T. Wright sees the play's frequent employment of hendiadys as functioning "not to resolve ambiguities but to assert them" ("Hendiadys and *Hamlet*," *PMLA* 96 [1981]: 168–93, p. 182).

43. Like his reaction to the blinding of Gloucester or to the ending of *Lear*, Johnson's famous reaction in calling the speech "too horrible to be read or to be uttered" has always seemed to me far more sensitive to the text than most of the opinions arrayed against it.

"How the wheel becomes it!"

It is true that characters in Shakespeare's plays are sometimes called upon to surrender their capacities for judgment, to give themselves up to powers beyond their conscious selves, to let the forest or time do the judging. Such lines must mean letting the play do the judging; yet a play, as the case of Hamlet's "tropological" trap suggests, is hardly trustworthy as an open clearing in which to watch the ebb and flow of a trial by event. In part the play must be, perhaps even when modern experimental theatre takes up the challenge, finished before the playing starts. Like certain versions of Christian history, it represents the playing out of secret judgments already closed and decided. Seen from this angle, Hamlet's account of the "purpose" behind playing allows itself another interpretation, for playing's purpose is, like that of living for Calvin, always both now *and* before, prospective and retrospective: "both at the first and now, was and is." And playing's purpose, again using Hamlet's definition, is to some extent locked in tautology, displaying, as do the mirrors of the medieval didactic tradition, a mirror in which the images have already been pre-disposed— showing "virtue her own feature, scorn her own image." The process of the theatre might appear to parallel a version of the ideally open process of the courtroom—one, no, judgment—only if one forgets that the character is already an emblem, a "living monument" (5.1.285), before the curtain goes up, our judgment only a re-judgment that follows from earlier series of isolations and dispositions.[44]

44. Virgil Whitaker realizes that perfect observance of Hamlet's rules for playing would lead the "judicious" among the audience inevitably to a "judgment," but his attribution of Hamlet's Sidneyan principles to Shakespeare fails to do justice to the

But what if the playwright were not only supremely sensitive to the capacity of judgment to deceive itself, having written a number of plays that hinge on the judge's being judged, but were also utterly conscious of his own poetic ability to give the uncertainty and motion of the empirical world the apparent stability and shape of a monument through his figures, through his capacity to embody in things for us his own fears, angers, desires, and prejudices? What if, in other words, the poet of Sonnet 76 had grown weary and wary of the fact that his own charactery could so effectively limn out the characters of our present world for us—like a camel, say, or weasel, or even very like a whale (3.2.361–67)—while remaining for him merely a too predictable retracing of his loves, his hates, his past written again? Might it not follow that the unhappy consciousness, seemingly so free and yet so doubly bound, might turn alternately to violence directed outward against images of its gaping audience—Hamlet against his many watchers, the play against its own—and inward against a version of itself—prince and play against Hamlet?

---

divergence between Hamlet's pronouncements and the play's ironies—something he elsewhere sees fully (*The Mirror up to Nature* [San Marino, Calif.: Huntington Library, 1965], 91). Harold Rosenberg's discussion of the role of judgment in legal and dramatic contexts is extremely useful, reminding one that the "dramatic identity" is born in an act of judgment (*The Tradition of the New* [New York: Horizon, 1959], 140). Compare contemporary attacks such as that of Stephen Gosson, which rejects the claim that the theatre could be a proper place for judgment, since, after all, the playwright inevitably distorts the truth as he follows his own desires and hatreds, contriving to pass off parts for wholes and wholes for parts (*Playes Confuted in Five Actions* [London, 1582], "second action").

IV

Given the gloomy suspicion, so often borne out in this play, that all representation, even quotation, amounts to violent usurpation, it would seem only a short step from the depiction of the quest for truth as pursued in the playwright's attempt at a self-denying fidelity to the multiple historicizing perspectives of Plutarch, to the gesture, defiant or despairing, that denies truth's place in the external world and relocates it within the willful self: usurpation triumphant. So Hamlet's "there is nothing good or bad but thinking makes it so," with its parricidal denial of the father and his revelations of truth might prepare us for the further denials enacted in Hamlet's struggles with Laertes at Ophelia's grave. There, furthermore, the hollow violence of the free play that follows from renouncing the quest for truth appears all the more shocking because the grave itself might otherwise furnish, as the sexton's joke suggests, a truly lasting "frame," one ultimate image, into which the problems that we have been discussing may at last be fitted.

The hero's graveyard perspective, with its visions of futile indiscrimination—in time Alexander become a bung-hole stop; fat king, lean beggar, emperor, and Diet of Worms, all become one diet for worms—might seem oddly out of place in a text that contains a very individual ghost and frequently takes revenge with high seriousness. In this self-contradiction, this answering its own *one* with its own *no*, the play at large dares the same fate as does Hamlet's own play within the play. In the prince's play, both murder and revenge are enacted through the same image, Lucianus, as if their difference were arbitrary or unimportant, and both acts are placed as well in a context rich with reference to the larger enveloping turn of time and event, wherein both acts appear, paradoxically, one thing after all. The player king's aged infirmity, his resignation of life and wife to the anonymous, inevitable turn of the common wheel, makes both supererogatory. It does not matter if Lucianus be brother or nephew, his cause revenge or murder, or even if he exists at all. To be or not to be is, from this perspective, not the question, since time, wherein everything—as the play frequently reminds us—both is *and* is not, will do one in well enough when it comes to it. And where, or rather when, does that leave judgment?

The "purpose" behind this boneyard vision, in which gravedigging inevitably commences with coming into being—whether of state or of individual (Hamlet and the state he would inherit born on the same day that Goodman Delver takes up his spade)—seems to be leading to some version of Hamlet's resigned "let be." This progress has ample Renaissance precedent. In Battista Fiera's *De Iusticia Pingenda*, for example, intense consideration of the proper means to represent true justice leads the discussion to the subject of death. The realization that perfect justice is uncircumscribable in total and only representable in limited and seemingly contradictory aspects leads Fiera's debating artists to turn their talk to death, since death's universal indiscrimination offers, paradoxically, the nearest approach to the absolute discrimination of perfect justice's unimageable truth.[45]

But instead of leading us through a *via negativa* to

45. Battista Fiera, *De Iusticia Pingenda* (Mantua, 1515), trans. James Wardrop (London: Lion and Unicorn, 1957). Cf. the end of Raleigh's *History of the World*, with its panegyric to Death.

such a culminating quietus in a resignation beyond judgment, the play continues to revolve even to the end. Hamlet's lines in the initial portions of the graveyard scene present, of course, a clear reversal of 1.2, as he reasons himself right back to Gertrude's "all that lives must die." His response to Laertes' declamations upon the loss of Ophelia, moreover, provides a distressing gloss on his earlier grief; for even as Hamlet echoes his mourning from 1.2 in the claim to have loved the departed one more than anyone else, one hears the absurdity of his protestations. Furthermore, the swings from violent self-affirmations, "This is I, / Hamlet the Dane" (5.1.245–46), to equally insistent disavowals of that self and its chosen deeds, "Was't Hamlet wronged Laertes? Never Hamlet" (5.2.220), demonstrate all too clearly how, in Hamlet's case, the self, in demonic fulfillment of Polonius's platitude, may end up true only to itself. And ironically, that self, stabilized neither by its being bound by nature and natural demands, as is Laertes, nor by its pursuit of its own cognitive truth, as Hamlet had once hoped to be, appears reduced to being a function of momentary circumstance. Its "that within" seems dictated by any and every that without; that which hinders the self or indulges it taking over the role of motive and motor in its circular whirl.[46] And what about us?

46. The exact sense of Hamlet's abstract truism "There's a divinity that shapes our ends, / Rough-hew them how we will" (5.2.10–11) makes me very uncomfortable considering the "ends" that have been shaped for Rosencrantz and Guildenstern and that are a-shaping for Hamlet. One balks at the announcement that the double murder, "Not shriving time allow'd," truly "serves [Hamlet] well" (5.2.8).

For Hamlet there lies beyond an experience of the futility of judgment not "no" but "play." But this is not free play; it costs. Doubt truth, doubt that truth is obtainable, and in that willful act one opens the place for play; but as the rest of the line might warn us—"Doubt truth to be a liar"—in the act of such doubting, one risks becoming, as does Hamlet, the liar one had hoped to uncover by first subjecting truth to the scrutiny of judgment. Judge for one must, and judge not because one cannot—this is the secret threat that lurks in the playwright's play on the name of father, son, and play:

I'll make a ghost of him that lets me.

(1.4.85)

The line is threatening enough to the lives of the characters who surround Hamlet and must necessarily, given his task, either "let" him in one sense of the word or the other, by furthering or retarding his cause. But in that "ham" is an archaic form of "him," this line takes on wider resonance. Him-that-lets, what better name for the father, son, and play, given the manifold, disturbing ways in which all three both hinder *and* permit? More ominously, what better name for him who, doubly inscribed in his own threat, both wrote the part of the father and son and then acted the part of the ghost? Still better and still worse, what better name for those of us in the audience who have found and still find in the play's nutshell our infinite scope and our prison's bounds, allowance more than ample to permit us to reveal ourselves through our judgments and hindrances sufficient to compromise every one of them? Our one *and* our no, turn and turn about. As Freud discovered when thinking about *Hamlet* in relation to the "that" within, we are in the play, and play is in us:

Oh, how the wheel becomes it! It is the false
steward, that stole his master's daughter.[47]

(4.5.167–68)

47. On Shakespeare as ghost see E. K. Chambers, *William Shakespeare: A Study of Facts and Problems* (London: Oxford University Press, 1930), 1: 84. Both Hamlet's play and man himself are termed "piece of work" (2.2.300; 3.2.44), suggesting comparable construction. Cf. Lacan, "Desire and the Interpretation of Desire in *Hamlet*," 34, on play. For Freud and *Hamlet*, see Lyotard, "Jewish Oedipus." Baret's *Dictionarie* (1580) suggests near synonymousness of "steward" and "disposer" (cited in the Variorum *Troilus and Cressida* note to 3.1.84).

5

"Turn our impressed lances in our eyes":

EMBLEM AND ICONOCLASM
IN *King Lear*

> [*Enter Lear, with Cordelia in his arms*]
> LEAR: *Howl, howl, howl! O! you are men of stones:*
> *Had I your tongues and eyes, I'd use them so*
> *That heaven's vault should crack. She's gone for ever.*
> *I know when one is dead, and when one lives;*
> *She's dead as earth. Lend me a looking-glass;*
> *If that her breath will mist or stain this stone,*
> *Why, then she lives.*
> KENT: *Is this the promis'd end?*
> EDGAR: *Or image of that horror?*
> ALBANY: *Fall and cease.*
>
> (5.3.257–64)

If Kent, Edgar, or Albany could control *King Lear*, the play would end with a striking visual image, a secular pietà, that would be a final meaningful emblem of the suffering the play represents. Suspended in Lear's speech are all the elements that might be used to form the commentary on this ultimate tableau. One waits for the unspoken lines to come: death the end of earthly greatness, the indifference of the heavenly vault, the mirror of tragic suffering that holds up to human life the final truth of its essence.

But the play does not end here, despite the fact that it has seemed on the verge of ending itself since the fourth act.[1] Kent makes an effort to close with a traditional reflection on "Fortune" and Albany attempts a final summing up:

1. In his *The Sense of an Ending* (New York: Oxford University Press, 1967), Frank Kermode remarks that everything in the play "tends toward a conclusion that does not occur, even personal death, for Lear, is terribly delayed" (82). And in Kermode's reading of the last scene "universality is explicitly disavowed." Perhaps the best treatment of the play's attempts at conclusion is Nicholas Brooke's "The Ending of *King Lear*," in *Shakespeare 1564–1964*, ed. Edward A. Bloom (Providence, R.I.: Brown University Press, 1964), 71–87. Brooke sees that the "greatness of *King Lear* is in the completeness of its negation" (87), but he agrees with Johnson that there is a kind of resolution nonetheless in the last scene, maintaining that "Lear dying with the dead Cordelia in his arms" provides "the one fixed and final image, in this case an emblem which sums up all" (78). In this he agrees also with Robert Egan's view of the scene as expressed in Egan's chapter on *Lear* in *Drama within Drama* (New York: Columbia University Press, 1975), esp. 113–14. For the lines of continuing debate on the ending of the play, contrast the opposing readings of Walter C. Foreman in his *The Music of the Close* (Lexington, Ky.: University Press of Kentucky, 1979) and Duncan S. Harris in "The End of *Lear* and a Shape for Shakespearean Tragedy," *Shakespeare Studies* 9 (1976): 253–68. Harris believes that in the final scene "The limitations of language and the limitations of man for which they stand are momentarily rescinded through art" (265). For a discussion of the way *Lear* resists closure even on the level of critical formulation see Kermode's *Shakespeare, Spenser, Donne* (New York: Viking, 1971), 39–58. Brooke's book on the play, *Shakespeare: "King Lear,"* Studies in English Literature, no. 15 (London: Edward Arnold, 1971), has influenced my reading.

You lords and noble friends, know our intent;
What comfort to this great decay may come
Shall be appli'd: for us, we will resign,
During the life of this old Majesty,
To him our absolute power: [*to Edgar and Kent*] you, to
    your rights,
With boot and such addition as your honours
Have more than merited. All friends shall taste
The wages of their virtue, and all foes
The cup of their deservings. O! see, see!

                    (296–304)

He breaks off. His sweeping distribution of poetic justice
is halted by the fact that the pietà will not be still, will not
be silent, will not be content in the role of public exem-
plum, but persists in *acting*. The scenic center of the stage,
which was to have been the incontrovertible emblem of
all the suffering that has gone before, refuses to be reduced to the emblematic meaning the other characters
wish it to embody. Lear's voice does not cease in deference to his role in a "speaking picture" of grief for fallen
majesty. Instead, Lear would use the otherwise emblematic mirror as a merely physical tool to determine whether
or not Cordelia breathes; he will not listen reverently to
any cosmic message from Cordelia's death, but insists he
hears her voice; he focuses on buttons and lips.

And my poor fool is hang'd! No, no, no life!
Why should a dog, a horse, a rat, have life,
And thou no breath at all? Thou'lt come no more,
Never, never, never, never, never!
Pray you, undo this button: thank you, Sir.
Do you see this? Look on her, look, her lips,
Look there, look there.

                    (305–11)

His attention to the broken particulars of physical existence profoundly subverts the decorous generalizations
of emblematic vision, which would seek to enwrap the
scene in meaning and so solidify living flux into significance. Lear must be dead, must be silenced before the
characters can make their final closure of the play with
commonplaces of "general woe" and "sad time." By this
time, though, such attempts have failed so often that they
are robbed of any credibility; we know that if Lear were
not dead, his utterly naturalistic voice would rise again in
subversion of Albany's decorum. Only Lear's silenced
corpse can provide safely manageable visual material for
Albany's emblematic treatment.[2]

The radical nature of this dramatic repudiation of
emblematic formulation may be more fully appreciated if
this scene is compared with a scene from a much earlier
play in which Shakespeare allows emblem and commonplace to go unchallenged. In the second part of *Henry VI*,
young Clifford discovers his dead father and is allowed a
lengthy speech:

> O,
> let the vile world end,
> And the premised flames of the last day
> Knit earth and Heaven together!
> Now let the general trumpet blow his blast,
> Particularities and petty sounds
> To cease! Wast thou ordain'd, dear father,
> To lose thy youth in peace, and to achieve
> The silver livery of advised age,
> And, in thy reverence and thy chair-days, thus
> To die in ruffian battle? Even at this sight

2. Similarly, it is the *silent* figures of Kent, Edgar, and Albany,
who offer Lear material for his metaphor "men of stones."

My heart is turn'd to stone; and while 'tis mine,
It shall be stony. York not our old men spares;
No more will I their babes. Tears virginal
Shall be to me even as the dew to fire,
And beauty, that the tyrant oft reclaims,
Shall to my flaming wrath be oil and flax.
Henceforth I will not have to do with pity.
Meet I an infant of the House of York,
Into as many gobbets will I cut it
As wild Medea young Absyrtus did.
In cruelty will I seek out my fame.
Come, thou new ruin of old Clifford's house.
As did Aeneas old Anchises bear,
So bear I thee upon my manly shoulders;
But then Aeneas bare a living load,
Nothing so heavy as these woes of mine.

> [*Exit, bearing off his father*]
> (5.2.39–65)

Clifford longs in his grief for the last day, as do the observers of Lear's tragedy. He, too, wishes for the cessation of mere "Particularities and petty sounds" and launches into commonplace pronouncements over the "ruin" of majesty. He is quick to proclaim his notion of justice, and his final action provides the audience with a classical emblem of his grief, as he bears his father from the stage the way Aeneas bore Anchises. Thus, his pain is quickly assimilated into art through its formal expression in metaphor, simile, and emblem; and there is no threat to the sufficiency of these artful means of imposing order on dramatic action.

The contrast between this scene from an early play and the final scene of *Lear* draws attention to the particular position of the later play when it is regarded with reference to the tension between formalism and naturalism in Elizabethan-Jacobean drama.[3] The insistent refusal of this final scene to halt its action around a significant figure or a metaphorical summing up is the last struggle of a conflict between action and emblem apparent throughout the play. Criticism has often called attention to the play's use of commonplace formulations and to the way it stages a number of obviously emblematic tableaux, but the fact is that these attempts to contain the action in manageable form are inadequate to their task.[4] This demonstrable inadequacy of emblematic schemata to the containment of the action of *King Lear* is evidence not of the dramatist's failure but of a fundamental iconoclasm, a force at work from beginning to end of the play and so pervasive in its effect that it works to undermine audience complacence even at that moment when commonplace, the emblematic embodiment of that commonplace, and the dramatic action seem to be in complete accord with one another—Lear's confrontation with the storm.

3. On this tension, see Introduction above.

4. See, for example, T. W. Craik, *The Tudor Interlude* (London: Leicester University Press, 1958), 95; also Emrys Jones, *Scenic Form in Shakespeare* (Oxford: Clarendon Press, 1971), and John Reibetanz, "Theatrical Emblems in *King Lear*," in Rosalie L. Colie and F. T. Flahiff, eds., *Some Facets of "King Lear"* (Toronto: Toronto University Press, 1974), 39–58. Reibetanz argues that "Shakespeare projects his own abstract statements into dramatic realities in the course of *King Lear*" (48), and he compares this dramatic projection of ideas to that of Chapman in *Bussy D'Ambois* and Fletcher in *The Faithful Shepherdess*. It is true that Edmund's speech lays out the action for the audience, but the point is that this glibly general formula is really a challenge to the audience to recognize the inadequacy of the formulation, even if objectively "true," to the realities of lived experience.

The audience is prepared for the emblematic significance of the storm scene by an anonymous "Gentleman,"
who claims that Lear "Strives in his little world of man to
outstorm / The to-and fro-conflicting wind and rain . . . /
And bids what will take all" (3.1.10–15). In other words,
we are prepared to see microcosm confront macrocosm,
and Lear's language conforms to this expectation:

Blow, winds, and crack your cheeks! rage! blow!
You cataracts and hurricanoes, spout
Till you have drenched our steeples, drown'd the cocks!
You sulph'rous and thought-executing fires,
Vaunt-couriers of oak-cleaving thunderbolts,
Singe my white head! And thou, all-shaking thunder,
Strike flat the thick rotundity o' th' world!
Crack Nature's moulds, all germens spill at once
That makes ingrateful man!
. . . .
Rumble thy bellyful! Spit, fire! spout, rain!
Nor rain, wind, thunder, fire, are my daughters: I tax
　　you not, you elements, with unkindness;
I never gave you kingdom, call'd you children,
You owe me no subscription: then let fall
Your horrible pleasure; here I stand, your slave,
A poor, infirm, weak, and despis'd old man.
But yet I call you servile ministers,
That will with two pernicious daughters join
Your high-engender'd battles 'gainst a head
So old and white as this. O, ho! 'tis foul.
. . . .
　　　　　　[*Enter Kent*]
No, I will be the pattern of all patience;
I will say nothing.

　　　　　　　　　　(3.2.1–38)

To emphasize the significance of his encounter with the

elements, Lear would have the world stripped bare of dis-
tinctions, of particularities. Upon a world reduced to
mere indeterminate ground, a stage "struck flat," he
would image his condition.[5] One fully distinct figure
would stand in contention with the "all" of elemental violence in which daughters and universe participate. According to his conceit, his "white head," that "head / So
old and white," would stand as the single fixity challeng-
ing a world of force. Bearing this intention in mind, one
finds nothing surprising about his sudden turn to silence
when Kent enters on the scene; for if Lear is to be part of
an emblem, as he obviously considers himself to be, he
cannot enter into the mediated exchange of dramatic dialogue. Emblems have only *their* significance to proclaim.[6]
That Lear's very identity is constituted in such emblematic fashion is underlined by his assertion "Here I stand."
That it is not so conceived in the final scene, but is rather
lost in attention to the physical presence of Cordelia is
clear; the way he attempts to live in emblems throughout
the remainder of the play requires demonstration.

Lear's characteristically emblematic behavior is evident in a scene just prior to that of the storm. He replies
to Regan's suggestion that he be reconciled with Goneril
by enacting a little tableau.

LEAR: Ask her forgiveness?
    Do you but mark how this becomes the house:
    "Dear daughter, I confess that I am old;

5. In his "On Shakespeare's Tragedies" (1808), Charles Lamb
calls attention to the inadequacy of limited stage machinery to
the demands of Lear's invocations. See Helmut Bonheim, ed.,
King Lear Perplex (Belmont, Calif.: Wadsworth, 1962), 14–15.

6. On the dialogue/monologue problem, see the *Caesar* chapter above.

[*Kneeling*]Age is unnecessary: on my knees I beg
That you'll vouchsafe me raiment, bed, and food."
REGAN: Good sir, no more; these are unsightly tricks.
Return you to my sister.

(2.4.153–59)

To make his point, Lear schematizes for Regan what he considers to be the essence of her request. He reduces a complex situation to a visual spectacle in which "Age" begs youth for mere physical necessities. The difficult political issue of the knights, with their ambiguous status and hence their possibly unsettling effect on a divided kingdom, is left completely out of the picture. In other words, a dispute, in which there might be more than a little justice and wrong mixed into both sides of the question, is embodied in a mode of representation that can only call forth sympathy for one side. Consequently, it is only with great difficulty that one can force oneself to recognize the inadequacy of this allegorical enactment to the complexity of Lear's situation. Such recognition demands an attention to the temporal context out of which this scene has evolved— something that the immediate visual impact of the emblem works against. This questioning of the emblem by placing it in context prepares one to perceive the storm scene in a new way.

The storm, after all, does not just happen to Lear; his language calls for it before the event. In rejecting Regan's suggestions, Lear makes use of a commonplace description of natural existence:

No, rather I abjure all roofs, and choose
To wage against the enmity o' th' air;
To be a comrade with the wolf and owl,
Necessity's sharp pinch!

(2.4.210–13)

In his terms, to leave his daughters means to leave all civilization and to choose the realm of necessity, where life itself is a conflict with the elements. The storm, then, when it does come, seems to flesh out his fore-conceit by providing it with physical realization. His ecstatic orchestration of its violence is a reveling in the satisfaction of a fulfilled prophecy: he had told Regan it would be so. But the problem for him is that the storm, like his own voice in the play's final scene, will not stop in deference to the proper limits of its emblematic role; instead, it becomes for him an annoying physical presence.[7]

This change in his perception of the storm is markedly apparent in one of his mad speeches to the blind Gloucester:

> Ha! Goneril, with a white beard! They flattered me like a dog, and told me I had the white hairs in my beard ere the black ones were there. To say "ay" and "no" to every thing that I said! "Ay" and "no" too was no good divinity. When the rain came to wet me once and the wind to make me chatter, when the thunder would not peace at my bidding, there I found 'em, there I smelt 'em out. Go to, they are not men o' their words: they told me I was every thing; 'tis a lie, I am not ague-proof.
>
> (4.6.97–108)

When the storm had seemed the emblem he desired, his every word had been aimed at inciting further violence from his universal opposite; now he speaks of the wet,

---

7. Thus to some extent the storm becomes a typically Shakespearean "character" in tension with its "role." Peter Ure explores the problematic of character and role in his "Character and Role from *Richard III* to *Hamlet*," in *Hamlet*, ed. John Russell Brown and Bernard Harris (London: Edward Arnold, 1965), 9–28.

the chattering teeth and agues—the concrete physical effects of the storm, instead of its emblematic qualities. His
new voice is no longer that of majestic challenger but that
of a sufferer worn down to the point of bidding the once
welcome thunder cease. His new emphasis is on the temporal rather than the figural aspects of experience—a fact
underlined by the perplexing remarks concerning his
white beard and the equivocations of his daughters. Telling him he had his "white hairs" before he had the black
ones is a way of telling Lear that his authority, his majesty, is inherent in him as an essential quality, independent of temporal existence (so elsewhere, Kent, in his
characteristically emblematic voice, sees "Authority" in
Lear despite the fact that circumstance has negated his
actual authority). The remarks about "ay and no" make it
clear that Lear recognizes, as he had not in the first scene
of the play, that speech is not any simple manifestation of
the speaker's essence; he admits the necessity of interpretation.[8] In sum, mad Lear is aware of his timebound,
physical, ague-prone existence: he is not "everything."
What it means to be "everything" is most apparent in the
first scene, where emblem dominates action, but also
where the play begins its pointed questioning of sight—
the emblematic sense.

　　Britain is divided before the first scene begins:
Gloucester's comments let us know that much. What we

　　8. Before his tragedy, Lear's speech is in the imperative, as
Maynard Mack points out in *"King Lear" in Our Time* (Berkeley
and Los Angeles: University of California Press, 1965). See also
Paul A. Jorgensen, *Lear's Self-Discovery* (Berkeley and Los Angeles: University of California Press, 1967), 70ff.; and Sigurd
Burckhardt's chapter on *Lear* in *Shakespearean Meanings* (Princeton: Princeton University Press, 1968).

see in that first scene, therefore, is meant to be ritual rather than contest. Royal Lear would incorporate even family ties into public performance: each daughter will respond according to the fore-plan when Lear indicates her place in the liturgy. This performance, moreover, is intended to correspond to the directions of a pre-existent visual model—the map.

Standing before his map of Britain, Lear confronts a bounded and ordered representation of a world fully under his control. This sense of control is heightened by the fact that the map, by its very nature, claims to represent Britain absolutely; that is, in a mode free of the conflicting partiality of merely situational perspectives. The map claims to signify Britain as absolutely as does the name "Britain," and Lear would know the map the way a god would see Britain—as subject viewing object. It provides conceptual clarity to Lear's "darker purpose": his plan to divide the kingdom in order to avoid future dissension looks orderly, reasonable, and effectual on the map's version of reality. It is as if the course of events could be closed around the structural certainty the map offers; as if the temporal forces of avarice, faction, and ambition that interpenetrate the human reality within the Britain the map represents could be effectively neutralized through spatial distribution.[9]

There is a blindness to the forces of human interac-

9. The interaction of map and fore-conceit here and their role in Lear's idolatry help make it understandable that during the iconoclastic controversy the plan of a future undertaking could be considered an "image." See Leslie Barnard's discussion of John Damascene, in Anthony Bryer and Judith Herrin, eds., *Iconoclasm* (Birmingham: Center for Byzantine Studies, 1977), 11.

tion in this human engineering, but there is also a conception of self implied in Lear's manipulation of the map that
corresponds to conceptions of self evidenced in the ritual
speeches of Goneril and Regan. Goneril declares her love:

Sir, I love you more than word can wield the matter;
Dearer than eyesight, space, and liberty;
Beyond what can be valued rich or rare;
No less than life, with grace, health, beauty, honour;
As much as child e'er lov'd, or father found;
A love that makes breath poor and speech unable;
Beyond all manner of so much I love you.

(1.1.55–61)

In the *topoi* of love beyond speech, Goneril arranges one
proportion after another (more than, dearer than, beyond), leading up to a final, ultimate summing-up—"Beyond all manner of so much." As the map presents a total
Britain outside time, a Britain that claims to surpass all
possible limited perspectives—is the thing itself, the
Idea, while mere experience only presents an infinite series of aspects of its "all"—so Goneril claims a love sur-
passing limited measure and situation. And the language
of "all" is a feature of Regan's speech as well:

I am made of that self metal as my sister,
And prize me at her worth. In my true heart
I find she names my very deed of love;
Only she comes too short: that I profess
Myself an enemy to all other joys
Which the most precious square of sense possesses,
And find I am alone felicitate
In your dear highness' love.

(69–76)

Regan not only dismisses partial degrees from her love, but asserts her very existence to be antagonistic to "all other joys" that lie outside the borders of that love.

When Cordelia's speeches are heard against those of her sisters, one recognizes more than the mere absence of flattery and more than another instance of Goneril's "more than I can say" *topos*. Cordelia's responses to her sisters' speeches are tentative and partial reactions that develop in time. They have not been established before the scene begins. She alone speaks according to no "darker purpose," no fore-plan. And she explicitly rejects the "alls" of her sisters' rhetoric:

> Good my Lord,
> You have begot me, bred me, lov'd me: I
> Return those duties back as are right fit,
> Obey you, love you, and most honour you.
> Why have my sisters husbands, if they say
> They love you all? Happily, when I shall wed,
> That lord whose hand must take my plight shall carry
> Half my love with him, half my care and duty:
> Sure I shall never marry like my sisters,
> To love my father all.
>
> (95–104)

Cordelia's love has no analogous relationship to a figure against an excluded ground, has no identity of its own, but exists in a bipolar reciprocity of exchange within her "bond." It is not possible to think of her as possessing that love objectively and in entirety, since it has originated outside herself in Lear's own love for her; rather, the love she describes is a betweenness shared among persons. If this relationship may be described in proportional terms—"Half my love with him, half my care and duty"—its portions exist as demands carried *away* from her by loved ones. Thus, her love is presented in terms fundamentally antithetical to the gathering process by which Goneril and Regan's loves are said to be bounded against that which is not themselves. Cordelia's love, as it is described, then, can only be known over time and from within its relation; there exists no way to step outside of its partial perspectives and know it in simultaneously extant objective totality. It cannot be known, in other words, as one knows a map of Britain.

By contrast, Lear himself is supremely easy with the rhetoric of totality. He banishes Cordelia:

Let it be so; thy truth then be thy dower:
For, by the sacred radiance of the sun,
The mysteries of Hecate and the night,
By all the operation of the orbs
From whom we do exist and cease to be,
Here I disclaim all my paternal care,
Propinquity and property of blood,
And as a stranger to my heart and me
Hold thee from this for ever. The barbarous Scythian,
Or he that makes his generation messes
To gorge his appetite, shall to my bosom
Be as well neighbour'd, pitied, and reliev'd,
As thou my sometime daughter.

(108–20)

With as much certainty as he had presumed his division of the kingdom would finally "shake all cares and business" from him, he disclaims "all" relation to Cordelia by "all" the powers that funnel their might through his royal position. Nor is this resemblance an isolated one. Lear's division of the crown shows his royal actions to be of a piece, for the ruling assumption behind such a radical act is an absolute conflation of the symbol with the reality it signifies. By dividing the crown between the two new kings, Lear asserts that the essence of kingship is somehow totally and really present in the crown; so that to sunder it is not to completely destroy a *symbol* of kingship but to portion royalty itself. As he had confused the orderly portioning of a representation of Britain with effective management of Britain itself—now, and in the future—so he identifies the completed, orderly portioning of the symbol of authority with effective division of power. In both cases there is a magical valuation of representation over temporal, political process. One who is "everything" need not concern himself about any gap of adequacy between his conceptions of the essence of things—their totality in his representations—and their experiential, partially revealed and partially concealed, problematic reality for others. He assumes that Britain will somehow remain Britain though sundered, that its essence, like its map, will remain unchanged despite surface alteration. And his speech of banishment assumes that he can close the complexities of Cordelia's existence by equating her essence with that of cannibals of kin—those who are forever and unalterably what they are by virtue of their one defining act. Thus, the banishment of Cordelia, like that of Kent, is in perfect accord with Lear's idolatrous relationship to his representations, for banishment from his "sight" keeps his conception of them locked forever on what he considers their essential antagonism. As he sees it, one defining moment has revealed their essence; further touch, sound, or sight is unnecessary.

This insistent pursuit of completeness, here clearly exemplified, but evident throughout the play, makes it fitting that the sense of sight dominate in action and imagery.[10] Sight offers the strongest perceptual support for differentiating essences from the interconnecting flux of experience. Hans Jonas suggests the advantages and perils that accompany a privileging of the visual:

> The effortlessness of sight is a privilege which, with the toil, foregoes also the reward of the lower sense. Seeing requires no perceptible activity either on the part of the object or on that of the subject. Neither invades the sphere of the other: they let each other be what they are and as they are, and thus emerge the self-contained object and the self-contained subject. The nonactivity of the seen object in relation to the seeing subject is not impaired by the fact that, physically speaking, action on its part (emission of light) is involved as a condition of its being seen. The singular properties of light permit the whole dynamic genesis to disappear in the perceptual result, so that in seeing, the percipient remains entirely free from causal involvement in the things to be per-

10. Literature on the sight imagery of *Lear* is, of course, extensive. See, for example, R. B. Heilman, *This Great Stage* (Baton Rouge, La.: Louisiana State University Press, 1948). Particularly useful is Paul J. Alpers, *"King Lear* and the Theory of the Sight Pattern," in Reuben A. Brower and Richard Poirier, eds., *In Defense of Reading* (New York: Dutton, 1963). Alpers rejects the clichés of "sight replaced by insight" that predominate in critical writing on Gloucester's blinding. Instead, Alpers calls attention to the important relationships expressed in physical contact, arguing that the "significance of 'what Gloucester learns' is of a kind directly opposite to that proposed by the sight pattern, which takes truly perceived realities to be something like Platonic Ideas—both more abstract and more real than the mere phenomena of life." On the sight/touch opposition in the Renaissance see John Charles Nelson, *Renaissance Theory of Love* (New York: Columbia University Press, 1958).

ceived. Thus vision secures that standing back from the aggressiveness of the world which frees for observation and opens a horizon for elective attention. But it does so at the price of offering a becalmed abstract of reality denuded of its raw power. To quote from our own earlier account . . . the object, staying in its bounds, faces the subject across the gap which the evanescence of the force context has created. Distance of appearance yields neutral "image" which, unlike "effect," can be looked at and compared, in memory retained and recalled, in imagination varied and freely composed. Thus becomes essence separable from existence and therewith theory possible. It is but the basic freedom of vision, and the element of abstraction inherent in it, which are carried further in conceptual thought; and from visual perception, concept and idea inherit that ontological pattern of objectivity which vision has first created.[11]

For our discussion of *King Lear*, it is important to note what sight as the "least 'realistic' of the senses" tends to lose in its version of reality.[12]

Sight allows for a gain in objectivity over the information provided by the other senses; it alone allows a full-scale distinction between the thing as it is in itself as distinct from the thing as it affects the perceiver.[13] Self-contained subject faces self-contained object across a distance—a notable gain—but, in its very condition, the possibility arises that such a division may lose the experience of connecting activity between the two. That is to say, vision, when unsupported by information from

11. Hans Jonas, *The Phenomenon of Life* (New York: Harper and Row, 1966), 148–49.
12. Ibid., 147.   13. Ibid.

other senses, tends to lose sight of the causal connections of force between things. The act and its temporal context continually dissolve before one, though the actor remains present to the eyes. Given the image of the actor and a notion of the significance of his act, the visual memory and imagination carry the process of abstraction begun by visual perception one step further by reimposing form on the otherwise lost action. This new schema takes what is certain—the actor, his object—and organizes it around the perceiver's notion of the meaning of the action. In recollection, moreover, one tends to forget one's own role in this recreation of the world and to believe in the objective reality of the representation.

Consider intense experience, whether of passionate love, of encounter with the sacred, or of abject submission to the command of an all-powerful sovereign. How can one hold onto these events, how retain the experience through time? Poetry, narrative, or visual embodiment in portrait, cult image, or imperial emblem offer more permanence than merely personal memory. A world replete with force, context, and connection, in other words, is funneled down to its embodiment in significant schemata. But what must necessarily be lost in this process, if not the force with which the experience and oneself first encountered one another: one's resistance or acquiescence, one's fear or joy—the whole fragile complexity of a complete interaction in time? What remains, what can remain, but the small residue capable of containment in visual representation and language? Of these two media, language is at least able to provide a wider range of possibilities. It can be used by the prophets, for example, to speak of their hunger and thirst for confrontation with the divine and to express the burden and wandering through which the divine made its demands felt. Furthermore, language can present the various aspects through which the sacred demand manifests itself—variously, stern judge, jealous husband, or solicitous father—without affixing its account exclusively to any of these. In visual representation, on the other hand, the possibilities for suggesting the complex evolution of an interaction are severely limited; whatever aspect is chosen for the divine or the beloved can scarcely be qualified within the work by an acknowledgment of the other faces that show themselves through time.

In other words, the image of visual art, and more especially the emblem, tends to cut the interconnections of temporal existence in favor of a closing around what it judges to be essential.[14] It reduces the infinitely complex manifold that one encounters in another to the demands of a total concept like that of character. It abbreviates as if character were something accessible to objective knowledge, rather than a horizon forever altering and being realized in interaction. But the appeal of such an abbreviation is hardly surprising. How much easier it is for one to act with certainty if the map and crown are there to be seen and handled in place of the complex realities they represent. How reassuring if the divine totality is safely present in the idol. It is precisely the desire for total satisfaction that makes the idolatrous abbreviation so compellingly attractive. As Paul Ricoeur suggests, desire for the "all" makes idolatry possible:

14. This view is, of course, an ancient one. In his "Twelfth Discourse," Dio Chrysostom discusses the frozen aspect of visual art in opposition to the temporality of verbal art (*Dio Chrysostom*, trans. J. W. Cohoon [Cambridge, Mass.: Harvard University Press, 1939], 2: 73–74). The simplifications of this opposition have been explored by Gombrich.

Only a being who wants the all and who schematizes it in the objects of human desire is able to make a mistake, that is, take his object for the *absolute*, *forget* the symbolic character of the bond between happiness and an object of desire: forgetting this makes the symbol an idol.[15]

Idolatry of whatever variety (erotic, sacred, political) originates in a reach for a horizon—happiness, the holy—that the finite grasp cannot hold. At the limits of one's grasp, an arc is completed behind the idol. The idol is formed in the short-circuiting of a desire for absolute plenitude. Paradoxically, the only force strong enough to bind one over to an idolatrous relationship with an object is a desire that begins as an objectless aim at an "all." Lear would be everything, and it is this objectless desire that leads him to an idolatrous evaluation of the storm. His need to be all-important causes him to take it for all the antagonism of the natural world, present and ready for confrontation. But the storm is not *his* macrocosmic storm, rather, in the words of the Fool, only "the rain" that "raineth every day" (3.2.77).[16] Instead of leveling the world, it wets and chills, driving home to Lear his physical reality rather than supporting his emblematic pretensions. If he smells out his daughters in that rain, it is because the rain makes unavoidably present what the Fool's counterpoint had always insisted upon—the undeniable corporeal reality of Lear's ague-prone existence.

With the general direction of this development in

15. Paul Ricoeur, *Fallible Man*, trans. Charles Kelbley (Chicago: Henry Regnery, 1965), 200.

16. The note in the Fool's voice complicates what Erich Auerbach has to say about *Lear* in *Mimesis*, trans. Willard R. Trask (1953; rpt. Princeton: Princeton University Press, 1968), 323.

mind, the evolution of Lear's later speeches seems appropriate. One who accepts the significance of emblem undergoes a dramatic experience negating the assumptions that had grounded his notions of correspondence. Not that this process is simple or easily brought to completion. Lear's emblematic vision is still functioning after the storm; it leads him, for example, to find an embodiment of the human condition in Edgar/Tom, and he believes strongly enough in schematization to attempt the arraignment of Regan in the person of a joint-stool. But utterly mad Lear is incapable of keeping his emblems within the boundaries of decorous generality: they tap a reservoir of disgust and violence that makes full acceptance of any one of them impossible. Amid his images of carnality and physical disgust, in fact, he manages a rejection of emblem by posing an ultimate anti-emblem: "There thou mightst behold the great image of Authority: / A dog's obey'd in office" (4.6.160–61). The great image of Authority is, of course, the king who images the ultimate authority of God. Against this commonplace of Christian tradition, the iconoclastic fury of Lear's remark reveals itself. Lear has traveled his own *via negativa* to reach this absolute rejection of traditional, public imagery. His way out of emblem lies through its use: only the wrenching power of dissimilitude can free one who has been so dominated by the emblematic.

In the light of Lear's course through imagery to the final iconoclastic destruction of imagery, the subplot takes on heightened significance. In its progess, Lear's own evolution finds a parallel. The subplot exaggerates emblem and commonplace in order to confront the audience with its own idolatrous allegiance to such inadequate substitutes for the complexity of existence. By pursuing the desire for reductive simplification to the point of grotesque extremes, the subplot turns our own lances back in our eyes.[17]

The subplot begins with Gloucester's significant pun:

GLOUCESTER: His breeding, Sir, hath been at my charge: I have so often blush'd to acknowledge him, that now I am braz'd to't.

KENT: I cannot conceive you.

GLOUCESTER: Sir, this young fellow's mother could; whereupon she grew round-womb'd, and had, indeed, Sir, a son for her cradle ere she had a husband for her bed. Do you smell a fault?

(1.1.9–16)

Physical conception, like mental conception, may come to visible fruit without awaiting its proper time. Throughout the play, characters direct their intercourse with physical reality on the basis of conceits that forerun appropriate timing. They close events into significant configurations which subsequently prove, as does Edmund, to be untrustworthy bastards that usurp the place of truths that can only be known in particularity, partially, and through temporal experience.[18]

Typical of this premature conception is Gloucester's assent to Edmund's misrepresentation of Edgar. Despite his protestations that Edgar could never be such a "monster" as to seek his death, Gloucester remarks: "These

17. For an excellent analysis of the simplifications in the subplot see Bridget Gellert Lyons, "The Subplot as Simplification in *King Lear*," in Colie and Flahiff, *Some Facets of "King Lear*," 23–38.

18. Compare Dio Chrysostom on the power of the image to block further conception, *Dio Chrysostom*, 2: 59.

late eclipses in the sun and moon portend no good to us"
(1.2.107–8). He then proceeds to read his situation according to these cosmic portents: "This villain of mine
comes under the prediction; there's son against father"
(114–15). In other words, despite the talk about awaiting
"auricular assurance," Gloucester has all but solidified
his conception around the framing lines of an original
cosmic figure. Edmund merely provides a particular body
to fill the slot in a form that pre-exists the occasion. As the
storm seems to Lear to frame his version of his plight, so
cosmic phenomena reinforce Gloucester's evaluation.

But lest we think Gloucester's confusion a simple result of Edmund's deceptive villainy, there is the striking
parallel to this scene when Edgar takes Gloucester to
Dover cliff. Gloucester's suicide attempt resembles his acceptance of Edmund's indictment of Edgar in that the two
incidents (like Lear's division of the kingdom) are
grounded in a need for immediate resolution of uncertainty. In his commissioning of Edmund, Gloucester encourages his son to "frame the business after your own
wisdom. I would unstate myself to be in a due resolution"
(1.2.102–3). From this commission there follows Edmund's emblematic presentation of the skirmish between good and evil sons, and hence Gloucester's "due
resolution." Similarly, in his suicide attempt, Gloucester
is prepared quite literally to "unstate" himself in his desire for resolution. His suicide is intended by him to foreclose future possibilities.

O you mighty Gods! [*kneeling*]
This world I do renounce, and in your sights
Shake patiently my great affliction off;
If I could bear it longer, and not fall

To quarrel with your great opposeless wills,
My snuff and loathed part of nature should
Burn itself out.   (4.6.34–40)

By ending his life, he can enclose it, can keep it this side
of impiety. His intention represents another instance of
that insistent demand for closure that characters have
voiced in the play's other scenes. For instance, Goneril
would rid herself of Lear's knights to prevent future troubles (1.4.339–40), or Lear would pluck out his eyes lest in
future they weep (1.4.311–12). It is significant, then, that
Gloucester's suicide declaration echoes the very first
expression of the if-I-do-X-then-Y-will-*not*-follow formulation—Lear's "fast intent / To shake all cares and business" from his age. So the structural similarity of Lear's
division of the kingdom (a form of unstating himself) and
Gloucester's suicide attempt is emphasized. The similarity does not stop here, either. Edgar's fictionally created
space allows Gloucester a place outside the confusing
reality within Britain's manifold perspectives. From Edgar's vantage point, Gloucester may contemplate that life
going on within the map as a gathered whole. Like Lear
before his map, Gloucester may consider from the edge
of Edgar's space a version of "This world" that deceptively supports a view of the self conceived as capable of
acting singly, decisively, and with finality.

   In the maintenance of this illusion, Edgar's description cooperates fully with Gloucester's desire. His description of the view from the imaginary cliff has built
within it a powerful sense of perspectival diminution.
This diminution promises Gloucester the opportunity to
end his physical being in a single moment, rather than
over the slow remainder of his life:

The crows and choughs that wing the midway air
Show scarce so gross as beetles; half way down

Hangs one that gathers sampire, dreadful trade!
Methinks he seems no bigger than his head.
The fishermen that walk upon the beach
Appear like mice, and yond tall anchoring bark
Diminish'd to her cock, her cock a buoy
Almost too small for sight.
                    (4.6.13–20)

From level to level, Gloucester's body will fall like a me-
teor in the night sky, till infinitesimal and finally resolved
into nothing at all. Thus, Gloucester's conceit, his fore-
plan of total self-annihilation and Edgar's presented "visual" conceit complete a circuit that prompts Gloucester
to act. When evidence of the eyes (here Edgar functioning
as Gloucester's visual imagination) supports what one
has preconceived, the possibility of further thought may
be lost, since the evidence of further experience will be
less attractive than the completed significant figure.
Think how difficult it is to reject cosmic correspondence
once one has *seen* Lear face the storm one had been led to
expect. The most dangerous situation for the further life
of thought, then, arises when physical circumstance actually is congruent with fore-conception.[19] In such a case,
as Edgar observes, thought may truly have its end:

            Gone, sir: farewell.
And yet I know not how conceit may rob
The treasury of life when life itself
Yields to the theft; had he been where he thought
By this had thought been past.
                    (41–45)

When physical circumstance—the forged letter or Edmund's self-inflicted wound—is there for visual rein-

---

19. Cf. Freud on the fulfillment of a guilty wish, e.g., in "Dos-
toyevsky and Parricide," in *Collected Papers by Sigmund Freud*, ed.
James Strachey (London: Hogarth, 1952), vol. 5, esp. 232.

forcement of the conceit predicting "son against father," thought's further evolution may be cut off in the closure of the emblematic moment. From that instant, Edgar is no more than a corpse bearing an assigned meaning—the rebellious son. Like Kent after his typing and banishment, Edgar has to become someone else in order to go on living.

What makes the Dover Cliff incident so profoundly iconoclastic is that it is Edgar, the character who suffers under emblematic typing and denounces conceit, who generates a grotesque emblem to subdue his father:

EDGAR: Thy life's a miracle. Speak yet again.
GLOUCESTER: But have I fall'n or no?
EDGAR: From the dread summit of this chalky bourn.
    Look up a-height; the shrill-gorg'd lark so far
    Cannot be seen or heard: do but look up.
    . . . .
              This is above all strangeness.
    Upon the crown o' th' cliff what thing was that
    Which parted from you?
GLOUCESTER: A poor unfortunate beggar.
EDGAR: As I stood here below, methought his eyes
    Were two full moons; he had a thousand noses,
    Horns whelk'd and wav'd like the enridged sea:
    It was some fiend; therefore, thou happy father,
    Think that the clearest Gods, who make them
      honours
    Of men's impossibilities, have preserved thee.
                         (55–74)

Edgar will have Gloucester understand his life from this one moment. Absolute evil, embodied in laughably monstrous form, has been overcome through the interference of those "clearest Gods," who look down with total comprehension on the map of the world. Yet if this ordering of existence works for poor, befuddled Gloucester, the play makes certain that we remain distanced from his solution. The low comedy of the fall should assure that much at least.[20] Secure, then, in our feeling of superior knowledge, we watch Edgar's manipulation of Gloucester. Because we are able to accept Edgar's explanation for his treatment of the old man, we might be tempted to feel ourselves able to discriminate between emblematic moments proper to the action of the play and those that characters produce out of their own self-interest. So, perhaps, Edmund's staged combat and Edgar's demon could be judged as understandably artificial, while Lear's responses to Edgar/Tom might be judged fitting commentary on the action of the play. Two moments, however, challenge such nice discrimination. Gloucester's blinding and the duel of the brothers—both highly emblematic moments and neither the product of a character's rhetorical strategies—implicate the audience for its own idolatrous eagerness to accept visual schemata for the "all" of the action.

Gloucester's blinding takes place in the context of his identification with lechery. In the third act that identification is made certain by a remark from the Fool:

20. The treatment of blind Gloucester should be considered in the context of such comic treatments of the blind man's deception by his boy as that in the Tournai farce *Le Garcon et L'Aveugle* (ca. 1270). The tradition also survives elsewhere in Shakespeare in Launcelot's encounter with Old Gobbo in *The Merchant of Venice* (2.2).

Now a little fire in a wild field were like an old lecher's heart; a small spark, all the rest on's body cold. Look! here comes a walking fire.

[*Enter Gloucester, with a torch*]

(3.4.114–17)

The staging reproduces a specific emblem, but the meaning is clear without recourse to sources.[21] The second specific identification of Gloucester with lechery occurs in a remark of Lear's:

I remember thine eyes well enough. Dost thou squiny at me?

No, do thy worst, blind Cupid; I'll not love.

(4.6.138–39)

Again the allusion is to a specific emblem.[22] But by this time such usage has become offensive. It has become so because the *act* of blinding Gloucester has been too fully articulated on stage, in all its physical particularity, for its emblematic meaning to seem anything but cruelly inadequate. The pulling out of his eyes—capable of convincing staging as the storm scene is not—outruns all possible rhetorical or moralizing uses. So, when Edgar later makes the play's final use of the blinding—"The dark and vicious place where thee he got / Cost him his eyes" (5.3.172–73)—our discomfort is more than a result of any variation in taste over the centuries. His glib formula is another of those unsatisfactory attempts at closure that

---

21. The figure of cupid with a torch may be seen in Albrecht Schöne, *Emblematik und Drama im Zeitalter des Barock* (Munich: C. H. Beck, 1964), 140.

22. On the blind cupid, see Erwin Panofsky, *Studies in Iconology* (New York: Harper and Row, 1962), 95–128.

haunt the play with their desire to enwrap particular human reality in cosmic meaning.

A comparison of the way Gloucester's blinding is treated with the treatment of the other major stage violence reveals how insistently the play attacks our eyes. In the duel scene, action is covered with formula and emblematic significance to the point of absurdity. Bracketed from the rest of the action by Goneril's announcement—"An Interlude"—the duel unfolds in all its archaic trappings: challenge meets counter challenge, trumpet answers trumpet. And at center stage, Good confronts Evil. It is as if this moment were an attempt to gather up all the loose ends of the subplot and bring it to a finish with one culminating configuration. The simple confrontation seems to give us a map version of the complex whole. That we could ever take this contrived stage machinery for an adequate embodiment of the subplot is a function of our idolatry, our readiness to rest in the closure of the significant image. This duel, however, like the blinding, provides more than one wants—though this time there is too much meaning rather than too much action. But, as if the irony in the presumed significance were not quite sufficient to do its demystifying work, we get Edmund's change of heart. The character whose actions are most capable of explanation in Elizabethan commonplace reverses the essential public meaning he had affirmed from his opening lines. Characters, then, like the action of the play, do not find resolution in an end that grants them some fixed significance. Their actions stop with death; and that death comes not in a dying into significance at some emblematic moment—the storm, the cliff scene—but unexpectedly and when it will.

The play's iconoclasm spares neither emblematic

staging, nor type character, nor commonplace; but there are suggestions that it is at work in even profounder depths. The dramatist offers through Edgar's remark— "The worst is not / So long as we can say 'This is the worst' " (4.1.27–28)—the possibility that the simplest sort of language should be scrutinized for its idols. He reminds us of the basic disjunction between perception and signification. Perception, so long as it remains conscious of its own finitude, cannot claim for itself the divine *Übersicht* of a non-situated view, but must be content with partial aspects. Language, on the other hand, always transgresses this finite perspective.[23] According to Ernst Cassirer:

> Subjective reality is characterized by extreme individuality and concretion; while the world of words is characterized by the universality, and that is to say, the indeterminacy and ambiguity, of merely schematic signs. Since the "universal" signification of the word effaces all the differences which characterize real psychological processes, the road of language seems to lead us, not upward into spiritual universality, but downward to the commonplace: for only this, only what is not peculiar to an individual intuition or sensation, but is common to it and others, is accessible to language.[24]

To say "this is the worst" means being able to step back from one's condition, view it, employ judgment to compare it with others, and put one's percepts into publicly significant language. Lear in his abject misery cannot step

23. Ricoeur, *Fallible Man*, 42.
24. Ernst Cassirer, *The Philosophy of Symbolic Forms*, trans. Ralph Manheim (New Haven: Yale University Press, 1966), 1: 188.

back to view the flux of events in a significant, synchronically complete figure, and he cannot defend himself with commonplaces. Instead, every moment wrenches him about, demanding that he experience physical reality in all its particularity. In a situation that might otherwise elicit a formal stage lamentation, he abandons decorum to speak of rats and horses, as elsewhere he puns and repeats himself randomly. The worst, like Cordelia's love, can neither be formed into an image nor spoken about; it can only be experienced from within. The only adequate perspective on the pietà is Lear's own from within it, and his perspective is so lost in physical immediacy that it is incapable of the distance necessary for abstraction to shape suffering into significant figure. Edgar may exhort Lear with the appeal that brought the emblems of demonic temptation and divine interference into his intercourse with Gloucester—"Look up, my lord."[25] But Lear is beyond such comforts.

25. In light of the other echoes of Montaigne that have been found in *Lear*, I think it worth adding one more that resonates with this reading of Edgar's line. Montaigne claims to be as frightened of "transcending humors" as he is frightened of high places (*Montaigne's Essays*, trans. John Florio [New York: E. P. Dutton, n.d.], 3: 13.385); surely Edgar's attempt to reintroduce the transcendent appears in this place, at this time, as a chilling, if nevertheless humanly understandable, maneuver.

· Conclusion ·

"If a lie
may do thee grace":
The Winter's Tale

The final moments of *King Lear* are fragmented by tension between a formal pietà and the form-shattering force of living action. It seems fitting, then, that this study of Shakespearean iconoclasm consider another final scene in which a character assumes the fixity of a "dead likeness" while standing, in the Folio's stage description, "like a Statue." Criticism has often brought these two final scenes together, and in the process has frequently reminded us that Hermione is not just any statue.[1] By virtue of the play's imagery patterns as well as its express debate over the subject of art and nature, she appears as the iconic embodiment of a conceptual reality—the art that is itself natural, nature made better by itself. But if the features of this final scene suggest a relaxation or even

1. See, for example, Robert Egan's discussion of the statue scene in his chapter on *The Winter's Tale* in *Drama Within Drama: Shakespeare's Sense of His Art in "King Lear," "The Winter's Tale," and "The Tempest"* (New York: Columbia University Press, 1975). For a useful survey of criticism of the play and a discussion of the shortcomings of that criticism see Charles Frey, "Interpreting *The Winter's Tale*," *Studies in English Literature* 18 (1978): 307–29.

a transcending of the tensions that we have seen in earlier plays, nevertheless, it does not quite constitute a palinode. By examining that scene in the context of the play's own internal debate about art and nature, we shall see that the iconic clarity of the statuary scene is itself suspect. Like the red blood still reigning in the winter's pale, iconoclasm lives on, even in *The Winter's Tale*.

I

The place and function in a work of art of an iconic dimension have a long history of consideration in Western aesthetics, and Aristotle offers a useful starting place for a discussion of this dimension in *The Winter's Tale*. In arguing for the proper sort of incident to be employed in tragic plots, Aristotle provides a telling example of the kind of thing most likely to produce pity and fear:

> Even matters of chance seem most marvellous if there is an appearance of design as it were in them; as for instance the statue of Mitys at Argos killed the author of Mitys' death by falling down on him when a looker-on at a public spectacle; for incidents like that we think to be not without meaning. A plot, therefore, of this sort is necessarily finer than others.[2]

The special power of this incident for Aristotle lies in the fact that, considered as a whole, it seems to be "not without meaning." It emerges from an indistinct background of mere contingency precisely because its parts can be subordinated to that meaning. A murder, the cause, has led to what looks like revenge, the effect, and the two dis-

---

2. *Poetics* 1,452a, cited from *The Basic Works of Aristotle*, ed. Richard McKeon (New York: Random House, 1941).

tinct, symmetrical halves fit together in order to form a whole, the action, which, strictly by virtue of its own features, appears to be the embodiment of a concept—Justice. This concept gives the conjunction of character and event the sharp, clear borders of a thing and thereby contributes "an appearance of design, as it were in them." We might term this effect of setting off and ordering that occurs as a result of appearing to be "not without meaning" iconic augmentation.[3]

Some such principle may play, as Gombrich has argued, a necessary role in any naturally occurring act of perception, and certainly it has retained its interest as a concern of aesthetics since Aristotle.[4] T. S. Eliot, for instance, has argued that visual images take on more "intensity" by possessing a meaning.[5] Considered historically, however, Western opinions of the proper relationship between image and meaning have been far from stable. For most of its history, the West, according to Auerbach, has been dominated by a Judaeo-Christian tradition that has strongly favored the predominance of conceptual meaning over the perceptual image.[6] Yet figures as diverse as the Wakefield Master and Martin Luther remind one that Christian tradition is divided; the sensory

3. Paul Ricoeur uses the term "iconic augmentation" in a different sense in his *Interpretation Theory* (Fort Worth, Tex.: Texas Christian University Press, 1976), 40.

4. On the primacy of meaning, see E. H. Gombrich's 1965 essay "The Use of Art for the Study of Symbols," reprinted in James Hogg, ed., *Psychology and the Visual Arts* (Harmondsworth, Middlesex: Penguin Books, 1969).

5. *Selected Essays* (1932; rpt. New York: Harcourt, Brace, 1950), 228–29.

6. Erich Auerbach, *Mimesis*, trans. Willard R. Trask (1953; rpt. Princeton: Princeton University Press, 1968), 48.

particular has had its own champions. As I have argued, this conflict in that tradition is useful as an aid to understanding the special conflicts that rage in *King Lear*.

Such conflict is a matter of some reference in *Lear* itself. When the Fool turns on the audience with the joking threat that ends the first act, for example, one is more than warned about what to expect from the interplay of things and their meanings in the rest of the play:

She that's a maid now, and laughs at my departure,
Shall not be a maid long, unless things be cut shorter.

(1.5.53–54)

They are not cut shorter, of course. Things are not kept safely bordered within the formal bounds dictated by the very meanings that give them their intensity; instead they grow menacing precisely in proportion to the conceptual borders they violate. The violent way that the play employs word and action to turn the probings of our meaning-hungry vision back on themselves is tightly condensed into Edgar's reference to broken Lear's appearance as a "side piercing sight." In this reference to the interpretive task of Longinus—piercing the side of the crucified one in order to determine whether he belonged among the living or the dead—Edgar's line suggests how the lances of conceptualization rebound from the things that one sees in the play and make their furious way back to penetrate the looker-on.[7] And in that forcible penetration who is to say, to continue the play's own play on an equivalence between physical and mental conception, what offspring will quicken into life? What follows in an audience that has endured the force of those

7. For Longinus, see Jacobus de Voraigne, *The Golden Legend* (1941; rpt. New York: Arno, 1969), 191.

"things" that the play has refused to "cut shorter," such as the horrible icon of an obscene Justice in Gloucester's blinding for adultery or the "great thing" that is alternately forgotten and violated by the other characters before the play finally grants its grotesque "departure"?

But if the iconoclasm in *Lear* most typically takes the form of giving one too much of the sensory particular in proportion to the general meaning it should serve, this represents only one more working out of the diverse iconoclastic tensions that haunt the plays. *The Winter's Tale*, too, deserves consideration in a study of Shakespearean iconoclasm, not least because it engages in iconoclastic activity while appearing to invert the strategies of *Lear*. If *Lear* repeatedly makes particular words and actions round upon us, attacking the conceptualizations that it arouses, revealing them to be meager commonplaces (Hamlet's insight about readiness or ripeness reduced to the status of a lame truism by Gloucester's "That's true too") or offensive simplifications (Edgar's vision of justly punished lechery), then *The Winter's Tale* seems to raise commonplace to the status of the truth, while its action seems to be full of pretty "touches" that "angle" for our eyes (5.2.81–82) instead of trying to put them out. In its own scene of violence, *The Winter's Tale* puts "Exit, pursued by bear" in place of "Out, vile jelly." The brutal action of the great wheel rolling downhill becomes the gentle wheel of the seasons. The setting on the wild heath gives way to the "great creating nature" of pastoral Bohemia, storm and carnivore safely over the next hill. The inscrutable, perhaps cruel, gods are replaced by Apollo's unambiguous oracle. Instead of an unacceptable icon of lechery, there is a winged figure of "Time himself." Edgar's discordantly farcical deceptions of his father are replaced by repeated, genial references to the creaking dramatic machinery that keeps the romance "like an old tale still." In structure, the open-endedness of *Lear* is replaced by the precise symmetry of the romance's two halves. And in its concluding moments, the aniconism of *Lear's* fragmented pietà is opposed by the fixed icon of the thematic concern with art and nature that dominates the final scene of *The Winter's Tale*. In many ways the features of *Lear* that betray a suspicion of order, symmetry, and conceptual generality seem simply given over.[8] But to say many is not, as our examination of earlier plays has argued, to say all.

II

The odd treatment of the iconic element in *The Winter's Tale* is not expressed in *Lear's* opposition of naturalizing and iconizing perspectives; there is little to be considered naturalizing about the later play. Neither is there the mutilating violence of *Hamlet*, in which central character and audience undergo temptation by the partial congruence of imagery and truth. Nor is there the kind of historical alienation that occurs in *Caesar* largely as a result of the dramatized encounter between classificatory metaphors. The problem is much simpler and more obvious than these.

Certain minor things about the play seem designed to surprise: the displacement of embodied pastoralism from Sicily to Bohemia, for instance, or the reversal of expectations that occurs when Polixenes refuses to embody in action the artistic concept of crossbreeding that he ap-

---

8. Egan argues that *The Winter's Tale* "devotes itself to shaping an antithetically positive and confident solution" to the problems posed in *Lear* (*Drama Within Drama*, 57).

proves in theory. But these small lets no more detract from the coherence of the story's meaning than do the repeated reminders of the play's fictionality. If anything, these surface disturbances serve to direct one's attention through the details of the work toward the meanings it presents.[9] Even if Florizel and Perdita seem rather too good to be true and jealous Leontes rather too bad to be probable, the whole remains reconcilable with a Renaissance poetic compounded from positions taken by Sidney and Chapman.

When Sidney employs Plato's terms "eikastike" and "phantastike," he gives them a whole new ethical/conceptual axis of definition. Where Plato had employed the terms to name two varieties, both objectionable, of art — the one consisting of images derived from perception, the other of images originating in fantasy—Sidney uses the one term to mean "figuring forth good things" and the other for representing "unworthy objects."[10] Having divided images along the line of their ethical meaning rather than according to their relationship of proximity to a model, Sidney goes on to redirect the terms employed in one traditional religious rejection of images. The original form of this particular argument holds that because images have the power to form those who make and see them, they are to be considered dangerous; otherwise

9. Edward William Taylor in his *Nature and Art in Renaissance Literature* (New York: Columbia University Press, 1964), asserts, as have many before him, that "the improbable plots of the last plays invite symbolic interpretation" (23).

10. On the relevance of Sidneyan poetics to the romances see Howard Felperin, *Shakespearean Romance* (Princeton: Princeton University Press, 1972). Robinson discusses Sidney's modification of Plato in his notes to the *Apology*.

they would be merely nothing. Sidney takes the idea behind the scriptural attack—"Thei that make them are like unto them: so are all that trust in them" (Ps. 115:8)—and puts it positively. Because the eikastike image has such power to recast life itself as an image, it is good.[11] From one Cyrus many Cyruses may proceed. Taking such an idea seriously would go hand in hand with Sidney's ethical concern that the poet produce images possessed of the right sort of meanings, "figuring forth good things" rather than "unworthy" things.

When one approaches *The Winter's Tale* through an acquaintance with Sidney's concern about figuring forth and Aristotle's observations on the effectiveness of iconic augmentation, Shakespeare's additions to the play's sources make a kind of aesthetic and didactic sense. First, the introduction of the greatly elaborated art/nature theme provides an intensifying iconic augment for those two remarkable additions to the sources, the sheep-shearing feast and the statuary scene. Second, the actual debate upon that specific subject by Polixenes and Perdita would appear to be designed to insure that the audience not just sense the vague presence of some message but clearly understand the important meanings these scenes body forth.

Such a reading of the debate presents the problem, already noted, that Polixenes is hardly ready to engraft his noble bud onto the baser bark of Perdita. Yet while this

11. For Shakespeare's echoing of this biblical phrasing see Stephen Booth's notes to Sonnet 137 in his *Shakespeare's Sonnets* (New Haven: Yale University Press, 1977). The phrase is used by Richard Hooker in his *Laws of Ecclesiasticall Politie* (London, 1594), 67. Hooker, like Bacon, uses idolatry to stand for all manner of blindness (68).

seems to be little more than the usual sort of decentering device that Shakespeare so often employs, the more disturbing fact is that neither Perdita nor Hermione actually is what the terms of the debate need them to be if they are to be icons—Perdita no peasant, Hermione no statue. As Rosalie Colie puts it, Shakespeare "has chosen *not* to match his literary insight with an objective correlative within the play; the debate of kind is much ado about nothing."[12]

But while Colie's judgment seems clearly on target in the matter of Perdita as peasant, there remains a Renaissance means by which to save the case of Hermione as a work of art. In such instances in which the literal sense of a work seems self-contradictory beyond the possibility of reconciliation, one should, according to Chapman, follow a long-standing tradition of exegesis and look beyond the apparent absurdity and contradiction for an underlying sense.[13] The way in which Hermione might be truly considered a work of art is suggested to us by Paulina's seemingly metaphoric claim "the stone is mine" (5.3.58). The stoniness of Hermione is an artistic contribution; by virtue of this more than natural fixity, this remarkable temporal persistence, the statuary Hermione may rightly be considered a work of art. Paulina's "art" recasts Hermione's "nature" in a new mold, as an image that is not

12. *Shakespeare's Living Art* (Princeton: Princeton University Press, 1974), 278.

13. Chapman recommends this time-honored principle in the dedicatory epistle prefixed to *Odysses*; see *Chapman's Homer*, ed. Allardyce Nicoll (New York: Pantheon, 1956), 2: 5. On the agreement between the poetics of Sidney and Chapman see Miller MacLure, *George Chapman: A Critical Study* (1966; rpt. Buffalo: University of Toronto Press, 1969), esp. 168.

the natural Hermione insofar as it embodies pure patience and constancy of purpose.

This recourse to an allegorical level, an augmentary
meaning beyond the literal sense, has the further advantage of suggesting a way to get around what has been
perhaps the most frequently voiced objection to the
play—the lie about Hermione's death. To the extent that
she is taken over by the demands of Paulina's art, Hermione must not only be numbed (5.3.102) but be in fact
dead (5.3.106) to any other role (wife, friend, queen) besides that of "dead likeness" (5.3.15). No longer quite a
"lie direct," then, Paulina's apparent falsehood may be
taken as a "mean" to the presentation of an idea: to the
extent that nature is, in the phrasing of Sonnet 112,
"bred" to a "purpose" or intended meaning, to the extent
that it figures forth, it will appear dead to any but that
purpose.

If we follow this lead, stepping slightly beyond the
literal sense in order to give figural credit to the word of
Paulina, allowing that Hermione is both "dead" and a
work of "art," do we not simply proceed in the direction
in which the play has been pointing us anyway? A concern with art and artfulness in their widest senses would
seem to be built into a work that contains not only the
varied exploits of the multitalented impersonator, singer,
and sometime puppeteer Autolycus and the writing,
casting, and directing talents of Camillo, but also goes so
far as to make artists out of far less probable figures. Are
we not authorized to look for some deeper conceptual
purpose being suggested when we encounter, on top of
all the other instances of artistic activity in the play, such
improbabilities as Mamillius acting as tale-teller to the
adults, the servant writing poetry to honor Hermione,

and, beyond all this, the outright absurdity of Time's claim to be, in spite of the evidence of our senses, telling us the very story that we are watching in performance? Whether or not art is nature, it certainly is ubiquitous. The extent of that ubiquity poses a crucial problem for our "eikastike" reading of Hermione's statue scene.

If Paulina's work of art embodies the good news that art itself is nature, that nature is actually made better by no means but nature makes that means, it must also be observed that the means employed in making nature better are disconcertingly similar to those employed elsewhere to make it worse. Nor are the agents of bettering and worsening so easily differentiated as the usual critical oppositions, such as that between the bad art of Autolycus and the good art of Camillo and Paulina, would have it. The same sun shines on all, as Perdita is compelled to remind herself, and from its bright lamp, shadows also take their shape. If art should be as lawful as eating, then, one of great nature's laws, the structure of the play seems strangely insistent upon reminding us, is that for every eater—whether cormorant devouring time, the leonine tyrant, or the building kite—there must be something to be eaten, a law applying even to the gentlest subjects of Flora.

Good Polixenes, the critics remind us, to some extent repeats the evil mistakes of jealous Leontes in his own rejection of Perdita as well as in the possessiveness he exhibits toward Camillo.[14] That similarity might be troubling enough, not so much for what it does to the reputation of Polixenes but for the shocking suggestion that

14. See Ernest Schanzer's "The Structural Pattern," in Kenneth Muir, ed., "The Winter's Tale": A Casebook (Glasgow: Glasgow University Press, 1968).

the evil of Leontes might be somehow tied to the great cycle of the seasons, might be in some sense natural to the species. And, Paulina's remarks about his "unnatural" behavior to the contrary (2.3.112), Leontes' sickness is abundantly characterized with the language of nature: the opinion that does "grow" in him (1.2.431, 433), and takes there its deep, if rotten, "root" (2.3.89), is said to be the product of "unsafe lunes" (2.2.30) but as unopposable as the force that binds the sea to obey the moon (1.2.427). Yet such suggestions that mad Leontes might also have a place in the same "nature" as the others seem to me no more disturbing ultimately than are the play's hints linking Leontes' art to that of the others—specifically to that of young Florizel—when it comes to means.

Leontes' deadly art repeatedly takes the form of recasting characters and events from the world around him in images that figure forth his own fearful needs: the linked hands of Hermione and Polixenes betoken adultery and call to mind a whole history of actions that accord not only with that meaning but with the very need for evidence that has gone unsatisfied; the illness of Mamillius means an acceptance of the "shame" of his mother's dishonor (2.3.15), that he believes, in other words, what Leontes is unable to convince others to accept; the flight of Polixenes means that Leontes' groundless delusions are true, that "All's true that is mistrusted" (2.1.48). The dependence of such image making on his own needs rather than upon truth is further underlined for us at several points in the sad treatment of Hermione.

The hardness Leontes fears in his own brows (1.2.146) is perceived in the bosoms of his suspects (1.2.153). The fears of horns (1.2.123–24) recur in oddly subjectless reference to, as we believe, Hermione as

"Inch-think, knee deep; o'er head and ears a fork'd one" (1.2.186). The angling that he does for them (1.2.180–81) comes back in his fear of having had "his pond fish'd by his next neighbour" (1.2.195), an apt designation for one he has just acclaimed most "next" to him after wife and child (1.2.176). His fear that Hermione's belly might be letting "in and out the enemy, / With bag and baggage" (1.2.205–6) represents with painful exactitude precisely what Leontes fears himself to have done. The "thing," the "trick" or puppet manipulated by others that he fears himself to be furnishes him a mold in which to cast her, as he calls her "thing" (2.1.82) and "hobby-horse" (1.2.276).[15] More ominously still, the terms of Polixenes' vision of natural innocence betrayed by the embodied "temptations" born to them in the women become deadly earnest in Leontes' insistent representations of himself as foolish "nature" (1.2.151) or innocent "natural goodness" (2.1.164) betrayed to a state of sleepless panic by the "cause" that is embodied in Hermione (2.3.3).[16]

Most telling among many such instances, however, is the nearly incoherent set of lines uttered by Leontes in his attempt to envision the workings of the "cause" Hermione has enacted in her presumed defilement of his pure white sheets.

15. Compare Hamlet's assertion that he could interpret between Ophelia and her lover as if they were puppets, a violent assertion that simply transposes onto her his own fear of being sounded to the heart of his mystery by other interpreters.

16. Peter Berek's remarks on this passage point out the relation between the illusions of eternal boyhood and the reified devilishness presumed in Hermione; see " 'As We Are Mock'd with Art': From Scorn to Transformation," *Studies in English Literature* 18 (1978): 289–305, pp. 303–4.

Can thy dam?—may't be?—
Affection! thy intention stabs the centre:
Thou dost make possible things not so held,
Communicat'st with dreams;—how can this be?—
With what's unreal thou coactive art,
And fellow'st nothing: then 'tis very credent
Thou may'st co-join with something; and thou dost,
(And that beyond commission) and I find it,
(And that to the infection of my brains
And hard'ning of my brows).

(1.2.138–46)

The name he calls his entity is the right one in spite of his own intentions, for wrong as he may be about what Hermione means, he is correct about his own means to making her an image, affection being either the lust he believes threatening him through her or, as we can see it, the force of his own affected imaginings, which threaten indeed.[17] Threatening beyond all "commission," commission either by his own desires or through the committed acts of others, Leontes' art, after first stabbing the world's true center to death, has been "coactive," fellowing nothings and "co-joining" with the slightest of somethings in order to create a dead likeness, a second world neither green nor golden, that communicates only with his own "unreal" dreams rather than with living truth. The dependence of this art upon death is not solely evident in the case of Hermione, either. In the process of changing his mind about Perdita's fate, Leontes' progression from "Let it live" to "It shall not neither" (2.3.156–57) signals not his decision to actually kill her, but as in the case of Paulina's treatment of Hermione, a resolution

17. On "affection" as a synonym for "imagination" see the Variorum note for this passage.

to give her the deadly life of an image. Because her illegitimacy is feared, the baby will be cast out upon the waves "like to itself" (3.2.87)—i.e., into a homeless, friendless, wandering existence that is her true image. This art finds its similar in Bohemia.

Death's tracery is oddly woven into Bohemia's love language, even from the very first lines:

These your unusual weeds, to each part of you
Do give a life: no shepherdess, but Flora
Peering in April's front.

(4.4.1–3)

The "weeds" of art, even though formed out of the living substance of "great creating nature" in the flowers themselves, do give a life to their wearer only by taking another away. No shepherdess can be Flora, and Perdita through Florizel's disposing becomes not more like herself but instead like the image of the natural force, the cause, that she figures forth. True, Florizel the lover, unlike the tyrant Leontes, speaks as though capable of belonging utterly to another:

For I cannot be
Mine own, nor anything to any, if
I be not thine.

(4.4.43–45)

The faint hint of narcissism in Florizel's lines, of using Perdita as a way to possess himself, is further suggested in the words used by the shepherd to describe the young man's love: "for never gaz'd the moon / Upon the water as he'll stand and read / As t'were my daughter's eyes" (4.4.174–76). And as his pranking-up of her suggests, the

Perdita that Florizel needs as guarantee of his identity seems dangerously close to being an image double rather than the shepherdess, a work of dead likeness rather than living nature.

Perdita protests against the "extremes" that are though quite opposed in their direction—praising rather than condemning—a feature reminiscent in their extremity of Leontes' own language for Hermione (or of Paulina's language for her); and in the course of her protests manages to indicate some understanding of the violence in such extremes:

One of these two must be necessities,
Which then will speak, that you must change this
     purpose,
Or I my life.

                    (4.4.38–40)

Whether Polixenes discovers their love or not, the very transformation of Perdita according to Florizel's "purpose" means, as her lines on the change of "disposition" by her disguise recognize (4.4.133–35), the loss of her proper life. Furthermore, the odd tone of Florizel's reply to this worry—"Strangle such thoughts as these" (4.4.47)—might alert us to a possible tyrannical aspect to the act of shaping that paradoxical stillness, at once monumental and moving, into which he could cast her:

              What you do,
Still betters what is done. When you speak, sweet,
I'd have you do it ever: when you sing,
I'd have you buy and sell so, so give alms,
Pray so, and, for the ord'ring your affairs,
To sing them too: when you do dance, I wish you

A wave o' th' sea, that you might ever do
Nothing but that, move still, still so,
And own no other function.

$$(4.4.135–43)^{18}$$

    Nor does Perdita, for that matter, insistent as she is upon nature rather than art, entirely escape infection by such artful impulses; and in her case, the very improbability of such action underscores its dominant features. Having undergone the attempts of Florizel to prank her up, she responds with a vision in kind. While she never actually bedecks Florizel physically with weeds natural or otherwise, in her language he undergoes such a covering with flowers that his identity is momentarily obscured, leaving him "like a bank, for love to lie and play on," or more ominously:

Not like a corpse; or if—not to be buried,
But quick, and in mine arms.

$$(4.4.131–32)$$

Perhaps this is how an embodied natural force—no shepherdess but Flora indeed—should speak. But the images of Florizel as a passively inert bank for the sport of love to employ or as a corpse quickened only for the receipt of love's embraces lend frightening overtones to the idea of being a dead likeness with a single function:

Nothing but that, move still, still so,
And own no other function.

$$(145–46)$$

18. Berek, too, is bothered by the similarity between the isolation of the static moment in this instance and that which occurs in Leontes' mistreatment of Hermione ("As We Are Mock'd with Art," 302). For a more positive reading of the lovers' artfulness in these speeches compare Anthony B. Dawson, *Indirections* (Buffalo, N.Y.: University of Toronto Press, 1978), 150.

Conclusion

Love, even in its arcadian innocence, appears in this play to employ the means used by tyranny to recast living nature as a puppeteer's "trick." We need not spend time on other similarities between lover and tyrant, such as their being "better pleas'd with madness" (4.4.485) when reason complains, their mutual readiness to risk destroying everything when they cannot have their way—after all, it is Florizel and not Polixenes who actually repeats Leontes' act of putting Perdita to sea on the waves of "chance" (4.4.541), or their common willingness to wipe out their own succession in order to follow the dictates of "affection" (4.4.481–82). It is not our purpose to make lover and tyrant into the same thing. Rather, the point is that it makes no sense, in light of their similarity of means, to divide them from one another along the art/nature axis. The jealousy of Leontes, if one attend the language of the play and not simply take Paulina's word for gospel, is not any more or less artificial than is the love of Florizel, no matter how wrong Leontes' madness may be. If, in Florizel's elevating treatment of Perdita, one is to see nature made *better* by natural means, then no firm ground exists upon which to argue that in Leontes' treatment of Hermione and Perdita, nature is not made *worse* by means equally natural. Nature is made neither better nor worse by no means but nature makes that means. It is in some such odd admission that one might end up if one truly determined to take Paulina and the play as anything other than liars direct.

III

"One of these is true" we might insist with the single-mindedness of Perdita (4.4.576), believing it the duty of the "eikastike" artist to behave like Time the storyteller, who, if he "makes" us accept an error is still bound to unfold it for us by some mean.[19] Such is the double mode of E. K.'s model artist Stesichoros, whose evil Helen is revealed in time to have been merely a false image of the true wife sacred to the Spartan believers.[20] Yet the suspicious tendency of our observations does little more than add force to insinuations about art raised by the play itself. For just as the hyperbolic ornament of Autolycus's praises acts in transforming "knacks" and smocks into goddesses and she-angels (4.4.210–11), so the equally artificial attacks of Polixenes cast a goddess and she-angel into the role of "angle" (4.2.47) or "knack" (4.4.429).[21]

And which of these is true? There are among audiences of this play as among audiences of Shakespeare

19. Compare Robert Grene's complete title for *Pandosto*, with its use of his favorite truism, "*Temporis filia Veritas.*" Richard H. Abrams offers one of the most interesting readings of Time's strategies in relation to the play's iconoclasm in his "*The Winter's Tale*: Problems of Iconoclasm and Dramatic Agency," in *Literature and Iconoclasm: Shakespeare*, ed. Irving Massey and Brian Caraher (Buffalo, N.Y.: SUNY, 1976).

20. Stesichoros's famous palinode was known to the Elizabethans by reputation; see E. K.'s remarks in *The Shepheardes Calender* for "Aprill," *The Works of Edmund Spenser*, ed. Edwin Greenlaw et al. (Baltimore: Johns Hopkins University Press, 1932–57), 7: 42.

21. The point is Northrop Frye's from his "Recognition in *The Winter's Tale*," in Muir, *The Winter's Tale: A Casebook*. See also Barbara A. Mowat's discussion of Shakespeare's alternating between an undercutting of tragic emotions with comic devices and an injecting of pain into comedy. Mowat notices that Camillo's art is as much a means to his own ends as is that of Autolycus (*The Dramaturgy of Shakespeare's Romances* [Athens, Ga.: University of Georgia Press, 1976]).

generally, the party of suspicion and the party of faith. Faith may indeed apprehend more than cool (or hot) suspicion can comprehend, but along with its rewards, faith, even such an attenuated faith as that which believes in the clarifying value of an art that figures forth, demands its duties. To believe wholly, one must perform something like the generous self-effacement of Perdita, and by the pattern of one's own thoughts cut out the "purity of his" (4.4.384). Furthermore, also like her, we must, if we are to believe, be prepared to play a part, to undergo transformation. When Paulina requires that all do "awake" their faith and in a hushed stillness contemplate the statue, one may join in homage to the work of a master artist—how can one not? But one should also notice the way this work of art turns artist with its votaries. From admiring Perdita, it takes the spirits, leaving her standing "like stone"; Leontes it pierces to the soul, wringing from him the exclamation—"Would I were dead"—while reducing him to the part of a passive "looker on." From one dead likeness many may proceed. Perhaps it is an uneasiness about this fact that prompts the playwright to jog our attention with such impertinencies as the reminder of Hermione's grave or of Leontes' having seen her corpse. Such facts remind us of a truth best expressed in the case of a corpulent image of "vanity" long since risen upon the Shakespearean stage from the death of iconism that he momentarily suffers beside an infinitely thinner image of "honor" to assert that it is to death that such "numbness" rightly pertains, while any image of life indeed can only be an act of counterfeit. To know that we need lies even to do ourselves grace is a knowledge that goes a long way toward constituting whatever small difference there might possibly be between our own rapt attention to Shakespeare's art and that senseless worship which is shown Autolycus's art by the "herd" at the feast: "no hearing, no feeling, but my sir's song, and admiring the nothing of it."[22]

22. My reading should be contrasted with that of Egan, *Drama Within Drama*, esp. 78, on the play as a call for our "faith" in order that the artistic image be allowed to "reform in its own image the world we inhabit, since that image only bodies forth our world's inherent and original truths." Cf. the similar point of Richard L. Harris, *"The Winter's Tale*: An 'Old Tale' Begetting Wonder," *Dalhousie Review* 58 (1978): 295–308.

· Index ·

Index

Index

Index

Index

303

Index

Index

Pafford, J. H. P., 3n

Painting, Elizabethan, 37, 82, 140

Palindrome: and *Hamlet*, 185–188; and temptation, 227–229

Panofsky, Erwin, 144n, 274n

Patrides, C. A., 114n, 117n

Peirce, C. S., 151n

Perkins, William, 38, 45

Phillips, John, 33n

Picture, speaking, 8, 10, 24

Plato, 114, 141n

Plotinus, 56

Plutarch, 117–120; on Brutus, 167–169; on Caesar, 148–149; on portents, 126; and style, 210

Pope, Alexander, 179, 222

Portraits, Elizabethan attacks on, 55

Praz, Mario, 8n

Prince, F. T., 3n

Prior, Moody E., 172n

Prosser, Eleanor, 219n, 226n

Pseudo-Dionysus, 61n

Puttenham, George, 37–38; and icon, 16, 36, 91, 154n

Rabkin, Norman, 2, 22–23, 105n

Raleigh, Sir Walter, 205n, 242n

Rasperger, Christopher, 58n

Reformation: and ritual, 178; and world order, 140–141

Reibetanz, John, 251n

Representation: and judgment, 196–199, 212–217; and usurpation, 241

Ribner, Irving, 8n, 120n

Richmond, Ian, 191n

Ricoeur, Paul, 276, 280; on idol and symbol, 265–266

Ridley, Nicholas, 46

Rist, J. M., 176n

Ritual form, 76–77

Roberts, Preston Thomas, Jr., 32

Robinson, Forrest G., 117n, 129n, 284n

Roessner, Jane, 55n

Ronan, Clifford J., 115

Rose, Mark, 24, 74, 186n, 195n

Rosenberg, Harold, 240n

Rossiter, A. P., 23n, 29n

Rymer, Thomas, 2, 180–182

Sacraments: dispute over, 58–59; and history, 60–61; and likeness, 57, 62

Salutati, Coluccio, 46

Schanzer, Ernest, 23n, 210n, 288n

Schlegel, A. W., 4, 19, 21, 215

Schneidau, Herbert N., 104n, 117n, 144n, 146n

Schöne, Albrecht, 274n

Scofield, Martin, 232n

Scot, Reginald, 41, 86n

Scoufos, Alice-Lyle, 117n, 195n

Sebonde, Raymond, 65n

Senses, hierarchy, 35, 81, 262

Index

Index

Turner, Robert Y., 88n
Turner, Victor, 141–142
Tuve, Rosemond, 7n
Tyndale, William, 46, 48, 53, 55, 60–61, 156n
Typology, 195–198

Ure, Peter, 255n

Vergil, Polydore, 68
Vision, 261–265; and Protestant prejudice, 35

Walker, John, 141
Walley, Harold R., 88n
Walter, J. H., 3n
Warnke, Martin, 33n, 143
Watkins, W. B. C., 21n

Webster, John, 55n
Welsh, Alexander, 218
Whitaker, Virgil, 239n–240n
Whiter, Walter, 5n
Wickham, Glynne, 69n, 139n
Wilden, Anthony, 232n
Wilson, F. P., 67
Wilson, Thomas, 156n
Wimsatt, William, 121n
Wind, Edgar, 57n
Wittkower, Rudolph, 56
Woolf, Rosemary, 50
Wright, George T., 238

Yates, Frances, 30–31, 45

Zwingli, Ulrich, 57

Compositor:	Wilsted & Taylor
Printer:	Thomson-Shore, Inc.
Binder:	John H. Dekker & Sons
Text:	Palatino
Display:	Palatino